RM WADE

KEYS TO THE KINGDOM

RELEASE THE KINGDOM IN YOUR COMMUNITY

*Seven Keys to Building Strategic Partnerships
for Unlocking a Region*

TRILOGY

Trilogy Christian Publishers

A Wholly Owned Subsidiary of Trinity Broadcasting Network
2442 Michelle Drive
Tustin, CA 92780

10 9 8 7 6 5 4 3 2 1
Library of Congress Cataloging-in-Publication Data is available.
ISBN 978-1-64088-547-9 (Print Book)
ISBN 978-1-64088-548-6 (ebook)

DEDICATION

This writing is dedicated to two men of God. These men have had a profound impact on my spiritual walk with Christ. Yes, their physical time that they were able to spend influencing me for the cause of Christ was rather limited, but with God, who provides the increase, it was definitely quality time spent. What they sowed into my life will echo in eternity for those whose lives God will be touched through me.

With that said, this is a call out to Gary Grayban and his wonderful wife, Dottie. In February of 2018, the company that I was working for changed directions slightly. The job that I had been hired to do now had gone away. I quickly started the hunt for a new job; I remembered that Facebook was advertising about a job fair in Pascagoula, Mississippi, for designers at the shipbuilding company there. Timing is everything, so Laura and I planned for the trip down from Oklahoma. My attitude is that even if I were to find the perfect job there, if we could not find a perfect church that we could step right into and start serving our God, then no matter how much they paid me, it would not be perfect. I did a search on the computer and found two that might do the job. Their statement of faith was in line with ours, and so I called down and spoke with the receptionists there. I asked for the person who heads up the altar prayer ministries. At the Oasis Church, I was directed to Gary. Let me say, speaking with Gary was like we were at a class reunion! You would have thought we knew each other for decades. Although he was decades my senior, it seemed we walked out our spiritual and natural lives together. We both worked at Rocketdyne, just not at the same time, he in the '60s and '70s while me in the '80s and '90s. He also worked at Hughes Aircraft roughly during the time that my father had also worked there. In the late '80s, when I would commute on the Highway 101 to Rocketdyne, I would listen to Pastor Jack Hayford from The Church on the Way on the radio, Pastor Jack was Gary's personal pastor. Both of our current individual churches are in line with Pastor Robert Morris of the Gateway Church in Southlake, Texas. We would talk for hours about how God's grace is so powerful and His guiding hands were so strong but so gentile.

The time came to head down to Mississippi. The job listing that was posted, I felt that I was a shoe in. I know the software programs—hey, I have designed airplanes. I can design ships, and we just use different gauges of metal, right? I found a good church, and now all it took was to land the job. We drove down and met Gary and his wife, Dottie, for dinner; a bonus was meeting their daughter, Lori, and her husband and children. It just seemed like if you looked at Laura and I and projected us out in twenty years, this would be us, personified in the persons of Gary and Dottie! How could this be? Well, during dinner, it came out that both Gary and Dottie were from Patterson, New Jersey, the same hometown that Laura's father, Joe, grew up in. Just way too many coincidences for to be coincidence.

The next day was the interviews. I firmly believe that I nailed both that I had. Both hiring managers were impressed with the résumé and indicated that they were passing it on to the next level. We went to dinner with Gary and Dottie again—what a delight sharing life and life's stories with these saints of God. As we were departing for Oklahoma, Gary confided in us that he had not been feeling himself lately. We felt it an honor that such a man of God would confide in us, so quickly.

Well, back in Enid, Oklahoma, we received the sad news that I did not get the jobs. Never mind, we were very blessed to have found a brother and sister in Christ that we identified so well with. Over the course of the next few months, we continued to stay in contact with Gary and Dottie. Gary's health continued to decline, and the doctors were at a little of a loss as to what it was that was attacking Gary. We would pray with him on the phone, and I would text him scriptures that God gave me for him. No matter what his day was like, he continued to walk this walk of faith and would not give Satan any glory. He would not give in to the symptoms of the day. He continued confessing God's Word over his life and his body. This man of faith never wavered in his faith to his God, the Father and Creator of the universe. I am still in awe of his love for our Father. In life, he was known professionally as a nuclear physicist; we knew him as a strong man of God who never wavered in faith. Although we only met in person twice, we spent hours on the phone; he was truly a lifelong mentor to me, if only for a year on this earth together. In February we celebrated his passing on to Jesus. From one rocket scientist to a nuclear physicist, your life on this earth was but a segment, and my segment only overlapped your segment for a brief time, but with God, our individual segments are but just a brief moment on the ray that is our individual existence in eternity. I look forward in spending some of eternity with you my brother Gary Grayborn.

Godspeed, Gary. He won his battle against ALS and is dancing with Jesus!

There is an old TV commercial that went something like this, "When EF Hutten speaks, everybody listens." Well, when Rex Parnell speaks, even the demons listen! After we started attending World Harvest Church, we were invited to attend the prayer and healing class on Monday nights in February of 2016. There the matriarchs and patriarchs of the church taught on The Believers Authority from the book by Kenneth E. Hagin as well as others on healings and other miracles. The matriarchs and patriarchs like Anita Sewell, Don and Wanda Walker, Rex and Wilma Parnell, Martha Counce and Nelda Butkhreart were the primary sources of mentorship. During class we would hear of the tails of when Anita, Rex, and Wilma returned from Uganda after having spent three weeks preaching there. Hearing of the power of God working through these saints was very faith-building. Hearing of the healings of the blind, the lame walking, and even the raising of the dead was truly awe-inspiring. Listening to these pillars of faith became something that Laura and I long for each week and still do!

The main thing that this class was different from other classes—we learned and practiced as we went. We prayed each Monday for different people to receive healing, and God answered our prayers. But Rex...when he would speak, you had better listen. He (as far as we knew) was a quiet man, but when he spoke, you better listen, as you just knew wisdom and faith would come out. He walked with such a command of the Word of God. If he gave you a Word from God, you better take notes because it was something special that you needed right now or you were about to need it! Other times, he would just give you a scripture, and when you went home to look it up—wow, how did he know that? The scripture would be so on mark for whatever you were going through that day or that week.

Once, while in Uganda, he knew he needed to pray for a woman's vision; he just did not know the details. When he laid hands on her face, cupping where her eyes were, he felt movement under one hand. When he removed his hands, she could see. What he did not know was that the woman did not have an eye in one of the eye sockets. God was regenerating a new eye inside the socket! That is the movement that he felt under one hand! He felt God's regeneration of an eye in the eye socket, just incredible! Praise His holy name!

I knew this was a man of God that I wanted to sit under his anointing.

I wanted to one day go to Uganda and take part of the move of God over there. Again, Laura and I are in the middle of folks that are some twenty and thirty years our seniors, but one could not tell. We are family. I was asked to join Rex on an annual hunting trip up to Nebraska. This city boy from the suburbs of Los Angeles had never been deer hunting before, but I am up for any new thing. I drove both Rex and Wilma up to Nebraska to the Faith, Hope and Love Fellowship Church that they were responsible for planting. I heard many stories of how God had used them to plant this church and touch the lives of so many while in two deer stands in twenty-eight degrees with the wind howling.

This trip coincided with the observance of Veterans Day. As we were driving to the church on Sunday, we listened to a Joel Osteen broadcast on the radio while they were also observing Veterans Day. I knew that Rex had served in the US Army, so when it came time for me to speak, I called him up and paid honor to him as well as all others present who have served. I then called up Wilma to join her husband. I called up the elders of the church to pray over these two soldiers serving in the army of God. They have served Him low these forty-nine years in ministry. It is such a privilege to be serving alongside such strong man and woman of God.

On this trip, it became evident to me that Rex's health was also not doing so well. Being the man of faith that he is, he also, like Gary, refused to give Satan glory and refused to accept the symptoms. He continued to confess God's Word over life and his body. I was blessed to be able to minister alongside both Rex and Wilma while up there. Seeing the Holy Spirit move in both of them was a true blessing.

Back to the idea of when Rex speaks, you listen. Rex had these steel-blue eyes; when he looked at you, it was as though he was looking deep into your spirit. It was like you could hide no secret sin. The light that so shone brightly within Rex is just awesome. When you were around him, because he was so close to God, you just knew you were also in God's presence because you were in Rex's presence. As God abides in Rex, so Rex abides in God. I am blessed to have had Rex in my life. I am blessed that I was able to sit under his anointing for these last three years. I want to be like him when I grow up. If I am half the man of faith that he is, I will be a very happy man. I can't wait to see you on the other side, my brother and spiritual father, Rex.

PS. And a special thanks to Downey High School freshman English teacher, Mrs. Martha Martin. Yes, you were unique in your discipline with a ruler; my hand still remembers the sting of the ruler and other methods of unique discipline. I firmly believe that you saw something; you believed in this C-and-D student. This one is for you as well. Thank you for investing in the lives of us students; even though we might not have showed it at the time, we loved you because we knew you loved us. You just had your special way of demonstrating that to us. Today it probably would be called "tough love."

TABLE OF CONTENTS

FOREWORD

I remember with fondness the first time I met Ron Wade. I was asked to be a partner on a special move that God was unfolding in Enid, Oklahoma, called Open Heavens! Ron was serving as the leader over the intercessory prayer team for the event. In a meeting, I heard how the event was birthed, launched, and specifically how Ron had a powerful strategy to help prepare for the move of God that would happen.

Since that night at Open Heavens, Ron's strategy has spoken to me many times as I've prayed over the region in Oklahoma. In fact, a few weeks ago, I had reached out to Ron and asked if he would be willing to write an article that would help me and others understand the keys necessary for unlocking a region wherever God may be calling someone. It became what you are about to read.

This is the most practical, powerful, and impactful strategy that any minister, ministry, or church could employ to unlock the region God has positioned them to labor for the kingdom of God. Today, more than ever, there is a need for sons and daughters of God to rise up as warriors and take back their regions, counties, cities, and towns for the glory of the kingdom of God.

Ron proved that utilizing these Spirit-fueled steps, people from across denominational lines can work together and labor to see an unlocking in their region.

Ron's deep walk with Jesus and his passion to see transformation is evident in every word he wrote. Ron and his wife, Laura, are truly gifted and anointed leaders who are willing to take the Gospel anywhere at any time.

I am glad to call Ron and his wife, Laura, friends and colaborers in the kingdom. I hope that the concepts, illustrations, and experiences Ron shares will inspire and empower you to begin cultivating the kingdom wherever God has called you as it has done me!

For Christ kingdom,
Rev. Jason L Coffman
Destiny Churches and Ministries
Founder of the Soar Apostolic Network and the Oklahoma Intercessors
Empowering Believers
Cultivating Kingdom

PREFACE

So…this book started out as an article that Pastor Jason wanted me to write; he gave me a subject matter, but beyond that, no real guidelines or limitations. I started writing and in about two weeks. I presented it to Jason, and he said, "Wow, I was only looking for about a 450- to 500-word article and you give me 32 pages!" Well, as you can see, we are just a little beyond those thirty-two pages.

I do issue a warning: some may not like some of the contents here in. This is not a book that is a "feel-good" book where every line just exudes the positive. That being said, there are some comical sections where I relate life and ministry. Know this—the content of this book is designed to encourage, challenge, and motivate you to a deeper level of prayer life and, thus, a deeper walk with God. It is my desire that the reader of this writing takes this ball and runs with it. Score that touchdown. Just realize—if you look at what I am suggesting at face value, you can psych yourself out.

Picture this—I am asking you to run a marathon. Both of us would be foolish if we expected you to run one tomorrow. No, depending on your existing fitness level, that would determine where you would start with your training program. This concept is a significant challenge, but guess what, it is entirely possible, no matter what your current level of spiritual fitness may be. We cannot sit down and eat an entire elephant in one bite. But through time, we can eat that elephant one bite at a time. As you start operating within the Jericho Cross Prayer (JCP), start out small. As you are faithful with the little things, you can work up to greater levels. The more you exercise your faith, the greater your spiritual fitness will become.

Now, you must also be warned—this book is very scripture-intensive.

I provide an abundance of reference scripture, sometimes multiple translations of the same verse, to drive a point home. I hope you enjoy! I pray you prayerfully apply the contents herein.

Currently, in this day and age, we must give ourselves more fully to prayer. John Wesley said, "It seems that God is limited by our prayer life— that He can do nothing for humanity unless someone asks Him."

ACKNOWLEDGMENTS

Thank you to the following for investing in me during this process.

First and foremost, I want to thank our Heavenly Father for having the grace in sending His only begotten Son to pay the ultimate price for me and my sins. Thank You, Holy Spirit, for teaching me and guiding me through this process. Thank You for inspiring me and nudging me and sometimes hitting me upside the head with a four-by-four. All honor and glory be to the Father, Son, and Holy Spirit Who was and is and always shall be—the GREAT I AM.

Thank you to my gracious wife, Laura. Thank you for your understanding and for your input. I appreciate how God is living out in your life. Thank you for the encouragement when I was seeking my voice in ministry, should I have a preaching style like that of Billy Graham, or Joel Osteen etc., but you quietly and patiently encouraged me to be who God created me—my quirky, nerdy style and all. So if my style is different, well, you have God and my wife to blame or praise, whichever you deem appropriate. Laura, I am sorry for the sleepless nights when our Father would wake me up from a dream and give me a download; honestly, I do try to lie still so as not to wake you. Thank you for your prayers, patience, and support.

I could thank an entire group of ministers that have fed me through the years, but I do not want to kill too many trees in the process. I will list those pastors that I have been in attendance for messages that have had a major impact on my life and gave me wisdom through the years. As well as those pillars in the faith that I have grown to love so much.

Julee Anne Wade (sister)
Virta S. Winters (great-grandma, preacher's kid)
Kathryn Kuhlman
Dr. Billy Graham
Pastor John Ashcraft
Josh McDowell
Pastor Adams
Pastor Art Aragon
Pastor Zack Nazarian
Pastor Lance
Pastor Jack Hayford
Pat Cronkite
Pastor Robert Morris
Pastors Brad and Tamy Mendenhall
Pastors Mike and Tamara Sturgeon
Missionaries Rex and Wilma Parnell
Don and Wanda Walker
Missionary Anita Sewell
Martha Counce
Nelda Butkhreart
Rev. Jason L. Coffman
Pastors David and Jordan Miller

INTRODUCTION

In 2017, I was part of a team that brought Open Heaven in Enid, Oklahoma, into existence. My role in this was that of the prayer coordinator and leading the altar prayer team. Open Heaven was one night of worship at the Central National Bank Arena. The dream and execution of this three-hour event required multiple thousands of man-hours over the course of a year. Over 48 churches were involved from multiple denominations. Private and corporate finances were used in the execution of the vision. I coordinated the prayer with the prayer leaders of those different churches. With over 1,495 people in attendance, we saw over 33 documented salvations with just as many and more physical healings documented.

Here are a few:

1.   Laramie prayed for Josh's back and neck; warm and tingling was felt with movement inside. Pain was gone.

2.   Courtney was prayed for by Laramie. Her wrists had carpal tunnel syndrome. Warm and tingling was felt. She was able to hold a water bottle without pain, first time in six months.

3.   Laura saw a woman in a wheelchair that was laying hands on someone else. She asked her if she could pray, and she said yes; she was in pain. Afterward, the woman said thank you; it was what she needed, and she was no longer in pain.

4.   Lane from Ponca City prayed for a man with a back problem; warm and tingling was felt followed by no pain.

5.   A teenage boy named Mason came to Open Heaven having a bad panic attack. Bud prayed for him, and when it was over, he came running to Bud, saying it was gone!

6.   Dale, Tammy, Bud, and I prayed for Natalie's back to be healed. She said it was! Praise God!

7.   Pastor Teddy and wife both laid hands on those who had their hands up. Neither one of knew who type of healing was needed. They prayed over them and left it in God's hands.

8.   After services Robert and his wife came over for prayer. The Holy Spirit led me to pray for healing in Robert's body that he had been suffering with. "And all things whatsoever you ask in prayer, believing, you shall receive" (Matthew 21:22).

9.   A woman with a fifteen-year-old back problem being healed from a lady praying for her at Open Heaven.

10. Dusty prayed for a couple of people for healings but had nothing specific told to him.

In the natural, I have been a bicycle race promoter, ensuring a fun race but most importantly, I strived to protect the health and safety of both athletes and spectators alike. I am also an aircraft structures designer. I work hard to ensure the flying public is safe.

I do not know what your ministry vision and goals are, but praise God, our Father does! This book will not necessarily address the Open Heaven and how we did that, per se—what I will do is assume that you want to step into or already have a ministry reaching out to peoples for Christ. I believe, as you put into motion and apply these seven keys, they will assist you in unlocking many doors. Not only will doors open, but doors will be shut on the adversary as well: passion, perspective, prayer, planning, persistence, positivity, and people.

> *"But what about you?" he asked. "Who do you say I am?"*
> *Simon Peter answered, "You are the Messiah, the Son of the living*
> *God." Jesus replied, "Blessed are you, Simon son of Jonah, for*
> *this was not revealed to you by flesh and blood, but by my Father*
> *in heaven. And I tell you that you are Peter, and on this rock I will*
> *build My church, and the gates of Hades will not prevail against it.*
> *I will give you the keys of the Kingdom of Heaven; whatever you*
> *bind on earth will be bound in heaven, and whatever you loose on*
> *earth will be loosed in heaven." (Matthew 16:15–19, NIV)*

The revelation that Jesus is the Christ, the Messiah—this is what the foundation that the church is built on. We must never forget this.

All of us at one time or another has longed to be part of a true revival. Not the scheduled revival that we see on church marques, but true revival that produces miracles, signs, and wonders with the manifest power of the Holy Spirit in operation resulting in transformation. Resulting in the salvation of souls, the reconciliation and healing of the entire man, spirit, soul, and body. We are all called to pray. I believe that if enough of us humble ourselves and pray, we will see the manifest presence of God move throughout the region and land.

I got a download from God the other day about revival!

I was reading about this class action lawsuit that has been filed against The Boeing Company, alleging negligence tied to the Woolsey Wildfire. The suit alleges that The Boeing Company did not properly maintain the land by clearing the brush. Boeing bought Rocketdyne and the Santa Susanna Field Laboratory (SSFL) in 1996 from Rockwell International. On November 8, 2018, the fire started there on the SSFL property at 5:46 p.m. on that Friday evening, and by 9:50 p.m., it was already at the Pacific Ocean. The Santa Ana winds fanned the flames and literally blew it to the ocean some 30 miles away in just a few short hours. The Woolsey fire killed 3, burned about 100,000 acres, and destroyed 1,500 structures in and around Malibu and prompted the evacuation of more than 295,000 people. I sat there staring at the map of this Woolsey wildfire, and a flood of memories came, and then I received a download.

But first the memories and the context of the download.

Back in 1988, when I worked at Rocketdyne Division of Rockwell, I was working on the space shuttle main engine as well as other rocket engines. After the engines were manufactured, the engines would be acceptance-tested. These tests consisted of attaching the engine in a test stand; the stand had the propellant tanks, control valves and instrumentation. For the shuttle, the propellants were liquid oxygen and liquid hydrogen. Anyway, we would static hot fire them, basically a simulated launch with the exception that it was in a test stand. We tested them to validate the engines were operating within normal operating parameters. Within the industry, we are called "the fire and smoke guys." The SSME during operations produces some 477,000 pounds of thrust. Now that is a lot of fire and smoke! These tests were conducted at SSFL in the hills north west of the San Fernando Valley.

God is a fire-and-smoke kind of guy as well:

> And the LORD went before them by day in a pillar of a cloud, to lead them the way; and by night in a pillar of fire, to give them light; to go by day and night. (Exodus 13:21, KJV)

This pillar of a cloud by day and pillar of fire by night demonstrated His manifest presence before the nation of Israel in a very powerful way.

> When the Feast of Pentecost came, they were all together in one place. Without warning there was a sound like a strong wind, gale force—no one could tell where it came from. It filled the whole building. Then, like a wildfire, the Holy Spirit spread through their ranks, and they started speaking in a number of different languages as the Spirit prompted them. This is what the prophet Joel announced would happen:
> "In the Last Days," God says, "I will pour out my Spirit on every kind of people:
> Your sons will prophesy, also your daughters;
> Your young men will see visions your old men dream dreams.
> When the time comes, I'll pour out my Spirit
> On those who serve me, men and women both, and they'll prophesy.

*I'll set wonders in the sky above and signs on the earth
below,
Blood and fire and billowing smoke, the sun turning black
and the moon blood-red,
Before the Day of the Lord arrives, the Day tremendous
and marvelous;
And whoever calls out for help to me, God, will be
saved." (Acts 2:1–4, 19, MSG)*

And we know that about three thousand came to Christ that day.

When I was looking at map of the Woolsey wildfire, this is what I was getting on the download:

I firmly believe that these are the end-times and the end-time harvest is about to come upon us. It is incumbent on all believers in Christ to hit our knees and pray for revival. We need to be likened to the Santa Ana winds and fan the flames of revival in the land through our prayers. We need to be like Elijah in 2 Kings 1:10 and call down fire from heaven and bring revival to the land.

Elijah answered the captain,

*"If I am a man of God, may fire come down from heaven and
consume you and your fifty men!" Then fire fell from heaven and
consumed the captain and his men. (2 Kings 1:10, NIV)*

We see in James 3:2–10 about controlling the tongue. I have always thought of this from a negative connotation, with regard to all the damage negative words can do to others and this still is true. But now I am seeing the positive power that our words can really harness. I am seeing in James:

*Likewise, the tongue is a small part of the body, but it makes
great boasts. Consider what a great forest is set on fire by a small
spark. (James 3:5, NIV)*

Let us use our tongues to speak life and love to a lost and dying world. As we utter the words in prayer, we fan the flames of the Holy Spirit, and this revival will spread faster than the Woolsey wildfire. And just like in Acts chapter 2, signs and wonders will follow. It is interesting to note that what happened in the upper room and Pentecost that we read in Acts chapter 2 was after ten days of fasting and prayer. So will you join me and become "the fire-and-smoke" kind of believer in Christ?

I believe that implementing these seven keys will help usher in the end-time harvest of souls. I believe that I have a mandate to get this message out. Please take the time to read this and prayerfully consider applying some, if not all, into your spirit and into your life.

CHAPTER 1
KINGDOM—WHY ON EARTH WOULD YOU WANT KEYS TO THE KINGDOM?

Greetings! Thank you for embarking on this journey with me, so let us look at the kingdom and what that really means, first by defining what the kingdom really is. In the New Covenant we see that the kingdom is defined in two ways, first by referring to Jesus as Messiah, ruling in His domain, the hearts of His believers. In this current age, the kingdom of heaven is purely spiritual, and we see this in Luke 17:21. The second definition of the kingdom of heaven is in the physical realm. His kingdom will be manifest physically when our Lord Jesus Christ will rule and reign on His throne on this earth when He establishes it. We read of this in Revelation 11:15.

So just who has these keys? We read in Revelation that it is Jesus Who is the possessor of the keys, and we find out how He came to possess those keys:

> *I saw this and fainted dead at his feet. His right hand pulled me upright, his voice reassured me: Don't fear: I am First, I am Last, I'm Alive. I died, but I came to life, and my life is now forever. See these keys in my hand? They open and lock Death's doors, they open and lock Hell's gates. (Revelation 1:17–18, MSG)*

> *When I saw him, I fell down at his feet as good as dead, but he laid his right hand on me and I heard his reassuring voice saying: Don't yield to fear. I am the Beginning and I am the End, the Living One! I was dead, but now look—I am alive forever and ever. And I hold the keys that unlock death and the unseen world. (TPT)*

KEYS Definition

1. a small piece of shaped metal with incisions cut to fit the wards of a particular lock, which is inserted into a lock and turned to open or close it

2. a means of gaining or preventing entrance, possession, or control

Reach down into your pocket or purse, grab your key ring, and look at it. On this key ring are various keys—a car key or two, that one is the house door key, as well as the dead bolt key. Those keys allow you to gain access

1

to you home and to operate your car. If you were to go on vacation, you might give that key ring to a friend so they can water plants and feed a pet. For that brief period, that person essentially has rights and privilege to your home and car; but upon your return, they lose those rights. If you lent your truck to someone, and that person refused to give you keys back, you have the title deed (pink slip) to prove that the ownership of the truck belongs to you.

> *He shall have your uniform and title and authority, and he will be a father to the people of Jerusalem and all Judah. I will give him responsibility over all my people; whatever he says will be done; none will be able to stop him. (Isaiah 22.20–22, TLB)*

> *I'll dress him in your robe. I'll put your belt on him. I'll give him your authority. He'll be a father-leader to Jerusalem and the government of Judah. I'll give him the key of the Davidic heritage. He'll have the run of the place—open any door and keep it open, lock any door and keep it locked. (MSG)*

KINGDOM Definition

1. a politically organized community or major territorial unit having a monarchical form of government headed by a king or queen

2. a realm or region in which something is dominant

First and foremost, we need to establish priorities. Jesus commanded us to go to Jerusalem, Judea, Samaria, and to the ends of the earth spreading the news of His kingdom. We see a clear pattern here with Jerusalem, Judea, Samaria. But I must add this. We need to apply these keys to our family first. As a husband and father, my Jerusalem is my wife and children. If I do not make a priority to be the priest of my household and lead them to Christ in love, then all else I do is for naught. I need to lead by example operating in the love, grace, peace, forgiveness, patience and self-sacrificial nature of God the Father. Then do the same for those in my immediate circle of friends (Judea)—and no, my in-laws are not my Samaria! First and foremost, this is my ministry; if I fail at that, am I not disqualified to minister elsewhere? The keys to the kingdom first must be used to unlock the kingdom in the hearts and minds of my family. These keys being applied daily toward my family. Then and only then can I apply them elsewhere.

When the disciples asked Jesus how to pray, this is detailed in Matthew

6:9–13. I would like to focus on verse 10.

> *Your kingdom come. Your will be done in earth, as it is in*
> *heaven. (Matthew 6:10, KJV)*

We see here that it all starts with prayer, having an attitude of prayer for the kingdom. Each morning my wife and I pray together and aloud two prayers, Psalm 23 and the Lord's Prayer, found in Matthew 6. Each day we begin and end the day praying for God's kingdom to come, thy will be done, in earth as it is in heaven.

What does it mean to pray for God's kingdom to be here on earth? So often, we as humans tend to limit ourselves in our thinking. We primarily think in our three-dimensional realm—what we can see, smell, and touch. The older we get, we start to expand in our thinking and add a fourth dimension, the dimension of time. Sadly, we limit our concept of time to just being linear time and not one of how God sees it, existence that has no beginning and no end; mathematically we call that infinity. As these days of our lives continue, time seems to change. Is it time that is changing, or is it something else? I believe it is our perspective of time that changes. I remember how at age six or so, summer vacation between first and second grades, those three months seem to take so long. I look at it this way, three months to someone who has only lived seventy-two months is a large percentage of that life. And if you really look at it from a cognizance level, at six, I probably really was only aware of the previous thirty-six months, so three months out of thirty-six, yes, a much larger slice of the pie. But now some decades later, having lived over six hundred and seventy-two months, a summer flies by; in fact twelve months seem to fly by. Time has remained constant; it is only my perspective of the passing of time that has evolved. This is demonstrated in the book of James.

> *Why, you do not even know what will happen tomorrow. What*
> *is your life? You are a mist that appears for a little while and then*
> *vanishes. (James 4:14, NIV)*

Our time on earth is so brief, and we as believers must not have the attitude like that of the world, "Eat and drink for tomorrow we die." We as believers know of another dimension.

As we become believers in Christ, an entire fifth dimension is revealed to us, and no, not the singing group. This fifth dimension, which is one that is in the spiritual realms, beyond the realms of men. Jehovah God sits on His throne in the heavenly realm transcending time and space; He is, has always been, and forever will be the Great I AM! It is His kingdom and His reign. It is God's Kingly Rule, His Lordship, His Sovereignty, His Solemn Word.

God is not constrained by the limits of matter, time, or space. He is infinity and beyond—way far and above what we can imagine even for Buzz Lightyear! Any basic understanding that we may come up with does not even scratch the surface into the depths of His complexities. Even if you were able to get a large auditorium full of the greatest spiritual philosophers to come up with a comprehensive definition of Who and What God is and how He operates, that definition would come up lacking. I humbly submit my limited understanding based on His Word and what I have witnessed and share in this writing. As limited as my understanding is, I pray that our Heavenly Father uses these words.

But what of this kingdom? Who foretold of its coming? In the Gospels of Matthew, Mark, and Luke, we see that they all attest that John the Baptist was the messenger promised in Malachi 3:1–2. This can be found in Matthew 11:10, Mark 1:2, and Luke 7:27. So let's see what it says in Malachi.

> *Look! I'm sending my messenger on ahead to clear the way for me. Suddenly, out of the blue, the Leader you've been looking for will enter his Temple—yes, the Messenger of the Covenant, the one you've been waiting for. Look! He's on his way!" A Message from the mouth of God-of-the-Angel-Armies. But who will be able to stand up to that coming? Who can survive his appearance? He'll be like white-hot fire from the smelter's furnace. He'll be like the strongest lye soap at the laundry. He'll take his place as a refiner of silver, as a cleanser of dirty clothes. (Malachi 3:1–2, MSG)*

So what did John the Baptist actually say and who was he pointing to?

> *In those days John the Baptist came preaching in the wilderness of Judea, and saying, "Repent, for the kingdom of heaven is at hand!" For this is he who was spoken of by the prophet Isaiah, saying: "The voice of one crying in the wilderness: 'Prepare the way of the Lord; Make His paths straight.'" (Matthew 3:1–3, NKJV)*

4

Let us just pause for a moment and look at the context of the time and place from which this was all taking place. God's voice had gone silent to the nation of Israel for four hundred years. No words from prophets, the likes of Jeramiah, Isaiah, Micah, or Ezekiel. Even though a lot of the words from these prophets of God were very harsh, at least they were hearing from the God of Abraham, Isaac, and Jacob. No words from their God for four hundred years!

Now they were under the boot of the tyrannical Roman Empire. The taxes from the Roman Empire were oppressing; add to that the local tax collectors adding more grief by taking even more. Herod Antipas was the local ruler of Galilee and Perea, representing Emperor Tiberius Caesar Augustus of Rome. Herod Antipas exercised even more oppression over the peoples of Galilee and Perea. The peoples of Israel, as it were, their necks were under the boot (sandals) of the Roman Empire, and they were desperate for relief from the tyranny. They looked to the holy scripture for a political messiah. After all, God delivered them from the tyrannical Egyptians; why can He not deliver them from this oppression? So word spread very quick that there was this prophet out in the desert that was likened to that of Elijah and that he was preaching of the coming of the kingdom. Could it be that this man was the forerunner of a new political messiah?

This John, a direct cousin of Jesus and like Isaac, Samuel, and Jesus, was divinely conceived. To put John's divine conception in context, let's also take a brief look at the others in the Bible that were divinely conceived and remind us exactly why this is of extreme importance.

Isaac was the son of promise; this conception was the first of many signs of how God would honor His promise to the peoples we would come to know as the people of Israel. Isaac being conceived after both Abram and Sarai both being well beyond childbearing years! Not only was Isaac the fulfillment of the promise. In Genesis 22 we read of another event concerning him, which would foretell of the substitutionary sacrifice of Jesus Christ. What am I referring to? Well, God told Abraham to take his promised son up the mountain to sacrifice him. Abraham, being the man of faith that he is, did not question but took Isaac up the mountain to sacrifice. Isaac, being smart, asked his father, "Why are we not taking up a sacrifice, where is the lamb?" Abraham said in faith, "God will provide."

Abraham answered, "God himself will provide the lamb for the

burnt offering, my son." And the two of them went on together."
(Genesis 22: 8, NIV)

Isaac knew his father to be a man of integrity, so he did not question the word of his father; he continued to walk up the mountain.

> *When they reached the place God had told him about, Abraham built an altar there and arranged the wood on it. He bound his son Isaac and laid him on the altar, on top of the wood. Then he reached out his hand and took the knife to slay his son. But the angel of the Lord called out to him from heaven, "Abraham! Abraham!" "Here I am," he replied. "Do not lay a hand on the boy," he said. "Do not do anything to him. Now I know that you fear God, because you have not withheld from me your son, your only son." Abraham looked up and there in a thicket he saw a ram caught by its horns. He went over and took the ram and sacrificed it as a burnt offering instead of his son. So Abraham called that place The Lord Will Provide. And to this day it is said, "On the mountain of the Lord it will be provided." (Genesis 22: 9–13, NIV)*

This is a prime illustration that we needed a substitutionary sacrifice for our sins, and that sacrificial lamb was the Lamb of God, in the person of Jesus Christ, which ushered in the kingdom age.

Now let us look at Samuel. With Samuel, God answered the prayers of Hanna so she could conceive Samuel. Samuel became the pivotal person in the Nation of Israel. He became the mouthpiece of Jehovah God to Saul, the first king over Israel. At the time of Saul, the nation wanted a king; they looked at other nations, and they all had kings. They did not want a theocracy, which is a government ruled by God, but they wanted a government ruled by men. God, Who operates beyond time and space, obliged the men of Israel and made a way. He saw His hand servant Hanna, who wanted desperately to have a child. She was without a child, yet she was persistent in going to temple to pray for a child. So desperate in her praying, so persistent in her praying that Eli actually thought that she was drunk, not understanding her plight. Once the high priest understood her plight, he prayed that God would answer her prayers, thus God intervening in the lives of mankind to ultimately fulfill His master plan. Samuel would grow in wisdom and in the ways of God such that he could be the voice of God to King Saul—a prime example of God, Who knows the beginning from the end, knowing that Israel still needed a voice, a mouthpiece from the throne room of grace, placing Samuel to be just that for King Saul.

That now brings us to John. The priest, Zechariah and his wife, Elizabeth, descendant of Aaron, were without child. They both were righteous and blameless before the eyes of God, yet they remained childless. The text indicates that they were very old. It came about that the priest Zechariah was offering incense at the altar that God appeared to him. He was so frightened by it; he froze in fear.

> But the angel said to him: "Do not be afraid, Zechariah; your prayer has been heard. Your wife Elizabeth will bear you a son, and you are to call him John. He will be a joy and delight to you, and many will rejoice because of his birth, for he will be great in the sight of the Lord. He will bring back many of the people of Israel to the Lord their God. And he will go on before the Lord, in the spirit and power of Elijah, to turn the hearts of the parents to their children and the disobedient to the wisdom of the righteous— to make ready a people prepared for the Lord." (Luke 5:13–17, NIV)

As a side note, Zechariah was not such a man of faith that he understood and followed the Word of the Lord… He doubted a little and paid for his doubt.

> Zechariah asked the angel, "How can I be sure of this? I am an old man and my wife is well along in years." The angel said to him, "I am Gabriel. I stand in the presence of God, and I have been sent to speak to you and to tell you this good news. And now you will be silent and not able to speak until the day this happens, because you did not believe my words, which will come true at their appointed time." (Luke 5:18–20, NIV)

And we have confirmation that all this was the inner workings of a magnificent God, in that when John, while still inside his mother's womb, leaped with joy upon hearing the voice of Mary, the mother of Jesus! What at testament that an unborn child was the first to acknowledge the presence of Christ, the Messiah!

> When Elizabeth heard Mary's greeting, the baby leaped in her womb, and Elizabeth was filled with the Holy Spirit. (Luke 1:41,

NIV)

Like the many prophets in the Old Covenant, the prophet we know now as John the Baptist was called of God to urgently call all peoples to an attitude of repentance, to prepare their hearts for the coming kingdom. It was a bold message, one that both challenged the hearts of the hearers while also giving them hope.

But this John—who was he, what was he about? He was a person of the wilderness; his face was red and rutted from the sun. He definitely was not of an upper class as he came wearing a rough, dark camel-hair coat, the dress more suited for a homeless of the time. He ate dried locusts, and who knows, maybe they were sweetened with wild honey to help with swallowing of them, but still, locusts! Dried locusts, in all their crunchy goodness! Let us just get it all out in the open—John the Baptist was not politically correct! He was calling out all to repentance. Young, old, rich, or poor—it did not matter what your position in life was; he called sin, sin. You either heard his message and you repented, or you were condemned by it. John did not need Facebook or any other social media to get his word out; his word was a direct call of God on his life. This word he carried, he carried the anointing of God on his life that when he spoke, those words pierced into the hearts of men to the dividing of the soul and spirit.

This was a call to consecrate their hearts to be cleansed, and John's baptism was the outward sign of one's inward repentance and a turning away from sin to prepare them for the kingdom to come (shortly). The immersion in water was not a new or foreign concept to the Jewish people of the time. Yes, it was not a commonplace occurrence but at the same time not entirely new. In the ancient rabbinic interpretations of the law, there is an entire section detailing this. In the Bible we see this in Psalm 51:2, Jeremiah 4:14, and Isaiah 1:16.

> *Wash me thoroughly from my iniquity, And cleanse me from my sin. (Psalm 51:2, NKJV)*

> *O Jerusalem, wash your heart from wickedness, That you may be saved. How long shall your evil thoughts lodge within you? (Jeremiah 4:14, NKJV)*

> *Wash yourselves, make yourselves clean; Put away the evil of your doings from before My eyes. Cease to do evil. (Isaiah 1:16,*

NKJV)

John also preached that if true repentance had occurred in a life, then one would see the fruits it produced afterward. That it would not be a mere sacrifice or ritual, but this changed heart would produce someone who is kind to their neighbor, helping those in need, selling possessions to aid others who are far less fortunate. Not a works mentality that we can work our way to heaven but a mentality that the changed heart will produce good works because of their love for God and a love for His people.

John's baptism of repentance is noted several places in the Gospels as well as the book of Acts. We find this in Mark 1:4, Matthew 3:6, Luke 3:3. Then we see it twice in Acts, Acts 13:24 and 19:4.

> *I baptize you with water for repentance, but one who is more powerful than I is coming after me; I am not worthy to carry his sandals. He will baptize you with the Holy Spirit and fire. His winnowing fork is in his hand, and he will clear his threshing floor and will gather his wheat into the granary; but the chaff he will burn with unquenchable fire. (Matthew 3:11–12, NRSV)*

> *Then Jesus came from Galilee to the Jordan to John to be baptized by him. But John protested strenuously, having in mind to prevent Him, saying, It is I who have need to be baptized by You, and do You come to me? But Jesus replied to him, Permit it just now; for this is the fitting way for [both of] us to fulfill all righteousness [that is, to perform completely whatever is right]. Then he permitted Him. And when Jesus was baptized, He went up at once out of the water; and behold, the heavens were opened, and he [John] saw the Spirit of God descending like a dove and alighting on Him. And behold, a voice from heaven said, This is My Son, My Beloved, in Whom I delight! (Matthew 3:13–17, AMPC)*

Let us look at the events surrounding John baptizing Jesus in the River Jordan. John was reluctant to baptize Jesus. Why? Could it be that he knew that Jesus was not sinful? They were cousins, and given that both were conceived under other than normal circumstances, did he know of the immaculate conception? We do know that while John was still in his mother's womb, upon hearing the voice of Mary, also pregnant with Jesus, John leaped inside the womb. This causes me to believe that the spirit of John knew at that age; he knew and was able to identify the spirit of Jesus in Mary's womb. I can just picture John's mother, Elizabeth, sitting beside the fire along with Mary, mother of Jesus; they would be chatting away; one would reminisce about the day when John did summersaults inside Elizabeth's womb. John had to have heard these stories! Surely John had heard of his cousin Jesus, who at twelve years of age was able to confound the priests at the temple. I mean, most first cousins would be talking of these things. I believe that within John's spirit, he was able to see the spirit of Jesus, and he just knew. When you are in the presence of a man of God, you just know. John relented and obeyed Jesus and the request to be baptized by John. And with it, this was the start of signs and wonders as the Holy Spirit descended and landed on Jesus. With the voice of the Father confirming His delight in the obedience of both John and Jesus, but mostly Jesus. This was the start of the public ministry of Jesus. We know that the baptism occurred and then His reading of the book of Isaiah.

> *And there was delivered to him the book of the prophet Esaias.*
> *And when he had opened the book, he found the place where*
> *it was written, The Spirit of the Lord is on me, because he has*
> *anointed me to preach the gospel to the poor; he has sent me to*
> *heal the brokenhearted, to preach deliverance to the captives,*
> *and recovering of sight to the blind, to set at liberty them that are*
> *bruised, To preach the acceptable year of the Lord. And he closed*
> *the book, and he gave it again to the minister, and sat down. And*
> *the eyes of all them that were in the synagogue were fastened on*
> *him. And he began to say to them, This day is this scripture fulfilled*
> *in your ears. (Luke 4:17–21, NKJV)*

Just as when He was twelve in the synagogue when He confounded the priests, not only that He understood the subject, but he was able to ask questions and dialogue with the elders of the faith. They had heard this scripture read many, many times; they had even read it themselves many times, but this time it was different! Every eye in the synagogue was on Him in astonishment. He spoke those words with power and authority like no other man they had ever heard. But then, the flesh got in the way. Instead of rejoicing that they have seen this prophecy fulfilled, they began to become indignant. "Who does he think he is? Is this not Joseph's son, the carpenter?" And so they ran him out of town.

Just a little more about John the Baptist. As I sit here contemplating the magnitude of the ministry of this prophet of God, had he been in the Old Covenant, he probably would have had his own book; he might have been considered today as one of the "minor prophets" but still a prophet nonetheless. What he did do was set the stage for when Jesus would come on the scene. So in a classic supporting man's role, he bowed out when the leading man came on the scene! He said it best in John 3:30:

> He must increase, but I must decrease. (NKJV)

> This is the assigned moment for him to move into the center,
> while I slip off to the sidelines. (MSG)

With that introduction, we must now move on to considering the kingdom of God. Let us look at what Jesus himself said of the kingdom, shall we? There are seven parables that Jesus told about the kingdom of God, so let us take a quick look at them to see if we would be interested in this kingdom and want to possess keys to gain access to this kingdom for all.

The first parable is found in Matthew 13:44:

> Heaven's kingdom realm can be illustrated like this: "A person discovered that there was hidden treasure in a field. Upon finding it, he hid it again. Because of uncovering such treasure, he was overjoyed and sold all that he possessed to buy the entire field just so he could have the treasure." (TPT)

In the Christian Standard Bible, we see it stated like this:

> The kingdom of heaven is like treasure, buried in a field, that a man found and reburied.

This treasure was hidden or buried in the field; the impression that I have is that the person who had discovered this treasure was not just walking in the field and he/she just tripped over it. "Oh my gosh, look what I found!" But the impression I have is that this person was a searcher; they were actively seeking. He was looking for a treasure of great prize, and when he found it, what did he do? Well, for starters, he was so overwhelmed with joy! He was stunned. Did he faint from all the excitement, I do not know—the text does not say that—but I can imagine that he might have. We do know that he hid it away so he could later possess this treasure for himself! He hid this treasure, what does that mean? I believe that it means that when we find the kingdom of God, we must secure it for ourselves. The enemy is like a roaring lion, seeking who he may devour; once we find the kingdom, we must secure it for ourselves so that the thief cannot steal it.

I am reminded of in 1985 when I worked on the B-1B Bomber. Rockwell International gave each employee on the program a commemorative coin, commemorating the first flight of a production B-1B. This coin was a 99.99% pure silver coin. A coin of great monetary value and a coin of great sentimental value for me. Was I like this person who concealed the treasure, put it away for safekeeping? No, for some unexplained reason, I put this coin in the glove compartment of my 85 Toyota truck. Yes, on the way home from work, I showed it to my father (we carpooled together; he worked across the street on the B-2 Bomber at Northrop). Every time I cleaned out the glove compartment, I would look at the coin and remember the program and smile. But then I would put it back into the glove compartment. Sometime in 1994, a thief broke into the truck and stole that coin. Yes, I was out of the monetary value of the coin, but more than that, I lost a coin attached to my sentimental heart. All because I did not secure this "treasure" properly. Yes, today I probably could do an eBay search to try and attain a similar coin for myself, but it would not be the same thing; the coin has lost its luster.

Please, so not misconstrue what I am saying here, God does not conceal His kingdom so that those who are not seekers will not find His kingdom— no, He is not cruel like that! It is His will that all come to the saving knowledge of Jesus Christ. Later in Mark 15:43, we are encouraged to be a seeker like Joseph of Arimathea.

So let's get dirty and back to the field where that treasure was found! This person who found this treasure sold everything of value to purchase the land where this treasure was found. The implication here is that all he possessed, his treasure, did not compare with the treasure that he had found. He was willing to risk it all for this new treasure. What if someone else had found it between the time he found/hid it and sold his possessions then bought the field? If this had happened, he would have been out of everything. He sold everything so he could rightfully own the field, thus owning the treasure it contained. What do you own? What do I own? I believe this is a chance to examine what we have. Would we be like this person and sell everything to attain this treasure beyond measure? Now that we have this treasure beyond measure, is it ours to keep, or are we encouraged—nay, commanded to give it away?

We have this treasure beyond measure—*salvation*, everlasting life—and it is ours to give away.

This has been a basic traditional way of looking at that treasure found in the field. I would like to interject another possibility. I do not know if this is an original concept, but here goes. I believe another way to look at this passage is that we, you and I, are in that field. We are that treasure beyond measure. God is the seeker in that field. He finds us and is willing to give all to make a way for Him to have us as His. A little more on this later, after we look at the second parable.

The second parable is found in Matthew 13:45–46:

> Or, God's kingdom is like a jewel merchant on the hunt for excellent pearls. Finding one that is flawless, he immediately sells everything and buys it. (MSG)

> Heaven's kingdom realm is also like a jewel merchant in search of rare pearls. When he discovered one very precious[y] and exquisite pearl, he immediately gave up all he had in exchange for it. (TPT)

Yes, this parable is very much like the first, although with some exceptions. As in the first, both were seeking and searching. Now the first one, the impression that I have is that he was a common individual; contrast that with the second individual. He was a merchant who deals with pearls daily; he knows what he is looking at based on years of experience. He has spent years of examining gems and precious metals and pearls, and as with any profession, he probably made a few mistakes here and there. In my mind's eye, I see him with the jeweler's eyepiece looking over this pearl. When he recognizes it for the rare item that it is, he pauses, puts it a little away from his face, and looks around to see if anyone is watching him. No, coast is clear; he now wonders if the person he is to buy it from knows the value of this pearl. He sizes up the seller. He indicates that he wishes to buy it and asks if he can have some time to arrange the finances for the purchase. He sells all so that he can possess this pearl of great prize.

Why did Jesus use a pearl and not a nugget of gold or maybe even a diamond? Well, each of those items, although can be very valuable, both need man's hands to increase the value—that is, the melting of the gold to purify it or a master diamond cutter to cut it just right. But the pearl has already gone through the natural process of refinement.

Could it be that like we are likened to the oyster, in that a grain of sand placed in the oyster causes irritation but it is through that very irritation that God transforms it into a pearl of great prize. We have our scars in our lives, but with those scars, God can transform us into a pearl of great prize. When the kingdom of God comes to us, are we in it on our own efforts to improve on it, or we are made perfect in Christ through the power of His Holy Spirit? God does not see us as we are; He sees us through the blood of Jesus Christ. We are the righteousness of God in Christ.

I would suggest looking at these two similar kingdom parables through the lens of another set of parables that Jesus introduced:

Jesus is the good Shepheard and leaves the ninety-nine to find the one who is lost. Jesus left His heavenly throne and became a man. He gave up all so that He could possess us, a treasure beyond measure. We see that illustrated in the story in Luke 15:

> *Suppose one of you had a hundred sheep and lost one. Wouldn't you leave the ninety-nine in the wilderness and go after the lost one until you found it? When found, you can be sure you would put it across your shoulders, rejoicing, and when you got home call in your friends and neighbors, saying, "Celebrate with me! I've found my lost sheep!" Count on it—there's more joy in heaven over one sinner's rescued life than over ninety-nine good people in no need of rescue. (Luke 15:4–7, MSG)*

> *There once was a shepherd with a hundred lambs, but one of his lambs wandered away and was lost. So the shepherd left the ninety-nine lambs out in the open field and searched in the wilderness for that one lost lamb. He didn't stop until he finally found it. With exuberant joy he raised it up and placed it on his shoulders, carrying it back with cheerful delight! Returning home, he called all his friends and neighbors together and said, "Let's have a party! Come and celebrate with me the return of my lost lamb. It wandered away, but I found it and brought it home." Jesus continued, "In the same way, there will be a glorious celebration in heaven over the rescue of one lost sinner who repents, comes back home, and returns to the fold—more so than for all the righteous people who never strayed away." (TPT)*

14

Jesus is the good Shepherd, as we know from Psalm 23, "The Lord is my Shepherd." I believe that we are the treasure beyond measure in that field that the Lord Jesus found and gave His all so that He could possess us.

God is the master jeweler. He knows exactly what He is looking at; in the world's judgmental eyes, we are of no value. But in God's eyes, we are highly valued. Let us look at the companion scripture to the one mentioned previously in Luke.

> Or imagine a woman who has ten coins and loses one. Won't she light a lamp and scour the house, looking in every nook and cranny until she finds it? And when she finds it you can be sure she'll call her friends and neighbors: "Celebrate with me! I found my lost coin!" Count on it—that's the kind of party God's angels throw every time one lost soul turns to God. (Luke 15:8–10, MSG)

> Jesus gave them another parable: "There once was a woman who had ten valuable silver coins. When she lost one of them, she swept her entire house, diligently searching every corner of her house for that one lost coin. When she finally found it, she gathered all her friends and neighbors for a celebration, telling them, 'Come and celebrate with me! I had lost my precious silver coin, but now I've found it.' That's the way God responds every time one lost sinner repents and turns to him. He says to all his angels, 'Let's have a joyous celebration, for that one who was lost I have found!'" (TPT)

Like before, I believe that an alternative way to look at that jeweler is that he is, in fact, God. God is searching for those of us to follow Him. And of course, we cannot look at the first two without looking at the last one in Luke 15, and that, of course, would be the parable of the prodigal son. After the son had left his father's house, I envision, the father every day scanning the horizon for his long-lost son. From dawn to dusk, he was scanning for his son to return. If sitting down for dinner, he was looking out the window. If at the well to draw water, he was always looking up to see if his son was returning. Finally, one day he looked up and saw his son on the roadway; he dropped everything his was doing and ran to his son! And though his son was dressed in the wares of a beggar and he smelled like hog poop when he got to his son, he picked him up and gave him the biggest hug. His son has returned! Let us look at his response in the Passion translation for Luke

15:22–24.

> *Turning to his servants, the father said, "Quick, bring me the*
> *best robe, my very own robe, and I will place it on his shoulders.*
> *Bring the ring, the seal of sonship, and I will put it on his finger.*
> *And bring out the best shoes you can find for my son. Let's prepare*
> *a great feast and celebrate. For this beloved son of mine was*
> *once dead, but now he's alive again. Once he was lost, but now he*
> *is found!" And everyone celebrated with overflowing joy. (Luke*
> *15:22–24, TPT)*

Total forgiveness was demonstrated to the son that day. Not only forgiveness but full restoration as a son of the father. The father's robe, his covering, his anointing were laid back on to the son. The family ring signified that the son had the full authority of the father. The sandals communicated that he was a son and not a servant.

Yes, I explained two parables of the kingdom by referencing three other parables that Christ told. The three parables concerning the lost sheep, the lost coin, and the lost son, I believe they refer to the Trinity. Jesus is the good Shepherd, often in scripture; the Holy Spirit takes on more feminine comforting nature, and so the widow (Holy Spirit) is searching for the coin; and God the Father is the father searching for the son. We are the sheep, the coin, and the long-lost son. In each case, highly valued by the Shepherd, the Widow, and the Father. And in each case, a party was thrown in honor of finding the sheep, coin, and son.

We find the treasure in the field; we find the pearl, and we sell all so that we can possess this treasure beyond measure.

Likewise, the full Godhead is seeking who they might find, and God, in the form of Jesus Christ, humbled Himself and died on the cross. He paid the ultimate price so that He could possess this treasure in us, you and I.

And may I reference one more scripture that reinforces God's attitude toward us being a treasure in His eyes?

> *But now, God's Message, the God who made you in the first*
> *place, Jacob, the One who got you started, Israel: "Don't be*
> *afraid, I've redeemed you. I've called your name. You're mine.*
> *When you're in over your head, I'll be there with you. When you're*
> *in rough waters, you will not go down. When you're between a*

*rock and a hard place, it won't be a dead end—Because I am God,
your personal God, The Holy of Israel, your Savior. I paid a huge
price for you: all of Egypt, with rich Cush and Seba thrown in!
That's how much you mean to me! That's how much I love you! I'd
sell off the whole world to get you back, trade the creation just for
you. (Isaiah 43:1–5, MSG)*

The third parable is found in Mark 4:26–29

*Then Jesus said, "God's kingdom is like seed thrown on a field
by a man who then goes to bed and forgets about it. The seed
sprouts and grows—he has no idea how it happens. The earth
does it all without his help: first a green stem of grass, then a bud,
then the ripened grain. When the grain is fully formed, he reaps—
harvest time!" (Mark 4:26–29, TPT)*

We are that man; we have been commanded to spread the Gospel, the too-good-to-be-true Good News to all mankind. The great commission is found in Matthew 28 and Mark 16. We are commanded to go and spread this Good News. Period, exclamation point, no need for further explanation. Well, yes, there is need for additional explanation; that just sounded kinda cool in my head when I was writing it. LOL. There is, in fact, need to explain this further because we clearly do not have enough laborers in the field spreading the seed.

We also see it in Romans:

*But how can people call on him for help if they've not yet
believed? And how can they believe in one they've not yet heard
of? And how can they hear the message of life if there is no one
there to proclaim it? And how can the message be proclaimed if
messengers have yet to be sent? That's why the Scriptures say:
How welcome is the arrival of those proclaiming the joyful news of
peace and of good things to come! (Romans 10:14–15, TPT)*

And once there is a field ripe for harvest, are there laborers available to reap that harvest? It would seem not!

*He turned to his disciples and said, "The harvest is huge and
ripe! But there are not enough harvesters to bring it all in. As you
go, plead with the Owner of the Harvest to thrust out many more
reapers to harvest his grain!" (Matthew 9:37–38, TPT)*

When he looked out over the crowds, his heart broke. So
confused and aimless they were, like sheep with no shepherd.
"What a huge harvest!" he said to his disciples. "How few
workers! On your knees and pray for harvest hands!" (MSG)

We need to be very purposeful in the spreading of the seed, the Word of God! We cannot be oblivious to the power in the Word of God from which we speak of.

So shall My word be that goes forth from My mouth; It shall not
return to Me void, But it shall accomplish what I please, And it
shall prosper in the thing for which I sent it. (Isaiah 55:11, NKJV)

When we spread His Word, that word will take root, and there will be a harvest. Some will sow the Word, others will water it, and still others will harvest it. At any given time, we can and should be doing one, if not all, these functions within God's timing for that individual soul from which we are led to minister to.

See Matthew 13:1–23, Mark 4:1–20, and Luke 8:4–15.

The parable of sowing the seed—I have to be honest, growing up in the LA suburb of Downey, I did not have an appreciation for this parable. Although at one time prior to the 1960s it had been an agricultural area, Downey was transitioning away from AG while I was growing up. I remember some orange groves and cattle/dairy farms in the area, but they are very dim memories. My Mammy and Pappy had one of the old orange trees in their backyard. I was always tasked to climb the tree to harvest some oranges. Usually about once a week, I was tasked to harvest them, but it was worth the climb as they were very sweet oranges. As a side note, it was the only time that I was encouraged to climb a tree! So as a preadolescent, I was in heaven! So yes, I really did not have an appreciation for sowing and reaping. All I ever did was reap what another man sowed.

And I must admit, my understanding of this scripture was rather manipulated by what I saw on the silver screen. Hollywood, in trying to illustrate this parable, kind of misguided this young mind. In one of the many movies on the life of Christ, they had Jesus, while telling this parable, reach into a huge barley sack of seed. He grabbed a handful of seed, and while explaining how the seed is spread on the path and amongst the thorns and such, they illustrated this by Jesus tossing some seed in the aforementioned locations. I thought to myself, "Why would Jesus purposely toss good seed on the walking path or in amongst the thorns? Did He not know what the end result would be?" This misguided understanding did not prevent me from telling others of the Good News. I just filed the thought away, until now. As of this writing, the Holy Spirit brought back some memories as they apply to this.

Please bear with me on the next four or five paragraphs; there is truly a point beyond planting a front yard.

In 1992, I purchased my first home. It was in a new housing development in Wichita. The development was located on what was formerly a wheat field. The soil was rich, very dark in color, and you could smell the nutrients in it as you sifted your fingers through the dirt. When it came time put my first yard in, the ground needed some preparation work. As it had been a construction site, there was hidden construction debris in the ground. I bought a rototiller and proceeded to go over the soil of what would become my front yard and backyard. As I turned the soil over, whenever I saw a shard of glass or a chunk of concrete or any other type of construction debris, I would bend down and pick it up to throw it away. I did this over and over each day for close to two weeks. You would be surprised how much stuff I cleaned from the soil. Me, being the engineer that I am, wanted to design out opportunities for failure. I had toddlers at the time and did not want them to be playing barefoot on the grass and come up with a shard of glass in their foot or to stub a toe on a chunk of concrete. Now the soil was properly turned over and large clods of dirt broken; now was the time to plant. Fescue was the grass of choice for south central Kansas, and I would be planting in the fall. I rented a verticutter machine that cut grooves into the soil and then it would lay seed into the grooves.

Once planted, I was very excited to see the fruit of all my labor. I put up stakes with string stretched between to help prevent people from walking across the "grass." Remember, I was a newbie; after a week or so, I began to get discouraged, no sprouting yet. Each morning I would wake up to see what I could see, finally I started seeing one blade here and one blade there poking through the soil. And as if on cue, overnight the entire yard had these blades of grass sprouting, so much so that it looked like green peach fuzz all over the yard. You could see the paths that I took with the verticutter in the lines of the blades of grass poking through the ground. My yard was coming in. In Wichita, in the fall, there is just enough of a growing season before the freeze to get a good crop started; that crop can be wheat or, as in this case, Fescue grass. My lawn became established and then went dormant during the winter. But by spring, it came back to life and was flourishing. I made sure to water it and cut that grass. I got on a schedule of fertilizing it three times a year. In back of my mind (I wrongly thought), the measure of a man is in some ways gauged by the condition of his front lawn grass. I groomed (mowed) it twice a week in differing mow patterns to help stimulate growth. I also used a mulching lawn mower so as to recycle the grass clippings back into the yard.

The following fall, I teamed up with two other neighbors to care for our yards. Now was the time to "overseed" the yards. My neighbors were well-seasoned Wichitians, so I was learning proper lawn care from them. We mowed the yard at each level on the mower until we were down to level one. Each time we mowed the yard, we were bagging the grass instead of mulching. Unlike the first planting of the grass that required a rototiller and a verticutter seed spreader, this operation would require much more time and many more tools. We rented an aerator and verticutter while I also bought a drop spreader for the seed and fertilizer. With all three neighbors working together, one using the aerator on the first yard, then followed by the one working the verticutter followed by the drop spreader of the seed. Each yard received a very good coverage of seed. To be quite honest, the yards looked quite abused. The aerator would bore a hole into the ground and expel a round chunk of dirt that resembled dog droppings. My yard looked better before we over seeded. This time, within two weeks, the yard was definitely showing signs of growth. First in the holes the aerator bored; now you had multiple blades of grass shooting up out of the hole. Now to me they resembled that of the plugs that a man gets who is trying to reverse his balding. You know the ones where they take from the back of the head and transplant the hair to the front and plug them in—well, that is how my front yard looked. All these green plugs. Then the growth started happening in the grooves from the verticutter. By the end of fall, before the grass turn dormant, it was looking real good. So much thicker than before.

The next fall, my grandmother had died. I had been planning on using winterize fertilizer on the yard but had put it off. The last real opportunity to do it before it was too late in the season was the day I was leaving for the flight to Los Angeles for Mammy's funeral. I hastily ran the drop spreader with the fertilizer in the dim lighting of twilight. I thought I gave it some good coverage. Well, in the spring, it was very evident what my paths were with the drop spreader. Along the path of the fertilizer, the grass was very thick and healthy, but the areas that did not get the coverage were thin. With that new lesson, I purchased a broadcast spreader for the next application of seed and fertilizer. Well, the broadcast spreader has issues as well; when applying the seed or fertilizer, there is a lot of overspray of the seed onto the driveway or sidewalk as well as into the flower beds. By the fourth spring, I had a lawn that many would envy. I continued to mow it twice a week. When you walked on it barefoot, it was like walking on carpet.

To prepare the soil for the application of the seed, I used three different tools: rototiller for fresh soil and to overseed we used an aerator and verticutter. To spread the seed and later the fertilizer, we used both a drop spreader and a broadcast spreader. Looking back now, this all takes time. and to effectively do a good job, one needs to use the appropriate tool for the given task. It would not make sense to use the rototiller if you were wanting to overseed. As I learned, if you are going to spread fertilizer and do not have much time, use the broadcast spreader to ensure even coverage rather than the drop spreader.

We are all called to preach the Gospel of Jesus Christ to Judea, Jerusalem, Samaria, and to the ends of the earth. This is our mandate.

> *I planted the seed, Apollos watered the plants, but God made you grow. It's not the one who plants or the one who waters who is at the center of this process but God, who makes things grow. Planting and watering are menial servant jobs at minimum wages. What makes them worth doing is the God we are serving. You happen to be God's field in which we are working. (1 Corinthians 3:6–9, MSG)*

This is the lesson I am learning from this. When we are spreading the seed, the Gospel of Jesus Christ, we need to use the broadcast spreader. Its reach is far and wide and spreads the seed in small nooks and crannies. The broadcast spreader is pretty indiscriminant in the spreading of the seed. We should be likewise: do not go into a situation with any sort of bias presupposition that a given person would not be receptive of the Gospel. We do not know what kind of day they have had. We do not know what is going on in their lives. We are only called to indiscriminately spread the Gospel of

Jesus Christ. And we trust that God will provide the increase.

With the drop spreader, it delivers in a much-targeted area a high concentration of fertilizer. With proper planning, you can ensure that the nutrients needed for growth gets full coverage for the entire field. When we have an established believer, we can be like the drop spreader and be very targeted in nurturing in concentrated doses the Word to the disciple that we are mentoring. You may plant, I may water, but God causes the increase; and at other times, I plant, you water, but still God causes the increase. We are colaborers with God to advancing the kingdom of God!

So what kind of means or methods can we consider for a broadcast spreader and a drop spreader?

Well, a broadcast spreader really is an outgrowth of your lifestyle. When people see you and the change that God has made in your life, this is broadcasted to your Judea, Jerusalem, and some cases your Samaria. These are your personal contacts that you can interact face-to-face on a regular basis. In today's life, those who see us daily has increased now with social media, Facebook, Instagram, Twitter, and you name any other platform. These are natural platforms to take a stand for Christ. The message of Christ can be broadcast to the world from the comforts of your home on your smartphone. We can take a stand for Christ, standing on these platforms in the middle of the town square proclaiming the Good News, both in person and online.

The drop spreader, like the broadcast spreader, is face-to-face. This is the day in–and–day out opportunity to invest in the lives of other brothers and sisters in Christ through discipleship and accountability. Yes, we can use the social media for this as well, as long as it is in a private message when dealing with private matters. This is through sending encouraging scripture and messages to help build up that brother or sister in the Lord. By doing this, we are watering and fertilizing the seed; maybe we planted that seed, or maybe another, no matter, it is our responsibility to encourage others in the Lord, to edify them and build them up in the Word and in our prayers.

In December, Laura was upstairs and proceeded to walk down to speak with me. While still on the stairs, she informed me that she just had a vision. She stopped at the lower landing on the stairs and shared the vision. We were in the middle of a very large field where the soil was dry and hard. There was this very large and ominous plow in the field that would require two very large oxen to drive it. But no oxen was in sight to drive the plow. It was only Laura and I. The impression was that this is a time for work and not a time for jubilee. We were to work the field and turn the soil over to prepare for planting. After working the soil, it became very dark and rich with nutrients, so rich you could smell it. The field was planted resulting in a sea of golden wheat flowing in the wind with a deep, rich blue sky in the background.

On February first of 2019, just six days after having taken the Department of Corrections class to get the badge to go into the prisons, we were given the opportunity to facilitate Victory Bible College classes at a local prison. Every day Laura and I prayed, "Thy kingdom come, Thy will be done, in earth as it is in heaven." Well, it did not take us too long to realize that this was a divine appointment, and in reality, since we always pray for God's will in our lives, this was a slam-dunk, no-brainer yes! We will do this! Laura told the dream in class. One student asked if they were our dirt; Laura exclaimed no! Dirt has a bad connotation—no, they are the soil, rich soil from which to invest in.

> But how are people to call upon Him Whom they have not believed [in Whom they have no faith, on Whom they have no reliance]? And how are they to believe in Him [adhere to, trust in, and rely upon Him] of Whom they have never heard? And how are they to hear without a preacher? (Romans 10:14, AMPC)

The fourth parable is found in Matthew 13:31–32:

> Then Jesus taught them another parable: "Heaven's kingdom realm can be compared to the tiny mustard seed that a man takes and plants in his field. Although the smallest of all the seeds, it eventually grows into the greatest of garden plants, becoming a tree for birds to come and build their nests in its branches." (Matthew 13:31–32, TPT)

We know that Jesus is the sower of the seed; He plants the Word of God in our hearts. We know that the mustard seed is the smallest seed known of at that time. But with this, also when fully grown, it can reach to about ten feet tall. The mustard seed represents the Good News, the Gospel of Jesus Christ, first starting small but growing to reach literally millions throughout the world. It is in the spreading of the Gospel; we are spreading the kingdom of God. The symbolism of the tree being large enough to offer refuge to birds refers to us seeking refuge and life in the kingdom of God. Yes, I admit, no new revelation with this short interpretation of the mustard seed. But please remember, this writing is going out to whomever attains it; this could be, in fact, the first time they ever have read about it in Matthew 13… I just did not want the mustard seed to be overlooked. LOL. Okay, I just had to put this one in there: When Christ says that if we have the faith, that of a mustard seed, we can command the mountain to be thrown into the sea and it will happen. We have this mustard seed of faith when we come to Christ; we also have this mustard seed of faith to move mountains. It is a gift from God that will bear much fruit!

The fifth parable is found in the following verse:

> Then he taught them another parable: "Heaven's kingdom realm can be compared to yeast that a woman takes and blends into three measures of flour and then waits until all the dough rises." (Matthew 13:33, TPT)

Now, unlike other stories that Jesus told where the yeast is referring to the false teaching of the Pharisees, here we find that the yeast is directly referring to the kingdom of God. This parable foretells how the Gospel of Jesus Christ will spread throughout the world. The kingdom of God will be widespread through all the corners of the world.

I know in today's world, we have instant this and instant that; if we must wait more than three minutes in the drive-through at McDonalds, man, the world must be crashing in! I mean, we just must have our coffee and McGriddles in three minutes or less! So in a world that existed before Pillsbury Dough Boy, if you wanted your bread to rise, you needed a small amount of yeast. Yeast is microscopic in size, yet only a very little is needed to be kneaded into the dough. But give it some time, and that little yeast will spread throughout the dough. The kingdom of God is much like this yeast. The domain of Jesus started with the twelve, grew to seventy, and on the day of Pentecost, another three thousand was added. How about that for exponential growth! And now it has spread throughout the entire world. There is an old saying attributed to St. Francis of Assisi, "Preach the Gospel at all times. Use words if necessary." We need to live this Good News in our daily lives, day in and day out. The change that has been made manifest in our lives by the power of the blood of Jesus Christ should compel those around us to ask what has brought about the change!

The very nature of yeast is to change whatever it comes in contact with. This is the change to the culture that our lives need to be kneaded into our sphere of influence to bring about the kingdom of God. Just like yeast infects the dough, our lives and the change that Christ makes infect the culture around us. It is a slow transformation, but it will happen. And just like that yeast that causes the dough to rise, we will bring about the kingdom of God in a comprehensive manner, complete and with finality.

> *For the earth will be filled with the knowledge of the glory of the Lord as the waters cover the sea. (Habakkuk 2:14, ESV)*

We also can reference Psalm 72:19 and Daniel 2:25 for how complete the spreading of the Gospel will be, through our allowing Him to work in our lives. And like yeast, the change is made from within. Christ changes our hearts and lives from within our spirit and soul and, with that seed, changes the world. As we remain in our own world, sphere of influence, as God works His change within us, people see the change. We don't cuss like we used to. We don't go to the bars or whatever vice we were into. People notice. We are a witness for the kingdom through the change that is being worked in our life. All the while, the work that yeast does to the dough is an invisible work. God's work on us from the inside out and is invisible, yet His effect is most definitely evident to all who know us! His grace working in our hearts is very visible for all to see. This transformation that is happening literally before the eyes of those around us is described here:

> *And we all, with unveiled face, beholding the glory of the Lord, are being transformed into the same image from one degree of glory to another. For this comes from the Lord who is the Spirit. (1 Corinthians 3:18, ESV)*

I started thinking more about that Pillsbury Dough Boy can of biscuits—how when we peel off the outer wrapping of the can, I do it very carefully not to initiate the "pop." I then take the can in the hand, strike it on the kitchen counter, and I really look forward to hearing the classic "pop." I got to wondering why it pops—well, obviously it is under pressure, but it must not be under pressure when it was first packaged. My intuition was that when it was packaged, it had a certain small amount of yeast in it, and given the nature of yeast and how it expands, this must explain how it was now under pressure. When I got home, I continued my search for wisdom on all things yeast and looked to the all-wise google for assistance. This was to no avail.

The sixth parable is found in Matthew 13:52:

> He said to them, Therefore every teacher and interpreter of the
> Sacred Writings who has been instructed about and trained for the
> kingdom of heaven and has become a disciple is like a householder
> who brings forth out of his storehouse treasure that is new and
> [treasure that is] old [the fresh as well as the familiar]. (AMPC)

> He said, "Then you see how every student well-trained in God's
> kingdom is like the owner of a general store who can put his hands
> on anything you need, old or new, exactly when you need it."
> (MSG)

> He responded, "Every scholar of the Scriptures, who is
> instructed in the ways of heaven's kingdom realm, is like a wealthy
> home owner with his house filled with treasures both new and old.
> And he knows how and when to bring them out to show others."
> (TPT)

I am reminded of the passing of my grandparents and then ten years later
my parents. My brother had the household contents of both in a storage
shed. I was tasked with rummaging through all this "stuff" to consolidate it
from two storage rooms to one. I found love letters between Mom and Dad
when he was stationed in France. Family photos were hidden in all kinds
of boxes. I found boxes of old racetrack programs and wagering tickets. I
had asked my sister and cousins for assistance in the sorting, but no help
was given from the family. Such a task of consolidating two generations
of history of your family, what to keep, what to throw out. In the end, I
packed two loads into the five-by-eight trailer full of stuff off to the dump.
There were the obvious ones: these decorative shelves that Pappy made, I
found one each for the grandkids. In the end, I made some mistakes. I found
that the old racetrack programs and wagering tickets should not have been
thrown out for tax purposes. Mom's antique couch, I wish I would have
saved—would go well in my 1906 home. The lesson—one person's trash is
another's treasure. I do not think it fair that I was the sole determining factor
as to what was a family treasure and not. I was not the originator of some
of these family heirlooms, so how do I equate a value of this treasure? But
as it applies to this parable, I needed to operate in wisdom and discernment
and approach it in prayer. Yes, sometimes when we get to share the Gospel

with someone, we can get real excited! In this excitement we want to throw everything at them, including the kitchen sink. Being in a constant attitude of prayer, we can be ready to share because we have been praying for wisdom and discernment; we can share the Word as He determines because every fish requires a different bait to catch them.

> *Study to show yourself approved to God, a workman that needs not to be ashamed, rightly dividing the word of truth. (2 Timothy 2:15, NKJV)*

We as believers in the Lord Jesus Christ need to follow this in 2 Timothy while being led by the Holy Spirit as we are sharing the acceptable year of our Lord to preach the kingdom. We must operate in wisdom as we share the "treasures" of both old and new. This is in reference to the Old Covenant and the New Covenant, presenting the entire treasure of the Word of God in season at the right time as we share the Gospel of Jesus Christ. God is the same, yesterday, today, and tomorrow. It is our responsibility to share the Word in its entirety in wisdom and grace and love.

The seventh parable is found in Matthew 13:

> *Or, God's kingdom is like a fishnet cast into the sea, catching all kinds of fish. When it is full, it is hauled onto the beach. The good fish are picked out and put in a tub; those unfit to eat are thrown away. That's how it will be when the curtain comes down on history. The angels will come and cull the bad fish and throw them in the garbage. There will be a lot of desperate complaining, but it won't do any good. (Matthew 13:47–50, MSG)*

> *Again, heaven's kingdom realm is like a fisherman who casts his large net into the lake, catching an assortment of different kinds of fish. When the net was filled, the fishermen hauled it up on the shore, and they all sat down to sort out their catch. They collected the good fish in baskets and threw the bad away. And so it will be at the close of the age. The messengers will come and separate the evil from among the godly and throw them into the fiery furnace, where they will experience great sorrow, pain, and anguish. (TPT)*

We were told to be fishers of men. It is our responsibility to cast the nets. The net will catch all manner of fish, large and small. Fish of many differing types, regardless of their inherent value (tasty or foul). The Gospel attracts many types of people: those who desire to repent, turn from their wicked ways, and follow Christ, and it will also attract those who might be considered a false believer, one who is masquerading as a Christian for selfish gain. We are not to be judges between the good fish and the bad fish; that is to be left to the two messengers. The bad fish or false believers—they are these can be considered be likened to the hearers of God's Word, the seed that falls on rocky and thorny soil. In Matthew 12:5–7, to not be mistaken, God will not be mocked; there will be a day of reckoning when God the Heavenly Father will separate the true blood-bought believers in Jesus Christ from the wannabe pretenders, and those wannabe pretenders will be cast into the pit of hell. We see this again in Matthew 25:31–46. We will look at the Matthew 25:31–46 in more depth in a later chapter.

CHAPTER 2
PASSION | KEY ONE

Passion—you either have it or you don't; you cannot manufacture it. We might be able to fake passion for a little while. Fake it well enough to fool to those around us, but in all honesty, over time, the only one we fool with this fake passion is ourselves.

> *"Teacher, which is the great commandment in the law?" Jesus said to him, "'You shall love the Lord your God with all your heart, with all your soul, and with all your mind.' This is the first and great commandment. And the second is like it: 'You shall love your neighbor as yourself.' On these two commandments hang all the Law and the Prophets." (Matthew 22:36–40, NKJV)*

A true genuine love produces fruit. We see that in the natural. Think of springtime and new love between a man and woman; he is off buying flowers and little gifts and trinkets. She is making his favorite meal. Love produces fruit. It is no different with God. Our love for Him must produce fruit; if it does not, we are only faking and lying to ourselves.

> *As the Father loved Me, I also have loved you; abide in My love. If you keep My commandments, you will abide in My love, just as I have kept My Father's commandments and abide in His love. These things I have spoken to you, that My joy may remain in you, and that your joy may be full. This is My commandment, that you love one another as I have loved you. Greater love has no one than this, than to lay down one's life for his friends. You are My friends if you do whatever I command you. No longer do I call you servants, for a servant does not know what his master is doing; but I have called you friends, for all things that I heard from My Father I have made known to you. You did not choose Me, but I chose you and appointed you that you should go and bear fruit, and that your fruit should remain, that whatever you ask the Father in My name He may give you. These things I command you, that you love one another. (John 15: 9–17, NKJV)*

An interesting thing about fruit—the object, whether tree or man, does not consume one's own fruit. We produce fruit for others to consume and benefit from. What kind of fruit am I referring to? Apples, oranges…no, in Galatians we read the following:

> But the fruit of the Spirit is love, joy, peace, patience, kindness, goodness, faithfulness, gentleness, self-control; against such things there is no law. (Galatians 5:22–23, ESV)

So if we are not to consume them, who then? Ah, that is where our Judea, Jerusalem, and Samaria come in. When we die to self, allow the Holy Spirit to work in us to bring His love, His joy, His peace, His patience, His kindness, His goodness, His faithfulness, His gentleness, His self-control, then all men shall be drawn to Jesus.

> Do not merely listen to the word, and so deceive yourselves. Do what it says. (James 1:22, NIV)

> He replied, "Blessed rather are those who hear the word of God and obey it." (Luke 11:28, NIV)

> Pure and unblemished religion [as it is expressed in outward acts] in the sight of our God and Father is this: to visit and look after the fatherless and the widows in their distress, and to keep oneself uncontaminated by the [secular] world. (James 1:26–27, AMP)

> Anyone who sets himself up as "religious" by talking a good game is self-deceived. This kind of religion is hot air and only hot air. Real religion, the kind that passes muster before God the Father, is this: Reach out to the homeless and loveless in their plight, and guard against corruption from the godless world. (MSG)

These outward acts are a demonstration of the love for our Father in heaven. No, I am not saying that these acts save us. We do not get saved because of works. But I am saying that they are a gauge for what is happening inside our hearts. We see this reinforced by the following warnings in Matthew.

> When the Son of Man appears in his majestic glory, with all his angels by his side, he will take his seat on his throne of splendor, and all the nations will be gathered together before him. And like a shepherd who separates the sheep from the goats, he will separate all the people. The "sheep" he will put on his right side and the

"goats" on his left. Then the King will turn to those on his right and say, "You have a special place in my Father's heart. Come and experience the full inheritance of the kingdom realm that has been destined for you from before the foundation of the world! For when you saw me hungry, you fed me. When you found me thirsty, you gave me something to drink. When I had no place to stay, you invited me in, and when I was poorly clothed, you covered me. When I was sick, you tenderly cared for me, and when I was in prison you visited me." Then the godly will answer him, "Lord, when did we see you hungry or thirsty and give you food and something to drink? When did we see you with no place to stay and invite you in? When did we see you poorly clothed and cover you? When did we see you sick and tenderly care for you, or in prison and visit you?" And the King will answer them, "Don't you know? When you cared for one of the least important of these my little ones, my true brothers and sisters, you demonstrated love for me." (Matthew 25:31–40, TPT)

So I must ask: Are we, the body of Christ, doing this? Yes, some are, but really, are we doing it? I firmly believe that if the body of Christ were really doing what we should be doing, there would not be a need for government food stamps or (EBT) cards. The poor would not be living from day to day in tattered clothing. They would not go to bed hungry or thirsty. The orphanages would be empty. Hospitals would go out of business because His followers come in and pray under the authority that Christ gave them, and healings would be commonplace. The elderly would not be dying in "assisted living" facilities, having never had a visitor (60 percent never have one now). The prisons would be a location for revival, and the idea of repeat offenders would be a thing of the past.

But sadly, the church, the body of Christ, is not doing all that we can in obeying His commands to spread the Gospel to all peoples. Okay, now from the body of Christ down to the individual stakeholder. You and I, are we, as individuals, doing all that we can? At the end of the day, we will all individually stand before our King and hear one of two things coming from the mouth of the King: "Well done, my good and faithful servant, come, enter into the kingdom prepared for you." Or we will hear, "DEPART FROM ME, I NEVER KNEW YOU!" Which shall it be?

Let us take a look at another time in Matthew where Jesus says those same words, "Depart from me, I never knew you." This is found in the following verse:

> At the time my coming draws near, heaven's kingdom realm can be compared to ten maidens who took their oil lamps and went outside to meet the bridegroom and his bride. Five of them were foolish and ill-prepared, for they took no extra oil for their lamps. Five of them were wise and sensible, for they took flasks of olive oil with their lamps. When the bridegroom didn't come when they expected, they all grew drowsy and fell asleep. Then suddenly, in the middle of the night, they were awakened by the shout "Get up! The bridegroom is here! Come out and have an encounter with him!' So all the girls got up and trimmed their lamps. But the foolish ones were running out of oil, so they said to the five wise ones, 'Share your oil with us, because our lamps are going out!" "We can't," they replied. "We don't have enough for all of us. You'll have to go and buy some for yourselves!" While the five girls were out buying oil, the bridegroom appeared. Those who were ready and waiting were escorted inside with him and the wedding party to enjoy the feast. And then the door was locked. Later, the five foolish girls came running up to the door and pleaded, "Lord, Lord, let us come in!" But he called back, "Go away! Do I know you? I can assure you, I don't even know you!" That is the reason you should always stay awake and be alert, because you don't know the day or hour when the Bridegroom will appear. (Matthew 25:1–13, TPT)

We all bear fruit; it is just that we need to examine what kind of fruit are we bearing. Is it fruits unto righteousness or unrighteousness? Much like your car has an array of gauges on the dashboard. We can see how our oil level is, what percentage of life we have before that oil needs to be changed. There is a gauge displaying battery power life as well as engine temperature. I believe it is time that we need to look at the gauges on our internal spiritual dashboard. What does our battery life look like? How does our oil look? What is our temperature? What does Jesus say about our temperature in Revelation?

> I know you inside and out, and find little to my liking. You're not

*cold, you're not hot—far better to be either cold or hot! You're
stale. You're stagnant. You make me want to vomit. You brag, "I'm
rich, I've got it made, I need nothing from anyone," oblivious that
in fact you're a pitiful, blind beggar, threadbare and homeless.
(Revelation 3:15–17, MSG)*

*I know all that you do, and I know that you are neither frozen in
apathy nor fervent with passion. How I wish you were either one or
the other! But because you are neither cold nor hot, but lukewarm,
I am about to spit you from my mouth. For you claim, "I'm rich
and getting richer—I don't need a thing." Yet you are clueless that
you're miserable, poor, blind, barren, and naked! (TPT)*

So what am I saying? We, as the body of Christ, need to find our first love
again. We need the passion of Christ to drive us into love for Him and our
fellow mankind. We need to find our first love! We need to abide in Him
and He in us.

*If I speak in the tongues of men and of angels, but have not love,
I am a noisy gong or a clanging cymbal. And if I have prophetic
powers, and understand all mysteries and all knowledge, and if
I have all faith, so as to remove mountains, but have not love, I
am nothing. If I give away all I have, and if I deliver up my body
to be burned, but have not love, I gain nothing. Love is patient
and kind; love does not envy or boast; it is not arrogant or rude.
It does not insist on its own way; it is not irritable or resentful; it
does not rejoice at wrongdoing, but rejoices with the truth. Love
bears all things, believes all things, hopes all things, endures all
things. Love never ends. As for prophecies, they will pass away;
as for tongues, they will cease; as for knowledge, it will pass
away. For we know in part and we prophesy in part, but when the
perfect comes, the partial will pass away. When I was a child, I
spoke like a child, I thought like a child, I reasoned like a child.
When I became a man, I gave up childish ways. For now we see
in a mirror dimly, but then face to face. Now I know in part; then
I shall know fully, even as I have been fully known. So now faith,
hope, and love abide, these three; but the greatest of these is love.
(1 Corinthians 12:1–13, ESV)*

As I began writing this, it was the middle of January, and all the local fitness gyms were experiencing the same thing: waning attendance numbers. When January 1 rolls around each year, we all look at our midsections and regret those second servings of pumpkin pie. We make the New Year resolutions and sign up for a three-year contract with the latest trendy fitness craze. Spin classes, Zumba, CrossFit, and now it is the Hot Box... We get real amped up on the latest and greatest, spend all this money, and it is evidenced by how crowded the parking lot is outside the gym come the first weekend of January. But as I noted earlier, it is just mid-January; it is a lot easier now to find a spot in the parking lot. Why, because the passion for fitness has not held up even two weeks, because it was manufactured. The following is my post from FB dated ten years ago:

> Yesterday, I hit the treadmill in the morning for 30 minutes and hit the row machine last night for 30 minutes. Today I swam for 40 minutes and went .57 miles... Will hit the Firehouse Spin Session tonight for two hours. Consistency and mixing it up...to keep it fun in the winter months. It is working for me.

This effort did work. I went from 230 down to 190, and I kept it off for about five years. Sadly, I am back up to 230.

How do we keep the passion for what God has called us to do? Well, the answer is noted above—consistency. We are called to be consistently in an attitude of prayer.

> *Rejoice always, pray without ceasing, in everything give thanks; for this is the will of God in Christ Jesus for you. (1 Thessalonians 5:16–18, NKJV)*

> *But you, beloved, building yourselves up in your most holy faith and praying in the Holy Spirit, keep yourselves in the love of God as you await the mercy of our Lord Jesus Christ to bring you eternal life. (Jude 1:20–21, NKJV)*

As you pray and continue to pray, taking on the mind of Christ, His passion will become your passion. His desire that all men come to Him for salvation, this desire will become more of a driving force in your life. That desire will cause you to see more and more opportunities to share the love of Christ. More doors will open, and the easier it will be to step through that door to witness.

The more that I started contemplating the entirety of "passion," the more that I feel lead to watch Mel Gibson's movie, The Passion of Christ. Why, you might ask? Of all the movies about the Christ that I have watched, no other one has touched me as this one. His love for us was/is so deep. He freely volunteered to endure one of the most brutal deaths that hell has ever imagined. The death on the cross, but wait, there is more: because He endured the beatings—and by beatings, I am speaking to many different kinds of beatings. After the crown of thorns were pounded into his skull, they then blindfolded him. While blindfolded, they then would hit him in the face, in Matthew 26:67–68.

Then they spit in his face and struck him with their fists. Others slapped him and said, "Prophesy to us, Messiah. Who hit you?" (Matthew 26:67–68, NIV)

In high school, I walked away from several fights—yes, punches were thrown, and some I was able to dodge, the others that struck me, some I was able to deflect some of that energy. But the Christ was blindfolded. He had no ability in the natural to be able to anticipate and deflect the blows; He just stood there silently took each blow like the perfect lamb of God that He is and was. The beatings to his face were so brutal that it is said that He was unrecognizable as a human being. He was flogged and scourged. The flogging consisted of two individuals striking Him on either side of Him with thick rods of wood that was thick enough to cast a significant blow but thin enough to flex and snap like a whip. Once they were finished, the two "individuals" then switched to a cat o' nine tails. This whip had a strong leather handle with leather straps that extended approximately eighteen to twenty-four inches, and at the tip had shards of glass, stone, metal, and shards of bone woven into them. Remember, this execution and beating was under Roman law and infliction, not under the Israelite law of punishment. Jewish law required to limit the lashing with the cat o' nine tails to 39 lashings, but under Roman law, the lashings could go as high as 150. During these lashings, once the whip was laid on Jesus, the shards of glass, stone, metal, and shards of bone penetrated the flesh, grabbing ahold of it, then the executioner would rip it back, causing the shards of glass, stone, metal, and shards of bone to rip flesh off of Jesus. It is said that so much flesh had been pulled off of Him that ribs and spinal column were visible. I do not know how authentic the Shroud of Turin is, but those who have examined it indicate that there are at least 120 distinct lashings from head to calf, some wrapping around to the front of the torso. Our Messiah, the Christ, His love for us is so intense that He endured all the pain and brutal beating of the cross for us; that is the true definition of passion.

> *Do you see what this means—all these pioneers who blazed the way, all these veterans cheering us on? It means we'd better get on with it. Strip down, start running—and never quit! No extra spiritual fat, no parasitic sins. Keep your eyes on Jesus, who both began and finished this race we're in. Study how he did it. Because he never lost sight of where he was headed—that exhilarating finish in and with God—he could put up with anything along the way: Cross, shame, whatever. And now he's there, in the place of honor, right alongside God. When you find yourselves flagging in your faith, go over that story again, item by item, that long litany of hostility he plowed through. That will shoot adrenaline into your souls! (Hebrews 12:2–3, MSG)*

I suggest you do likewise if the movie is available. We need to put on the mind of Christ. I believe that to fully understand what that means, we need to also understand what His motivation was for going to the cross. That motivation was His passion for us. Read the accounts in all four gospels. We are also told in Matthew:

> *Then Jesus said to his disciples, "Whoever wants to be my disciple must deny themselves and take up their cross and follow me." (Matthew 16:24, NIV)*

Does that mean that we literally die in the physical? In most cases, I would say, no, we need to daily deny ourselves of all that this world has to offer (die to the flesh) and live for Him. This is a daily, moment-by-moment dying to self. It is a moment-by-moment basking in being in His presence. It is in the dying that we can really tap into His passion. This is the sustainable passion as long as our devotion to our Heavenly Father continues to grow and flourish. Being in His manifest presence will cause your passion to grow, as we abide in Him and He abides in us.

The other night, while going through the video-teaching series at the prison for Victory Bible College, I was given the following word about abiding in Christ. And so at the end of the teaching, I broke into some *Looney Tunes*!

"Th-th-the-th-th-the-th-th-that's all, folks!"

Here comes some *Looney Tunes* you will have to endure through some of my peculiarities—that is how God made me. The reference scripture was John 14:15

> *You may ask me for anything in my name, and I will do it. If you love me, keep my commands. And I will ask the Father, and he will give you another advocate to help you and be with you forever—* *(John 14:15, NIV)*

"If you love me, keep my commands." When the instructor was going through the definitions for "keep," he was saying it meant to "have or retain possession of." I had a vision of Daffy Duck in an episode with Bugs Bunny, "Ali Baba Bunny." Bugs and his strange friend Daffy were traveling in the desert. This is where Daffy finds a cave with riches beyond measure; a genie from a lamp casts a spell on Daffy and shrinks him down to about two inches. Later, on at Pismo Beach, Bugs finds a clam that had washed up on shore. He then opens the clam to find a pearl. Just then, the two-inch-tall Daffy is seen running up Bug's arm to the clam and grasps hold of the pearl with both wings (arms) and legs, screaming, "It's mine, mine, I tell you, it's all mine!"

As we abide in God, He abides in us. We need to be like Daffy with God! Grasp on to Him and say, "He's mine, mine, I tell you, He's all mine!" Now don't get me wrong—there is enough of God to go around for all of us. The "all" that I am referring to is the completeness of God: all that He was, all that He is, and all that He will ever be in the Godhead. That all is available to us as we abide in Him and He in us. His all in all, God the Father, God the Son, and God the Holy Spirit; three in one is available to us, in their full strength, power, and authority. Jesus says in John,

> *I give them eternal life, and they shall never perish; no one will snatch them out of my hand. My Father, who has given them to me, is greater than all; no one can snatch them out of my Father's hand. I and the Father are one. (John 10:28–29, NIV)*

As we abide in Him and He in us, we are tightly grasped inside the hand of the Creator of the universe! You are His, His, He exclaims to all, You are all His!

As we abide in Him and He in us, He is ours, ours, we exclaim to all, He is ours!

It is in this abiding that His manifest presence can be made known to us in all manner of manifestations—manifestations of healing of the entirety of our being (spirit, soul, and body) and the working of signs and wonders. This is the true source of the passion.

The other day, we were at the prison facilitating the VBC course on The Believers Authority. I was reminded of a task I had undertaken at home. We live in a house built in 1906. The tree that is on our property line is some 3.5 to 4 feet in diameter at its base. We do not know the age of the tree; it had been trimmed back some four years ago to just the stub of a trunk some fifteen feet tall. When we had bought the house in June of 2017; there were six to eight large branches that had grown out of the top of the stub trunk. These limbs were some six to fourteen inches in diameter. We had the tree trimmed back to the stub trunk in the fall of 2017. In mid-March, I decided to trim back the new growth. I thought it was a good time before the tree started to flow with sap. Once up on the stub trunk, I noticed that this tree was hollow on the inside. The outer layers of it were only about six to eight inches thick. Once I trimmed back the new growth, I stepped back to see this tree. By all outward appearance, this could be considered a dead tree. Even if you looked closely at the hollowed-out areas, one would not be impressed.

That was when it struck me, the outside world looks at my students in like manner. That there is no life in them, and their only worth is to be cut up and made firewood. But God! But God—as I was starting to clean up the small limb clippings, I noticed a fairly shocking thing. The cut limbs were bleeding a goodly amount of sap. He is the vine, and we are the branches, His life force flowing through us! My students are not dead; they are alive in Christ. Christ is transforming them into His image. His life is flowing in them!

I am the true vine, and My Father is the vinedresser. Every branch in Me that does not bear fruit He takes away; and every branch that bears fruit He prunes, that it may bear more fruit. You are already clean because of the word which I have spoken to you. Abide in Me, and I in you. As the branch cannot bear fruit of itself, unless it abides in the vine, neither can you, unless you abide in Me. "I am the vine, you are the branches. He who abides in Me, and I in him, bears much fruit; for without Me you can do nothing.

If anyone does not abide in Me, he is cast out as a branch and is withered; and they gather them and throw them into the fire, and they are burned. If you abide in Me, and My words abide in you, you will ask what you desire, and it shall be done for you. By this My Father is glorified, that you bear much fruit; so you will be My disciples. (John 15: 1–8, NKJV)

As we abide in Him and He abides in us, we will produce fruit! We will produce fruit in abundance! God's transformative power is manifest in these students at the facility. There is much life in them. I have learned that I am no better and no worse than they. I have had lust in my heart, means I have committed adultery; I have had hate in my heart, means that I have murdered. I revisit the cross at Calvary and really understand, or at least get a glimpse at the depths from which Christ paid the ultimate price so that I could have a relationship with Him. He suffered and died so that my grievous sins may be forgiven. How can I not love Him in return? And how can I not in turn obey Him when He commands me to go?

Even so, every good tree bears good fruit, but a bad tree bears bad fruit. A good tree cannot bear bad fruit, nor can a bad tree bear good fruit. Every tree that does not bear good fruit is cut down and thrown into the fire. Therefore by their fruits you will know them. (Matthew 7:17–20, NKJV)

My prayer for you today is this:

And may the Lord make you to increase and excel and overflow in love for one another and for all people, just as we also do for you, So that He may strengthen and confirm and establish your hearts faultlessly pure and unblamable in holiness in the sight of our God and Father, at the coming of our Lord Jesus Christ (the Messiah) with all His saints (the holy and glorified people of God)! Amen, (so be it)! (1 Thessalonians 3:12–13, AMPC)

May God our Father himself and our Master Jesus clear the road to you! And may the Master pour on the love so it fills your lives and splashes over on everyone around you, just as it does from us to you. May you be infused with strength and purity, filled with confidence in the presence of God our Father when our Master Jesus arrives with all his followers. (MSG)

And from the days of John the Baptist until the present time, the kingdom of heaven has endured violent assault, and violent men seize it by force [as a precious prize—a share in the heavenly kingdom is sought with most ardent zeal and intense exertion]. (Matthew 11:12, AMPC)

Let me tell you what's going on here: No one in history surpasses John the Baptizer; but in the kingdom he prepared you for, the lowliest person is ahead of him. For a long time now people have tried to force themselves into God's kingdom. But if you read the books of the Prophets and God's Law closely, you will see them culminate in John, teaming up with him in preparing the way for the Messiah of the kingdom. Looked at in this way, John is the "Elijah" you've all been expecting to arrive and introduce the Messiah. (MSG)

AROMA THERAPY

Back in about 1985, when I was working on the B-1B bomber, I was supporting the titanium weld shop. Because we were handling large plates of titanium, we were required to wear steel-tipped boots. These plates were three inches thick by five feet wide by about eighteen feet long. They were part of the wing-carry-through section of the plane that enables the wings to sweep back. To help keep my cloths clean, I also wore a work overcoat. One day, a female workmate of mine gingerly danced around a subject—well, I will put it bluntly: she asked if I showered each day because each morning, I came in very ripe-smelling. I was dumbfounded. I shower at least twice a day, in the morning and when I get home in the evening. Why would I stink? To add insult to injury, I kind of had a crush on her! It came down to one simple and overlooked habit. I came to work in one set of shoes, changed into the steel-tipped boots, then at the end of the day, I put the boots in my desk drawer along with my work overcoat. The overcoat absorbed the "aroma" of the boots. Problem solved: wash the overcoat and store the boots on the floor. I was glad that the workmate was bold enough to confront me. A lesson learned some thirty-four years ago, yet remembered today to examine aroma therapy.

Fast-forward a few years to the early '90s when the automotive industry was starting to explore the SUV market. I went on a test drive of an Isuzu Rodeo to see what the hype was all about. The local dealership in Santa Monica also sold other, more upscale auto brands. Given the neighborhood and the dealership, I had certain expectations about the test-drive. No, I was not expecting to be served Russian caviar and be given the royal treatment, but I was expecting a friendly, respectful (no pressure) salesman who knew his product well. Well, when I went on the test-drive, he sat in the front passenger side, and he explained quite thoroughly all the unique functions and features of this rodeo. The one thing that I did not expect was his bad breath! He had the worst case of halitosis that I had and have ever experienced in my life! It was so bad that even though I was enjoying the test-drive for the performance of the vehicle, I really had to cut the drive short and make a speedy return to the dealership! After some short pleasantries to shake the salesman off me, I quickly retreated to my own vehicle. In comfort of my car on the drive home, I was revisited by the odor of the halitosis, oh no! His breath permeated my clothes, and now I still smell him! In engineering terms, my clothes were "outgassing" whatever was absorbed from his breath. Once home, I quickly put the clothes in the wash…sat down to relax, and yet again, his breath was still there! His breath was in my hair! I quickly showered and frantically washed my hair several times. Still yet the smell lingered; it is embedded in my nostrils! I actually used a Q-tip dipped in some soap to clean my nose out. This finally did the trick; I was no longer haunted by the odor that invaded my space by this man.

A similar but opposite situation happened in '95. In the office where I worked, we had cubical partitions that would occupy four individuals with a center aisle connecting four or five cubicles. I sat in the second cubicle from the main aisle. There was this one administrative assistant who was into New Age religion. She had this unique perfume that she bragged about being customized to her biology. It was okay—I mean, it did not smell bad but was just a slight bit overpowering. She was also a smoker, so her sense of smell was altered by the smoking, so maybe she put on too much of this perfume. Either way, I would be sitting at my desk, with my back to the main aisle. I would smell her coming before she even turned down the connecting aisle to me sitting in the second cubicle. With my back turned and her being some twenty-plus feet away, I could anticipate her presence soon because of the aroma that preceded her from such a distance.

So by now, you are probably wondering just where I am going with this entire aromatic sensory overload. Well, if you are still with me on this one, I will get there eventually.

The first story of aroma therapy, in the natural, I stank, even though I showered a lot. I stank because of a habit I had developed. In the spiritual, I was washed in the blood; but because I was not renewing my mind daily, I was stuck in habitual sin, and so I stank in my sin.

The second story of aroma therapy, in the natural, as this man spoke, there was a transference of the chemicals from his mouth to my clothes, hair, and nose. I had to take drastic measures to eradicate the evidence from being in his presence. In the spiritual, what words are we listening to? What movies are we watching? What messages are we allowing into our being? These messages can be good, or they can be laced with poison. The popular culture is fraught with those final-days messages: what is good is evil and what is evil is good. Over and over these messages are bombarding us. Although, unlike in the natural that the halitosis is repulsive, in the spiritual the adversary's lies make it more enticing, more palatable. But in the end, it is the way of destruction. Just as I took drastic measures to eradicate the natural halitosis aroma, we also need to take drastic measures to eradicate the spiritual halitosis in our lives. This is done by replacement, replacing those messages with His Word and meditating on His promises to you.

I firmly believe that as we abide in Christ and Christ abides in us, His presence should be so permeating every fiber of our very being that His presence is known as we enter a room, His nature permeating our spirit, soul (mind, will, and emotion), and body. His presence is announced when we enter a room because He resides in us in power and in grace. Just as the guards that are beside the doorways at a Buckingham Palace, as they announce to all present that the queen is approaching, so to Christ living in us should be the announcement that the kingdom of God is at hand. As we continue to die to ourselves, our earthly desires, and pick up our cross and follow Him daily, we become more like Him.

> *I beseech you therefore, brethren, by the mercies of God, that you present your bodies a living sacrifice, holy, acceptable to God, which is your reasonable service. And do not be conformed to this world, but be transformed by the renewing of your mind, that you may prove what is that good and acceptable and perfect will of God. (Romans 12:1–2, NKJV)*

It is in obeying Him and dying to self that we become more transformed into His image and likeness. This is a living sacrifice, but to be a sacrifice, we must not keep slithering off of the sacrificial altar; we must stay there silent like a lamb. It is this sacrifice that we become a sweet-smelling aroma to our God. At the end of our lifetime, when we go before the judgment throne of God, what will it all matter? Will it matter who won this year's championship in whatever sport? Back in my day the question was, "Who shot JR?" or maybe today in GOT it would be, "Who killed the Night King?" No, you do not have to answer those questions there. But really, when we stand before God on that day, the only thing that will matter is, "What did we do with Christ, did we make Him Lord, did we obey Him?"

So now we look at that aroma therapy again; even though I showered each day, yet still I smelled. I do not know if that salesman brushed his teeth each day or if there were underlying health issues that caused the halitosis. That administrative assistant broadcast her unique aroma. I firmly believe that there is an example in the scripture of our lives being a pleasing aroma to our Heavenly Father. The answer is found in this house we are building, yes, that house, and it is called our life. How are we building our life? Do we want this house to survive the storms that will come? All depends on the foundation that we build it on and what our materials of choice are.

> Let each carpenter who comes on the job take care to build on
> the foundation! Remember, there is only one foundation, the one
> already laid: Jesus Christ. Take particular care in picking out your
> building materials. Eventually there is going to be an inspection.
> If you use cheap or inferior materials, you'll be found out. The
> inspection will be thorough and rigorous. You won't get by with a
> thing. If your work passes inspection, fine; if it doesn't, your part of
> the building will be torn out and started over. But you won't be torn
> out; you'll survive—but just barely. (1 Corinthians 3:11–15, MSG)

> For no one is empowered to lay an alternative foundation other
> than the good foundation that exists, which is Jesus Christ! The
> quality of materials used by anyone building on this foundation
> will soon be made apparent, whether it has been built with gold,
> silver, and costly stones, or wood, hay, and straw. Their work will
> soon become evident, for the Day will make it clear, because it
> will be revealed by blazing fire! And the fire will test and prove the
> workmanship of each builder. If his work stands the test of fire, he
> will be rewarded. If his work is consumed by the fire, he will suffer

great loss. Yet he himself will barely escape destruction, like one being rescued out of a burning house. (TPT)

How do we want our life to smell to God? Do we want it to smell like sweaty work boots or a sweet- and satisfying-smelling aroma that brings comfort and delight to God the Father?

Watch what God does, and then you do it, like children who learn proper behavior from their parents. Mostly what God does is love you. Keep company with him and learn a life of love. Observe how Christ loved us. His love was not cautious but extravagant. He didn't love in order to get something from us but to give everything of himself to us. Love like that. (Ephesians 5:1–2, MSG)

Be imitators of God in everything you do, for then you will represent your Father as his beloved sons and daughters. And continue to walk surrendered to the extravagant love of Christ, for he surrendered his life as a sacrifice for us. His great love for us was pleasing to God, like an aroma of adoration—a sweet healing fragrance. (TPT)

We see that burnt sacrifice is very pleasing to our Father. We need to live a life in sacrifice and praise for all that Jesus has done and is doing for us.

But he shall wash the entrails and legs with water. The priest shall offer all of it, and offer it up in smoke on the altar. It is a burnt offering, an offering by fire, a sweet and soothing aroma to the Lord. (Leviticus 1:13, AMP)

Aaron's sons shall burn it all on the altar upon the burnt offering which is on the wood on the fire, an offering made by fire, of a sweet and satisfying odor to the Lord. (Leviticus 3:5, AMPC)

The priest shall burn them on the altar as food, offered by fire, for a sweet and satisfying fragrance. All the fat is the Lord's. (Leviticus 3:16, AMPC)

Lord, I call upon You; hasten to me. Give ear to my voice when I cry to You. Let my prayer be set forth as incense before You, the lifting up of my hands as the evening sacrifice. (Psalm 141:1–2, AMPC)

God, come close. Come quickly! Open your ears—it's my voice you're hearing! Treat my prayer as sweet incense rising; my raised hands are my evening prayers. Please, Lord, come close and come quickly to help me! Listen to my prayer as I call out to you. Let my prayer be as the evening sacrifice that burns like fragrant incense, rising as my offering to you as I lift up my hands in surrendered worship! (MSG)

If we are living the life of sacrifice of praise, His presence precedes us as we go about our daily lives in this walk of faith. His presence enters a room as we enter the room because the same spirit that rose Christ from the dead lives and abides in us! As we abide in Christ and Christ abides in us, it will become very evident to those around us that they have encountered the divine one who lives in us! Wherever we go, the Holy Spirit will make His presence known, much like what is described in Psalm 65, dripping of the oil of the Holy Spirit.

You crown the earth with its yearly harvest, the fruits of your goodness. Wherever you go the tracks of your chariot wheels drip with oil. (Psalm 65:11, TPT)

CHAPTER 3
PERSPECTIVE | KEY TWO

Perspective is something we need to stand back and take a look at.

Then God said, "Let Us make man in Our image, according to Our likeness; let them have dominion over the fish of the sea, over the birds of the air, and over the cattle, over all the earth and over every creeping thing that creeps on the earth." (Genesis 1:26, NIV)

When we were created in God's image and likeness, we were created with creative capability. He gave us imagination, dreams, visions, intuition, critical thinking, and logic. He gave us dominion over all the earth. When Adam fell, he forfeited his dominion over to Satan. Let us gain some understanding and perspective on this dominion.

There is a FB posted photo of two men facing each other standing about eight feet apart. Placed between them on the ground is a number. One man says that the number is the number 6, while the other states that it is a 9. Who is right, and who is wrong? Both are correct based on their perspective. We need God's perspective. Moses sent twelve men to spy out the land; ten came back with a tale of men so large the Israelite spies felt like grasshoppers. While two came back and Joshua said that the Israelite army with the backing of God could take the land. Joshua had God's perspective while the ten others did not. Joshua knew from experience that putting his faith in God is not blind endeavor but one of certainty. God had already proved Himself to be faithful and trustworthy. Not blind faith but assured faith that God would follow through with His Promise, His Covenant with the nation of Israel.

When it comes to what you believe God has called you to do, do your homework, spy out the land. Just as Joshua sent spies into Jericho, we must gain as much knowledge as possible. After all, we read,

My people are destroyed for lack of knowledge. (Hosea 4:6, KJV)

In World War II, there were some seventy million people killed in just six years. The civilian-to-combatant fatality ratio in World War II lies somewhere between 3:2 and 2:1. It is estimated that some 60 to 67 percent of those were civilian deaths due to the Holocaust, ethnic cleansing, the

Bengal famine in India because of England fighting the war, and the use of the increasing effectiveness and lethality the day and night bombing of the industrial might of Germany. The carpet bombing of Germany resulted in a high civilian casualty rate because the war factories were located in heavily populated metropolitan cities. The targeting systems used are primitive by today's standard; they were effective at locating the target, but the delivery system was still hit-and-miss.

Today we have laser-guided "smart bombs," which resulted in a marked reduction in the civilian casualty rates in the Iraq War. American and Coalition forces killed at least 28,736 enemy combatants as well as 13,807 civilians, which resulted in a civilian-to-combatant casualty ratio inflicted by coalition forces of 1:2. The reason why I make mention of these two morbid facts is this: *perspective*. The better we understand what the problem really is, the better we can laser-target our prayers to be able to make deeper penetration into enemy territory for the kingdom.

Do the research to find out who is where in your city—mayor, city council, judges, police and fire chiefs, school board members, school principals, churches, pastors, etc.; this will then fold back into the JCP. Make a Word document detailing these facts. When you are able, I have found it helpful to include a small photo of the individual embedded into the document. This way, when you pray for them, you are able to see the face of the individual for whom you are praying. At the back of the book is my e-mail address. I will send you an editable version so you can add your region-specific data to it.

As you spy out the land, you will know who the movers and shakers of your region are. You are now regularly praying for them, and as you do and remain consistent in your prayers, your prospective will change. Your view on your regional leaders will start becoming more and more in line with God's perspective. You are developing within you the heart of God toward them.

Another aspect of spying out the land is to find out the demographics of the region. Things to consider are divorce rate, crime rate (churched/unchurched numbers), drug usage, foster care, domestic violence numbers, child abuse, and the list can continue. Feed those numbers back into your personal JCP manual. Be creative as to listening to the spirit to lead you in areas that He can target to use your specific gifting.

This is what I found for Garfield County:

The County has a population of 60,913 as of this year. I have heard it said that we have a combined seating capacity in our churches at about 12,000. We live in a post-Christian society these days. In a recent survey, in the United States, sadly, only 38 percent are connected to a church. If this percentage is true, my church and every other church in Enid should be busting at the seams seeing weekly attendance at around 23,400 precious souls. Yes, a handful of churches do have multiple services on a weekend, but not enough to even come close to fulfilling the 23,400-attendance requirement. I feel that this 38 percent number is not entirely accurate; I firmly believe that a large segment of that 38 percent would fall under the subgroup of Christmas and Easter attendees. Case in point, my church's regular attendance rate hovers around 500. This past Resurrection Day, we added two additional services on Saturday night, and praise God, we saw our attendance spike to 891, resulting in a 78 percent increase.

The Gallup Poll on April 18, 2019, US, "Church Membership Down Sharply in Past Two Decades" by Jeffrey M. Jones, details that we, the church, are not representing Christ as we should. Please do not get offended by that statement. Check out the numbers for yourself and draw your own conclusions.

In this report, they even have a subgroup considering party affiliation and found Republicans saw a relatively modest decline in church membership of eight points since 1998–2000 from 77 percent to 69 percent. Now contrast that with the Democrats showing one of the largest subgroup declines, of 23 points, from 71 percent to 48 percent.

And in yet another report, Generation Z, those born between 1999–2015, it indicates that 13 percent identify as an atheist, twice that of adults. This would explain the following dower information. Researchers at the Pacific Institute for Research and Evaluation in Maryland studied Millennial Generation and Gen Z mortality data from the National Center for Health Statistics. The results were published in the Journal of Studies on Alcohol and Drugs. What was found was that the death rates from drug overdoses for people ages fifteen to twenty-four rose by 19.75 percent from 2006 to 2015. Sadly, during the study period, 36,422 adolescents and young adults in the United States died of drug overdose and poisoning.

Most of those deaths were from drug overdoses from opioids and prescription and illicit drugs like heroin, as detailed in the report. Death rates from opioid use rose by an average of 4.8 percent annually during the study time period. Alarmingly, a steeper increase of 15.4 percent was seen between 2013 and 2015.

Digging deeper into the numbers, the researchers found that drug overdoses were the highest among whites and Native Americans at 11.9 deaths and 10 deaths for every 100,000 people, respectively. That compares with 2.6 deaths per 100,000 people for African Americans while seeing 4 deaths per 100,000 people for Hispanics.

New York State had the highest increase of drug overdoses with a death rate, up 9.4 percent each year during the period. Ohio, Massachusetts, and New Jersey trailed New York only slightly with 9.1 percent, 9 percent, and 8.7 percent increases annually, respectively, according to the researchers compiling the numbers. More Americans died from drug overdoses in 2017 than were killed during the entire twenty-year Vietnam conflict (November 1, 1955 to April 30, 1975. In 2017, there were 70,237 overdose deaths.

In my search of how we are doing as a society, one thing I did find is the following:

In 2010, we saw 480 marriages but 384 divorces in Garfield County. This is a sad state of affairs. And according to the American Psychological Association, in Western cultures, more than 90 percent of people marry by age fifty. However, about 40 to 50 percent of married couples in the United States divorce. There are some 411,444 people living in Oklahoma over fifteen years of age who are divorced. Or compare that to the 28,339,199 Americans who are already divorced in 2019. According to the 2013–2017 Community Survey, the overall divorce rate in Oklahoma is 13.2 percent, which compares to the US divorce rate of 10.9 percent.

In 2015, there were 638,169 abortions. This equates that for every 1,000 live births there were 188 abortions. The year 2015 was a far better year than in 1990, when there were 1,429,247 abortions. That equates that for every 1,000 live births, there were 345 abortions. So yes, the trend is going down, and we can be very thankful for that, but one abortion is too much.

The *Bulletin of the World Health Organization* recently published the following findings: 376 million new cases of gonorrhea, syphilis, chlamydia, and trichomoniasis developed among people between the ages of fifteen to forty-nine in 2016. It was found that syphilis alone caused some 200,000 stillbirths and newborn deaths in 2016. Syphilis is one of the leading causes of baby loss globally, second only to malaria.

Laura and I noticed that since moving to Enid, each April on the yard of the county courthouse, a display of small children figures is placed. Last year, Laura inquired as to what they represented. The display represented the number of child abuse cases for the past year. The display gripped our hearts as we counted; the sheer numbers drove a stake in our hearts, crying out to God for mercy for these sweet, innocent, precious souls. If my memory is correct, the number was in the high 200s. Last week we saw the display for 2019, and so we counted.

Of a population of 60,913 in Garfield County, Oklahoma, we saw 335 cases of child abuse in the last year, which is .55 percent of the general population. In Garfield County, there are 15,836 children under the age of eighteen, or 26.1 percent of the general population. This means the 335 cases of child abuse account for 2.16 percent of all the children in Garfield County. This is in the middle of the Bible Belt, with a number so high? I am saddened to even think what the number might be for Los Angeles County! And to think that these numbers presented only represent the reported numbers; sadly, the actual numbers may be quite higher!

While on the subject of child abuse, I recently ran across the following very sad statistics about childhood sexual abuse. One in every four girls and one in every six boys will be sexually abused before the age of eighteen. A full 90 percent of child sexual abuse cases are perpetrated by a trusted friend or member of the family. Of those, 30 percent will be perpetrated by a member of the family. Right now, there are over 42 million survivors of child sexual abuse. These numbers are grim and are completely exemplified by Larry Nassar. Larry Nassar, from 1992 to 2014, allegedly molested some 332 young girls as a doctor of medicine, from 1996 to 2014. He did this while representing the USA as the national medical coordinator for USA Gymnastics. He pleaded guilty of molesting ten girls; he also pleaded guilty to child pornography. He has multiple sentencing of 60 years, 40–175 years, and 10–125 years.

We see that Matthew 25:32–40 speaks to the basic needs of all mankind. Seniors are a large sector of society that is sadly forgotten, often neglected, and at times abused. We seek to make a difference and reverse the tide—

bringing God's grace, hope, forgiveness, and love to this generation, the greatest generation on earth.

From that Matthew text, the phrase that echoes in our hearts is this:

The King will reply, "Truly I tell you, whatever you did for one of the least of these brothers and sisters of mine, you did for me."

Family is family. What does it say about our "love" when we cart our family members off to a facility and never visit them? Out of sight, out of mind? Or is it like we are just sending Fido off to the pound to just let them deal with the end of days for Fido? Our moms and dads changed our diapers; they cleaned up the bloodied knees; and they kissed our tears away. Yet we ship them off to a facility and never visit them. Is that what Christ would do? Please, please, I beg you to not let this be the case for your elders. A full 60 percent of all who are put into an assisted-living facility will never have a visitor. Okay, I will get off my soapbox…for now.

One might be tempted to say that I am encouraging an overanalyzing aspect of all this, that I want to overintellectualize a movement of God and not allowing the Holy Spirit to flow easily. There is an old saying that I find to be very true: "If you have the Spirit without the Word, you blow up. If you have the Word without the Spirit, you dry up. If you have a balance of the Word and the Spirit, you grow up." I prefer to operate with all available knowledge. And then there is the knowledge dealing with the numbers and statistics to give an account of what the situation is and what dominion is over an area. The natural knowledge coupled with the words of knowledge from the spirit will lead to success. Joshua spied out the land; he also was allowed to see into the spiritual realms and proclaimed that Israel could take the land with the power and authority of God.

Now that we have taken a look at the state of affairs of our city, region, and nation, now let us focus back to the local level for knowledge—both whatever knowledge we can glean on the web about the local movers and shakers. Real knowledge, not the gossip that sometimes is out there. Again, using knowledge in the natural coupled with the words of knowledge and discernment, we can more effectively pray against the dominions over the region.

My people are destroyed for lack of knowledge. Because you have rejected knowledge. (Hosea 4:6, NKJV)

Study to show yourself approved to God, a workman that needs not to be ashamed, rightly dividing the word of truth. (2 Timothy 2:15, AKJV)

So study the lay of the land; find out where the enemy strongholds are so that you can target your prayers effectively. As you study, pray, then pray some more. Once you think you are finished praying, pray some more. Learn to be in such an attitude of prayer that you are constantly talking to God.

Now that you have spent time praying for the movers and shakers in your region, you are viewing them from God's perspective. Be open for God to operate in the gifts of wisdom and knowledge in your life. This will give you better insight on how to work with them to accomplish what God has called you to do. When in doubt, pray.

An interesting thing happened when returning from California to attend a funeral. We were on the flight from Denver to Oklahoma City. We were conversing with the flight attendant; I asked her where she was based out of, and San Francisco was what she indicated. She also said that she would be flying back there in the morning then fly to Kansas City. I asked how long a layover in KC, and if it was a day layover, that it would be advised for her to go to Arthur Bryant's BBQ. It is located near where the old municipal stadium once was, and as a result, pictures are on the wall of baseball greats like Babe Ruth and Joe Dimaggio. She had been looking away at the time, busy still serving another flyer; when I said that, her head swung around and rested in a slightly tilted position with a very inquisitive look on her face. When she swung her head around, she simultaneously covered up a lapel pin. She asked how I knew she was a big baseball fan. I answered that I did not know that. She then uncovered her pen to reveal a San Francisco 49rs pen. She indicated that she was a big baseball fan and one of her bucket list points was to visit each MLB stadium. She indicated she would love take some stewardess friends to go to Arthur Bryant's and was grateful for the tip.

Later, Laura and I were having a good conversation with two passengers behind us (they heard the interchange with the attendant). We learned that they were meeting up in Oklahoma City with a third woman to start a road trip to Michigan to get a fourth woman. I glibly said, "Sounds like you are going to have a Thelma, Louise, and Suzy road trip." Well, the woman adjacent to me on the other side of the plane looked at me with surprise and also tilted her head in disbelief. She almost screamed at me, asking how I knew her name was Suzy. I told her that I did not! We all just paused, in some disbelief—first the baseball story and now Suzy! A comment was made that I should accompany them to a casino or maybe that I should buy a lottery ticket. This was the first time that something like this has happened back-to-back so blatantly. I was given supernatural insight about these two strangers. Sadly, for me, I am still so new at operating in the gifting of words of knowledge that I was in such a state of shock that I did not realize the opportunity to share the Gospel with these individuals.

I am now more open to it happening again, and I see it as having great potential for opening up a dialogue about God. These types of words of knowledge could come in handy while dealing with those in authority in your region, not that is a parlor trick but as a key that can open doors. So pray and be open to however God chooses to use your individual gifting. Also pray to be open to be used of God in other giftings that are targeted for that given moment when they are needed to target the Gospel to a person.

After you have interceded for the regional movers and shakers that have dominion in the natural, after much prayer, now is the time to interject into those prayers, asking God that you may find favor in the eyes of those in authority. Just like Moses eventually found favor with Pharaoh.

We volunteer twice a week at a local prison—I say local, but in reality, it is some forty miles away. We get off work at four thirty, and the session at prison officially starts at six thirty—sounds like an easy trip, right? Well, for the most part, it can be, if the stars align just right. No, actually we pray for traveling mercies every day. Shift change at the prison is at six, so we like to arrive to go through security at five thirty so that we are not delayed by the guards also going through security. The forty-mile journey takes us right through our sleeper downtown during rush-hour traffic. We have to cross four different rail train lines on our way to the prison. The first one we cross twice because the rail line is the hypotenuse of a triangle where we also traverse the "a" and "b" of the triangle. We have a workaround to prevent that one from delaying us. But from that point forward, the trip really requires a heightened level of situational awareness. Driving with your focus, not just on the car directly in front of you, but also being aware of the traffic flow up to a quarter a mile ahead. Luckily with the second train rail crossing, the terrain cuts us a break; there is a fairly significant dip in the road (hill/valley), but really a dip—this is Oklahoma, after all, that allows us to see close to a half mile ahead to see if there is a train on the tracks. If so, we have a workaround underpass. It also pays to be aware of what is in the traffic ahead. If the rails are clear, but a tanker truck is a quarter mile ahead; it will have to stop at the tracks, so I will position myself in a lane that will not slow because of the stopped truck. The third and fourth rails do not have workarounds; if there is a train, we are delayed, and the shift change will delay us even more. If all goes well, we are through security by five forty-five, and now we can use that time in preparation for the day's class. We like to get into an attitude of worship, allowing the Holy Spirit to calm us prior to ministry to and with our students.

What does this all have to do with perspective, you might ask? Any task, any ministry that God has set before us will have challenges. These challenges can come from a multitude of directions. This journey we call life and ministry is on a path that God has set before us.

> Your word is a lamp for my feet, a light on my path. (Psalm 119:105, NIV)

His Word illuminates what is directly in front of us so we do not trip on something, or at the very least, we do not stub our toes. While His Word is also a light on the path to guide us along the way. That lit path helps prevent taking a wrong turn or to step off a cliff! A heightened sense of situational awareness, both in the natural and the supernatural, is required as we take these steps on our journey with Christ.

Okay, in an effort to be fully transparent, yes, these examples that I give are real-life and are a means to convey the concept that we must be very situationally aware because our adversary is like a lion, seeking whom he can devour, but…you have permission to laugh or chuckle a little, but only a little. Okay, am just being authentic here. Last night when we were headed to the prison, on that last stretch of highway—it is a ten-mile country road with no stop signs—well, I let my guard down. I was not very aware of my situation. I was not aware of my speed, and yes, I got pulled over for exceeding the speed limit of 65. In typical fashion, "Do you know why I pulled you over?" in a very stern voice, and then me, "Yes," I said very sheepishly. I indicated that we were headed to prison to volunteer there. When he stepped back to our car, he went to the passenger side, looked at me again, and sternly said, "SLOW DOWN!" and "CRUISE CONTROL!" Then he also followed by looking at Laura and said, "I am letting you off with a warning today." Then he looked back to me, pointing his finger at me, and saying, "SLOW DOWN!" and "CRUISE CONTROL!" We told him thank you and that we were trying to get there before shift change. He said, "Yeah, you gotta be there before shift, otherwise you will be waiting forever."

God, through this officer, extended me some grace! Praise God! Oh, and yes, we did make it in time right before shift change; no matter, they did not have a female to pat Laura down, so we waited a little longer than usual. Five minutes can make the difference of fifteen or twenty when processing through security.

Usually I am able to spot a law enforcement officer from great distances; this day I let my guard down. We must stay vigilant and situationally aware. You never know where and when the adversary might pop up.

As a side note, I am not by any means implying that law enforcement are our adversaries, so please do not read that into the above story. I hold our military and law enforcement in high esteem and pray for them regularly, both in my prayer closet on a JCP and at times in person.

In the months leading up to the Open Heaven, we had several close calls. We were doing the JCP prayer regularly, knocking on the gates of hell and coming against them in the power and authority of Christ. So it would be very natural that the adversary would try to fight back. He is, after all, like a roaring lion. Just like if we were in the deepest savanna of Africa, we would naturally be very situationally aware looking out for a real lion—well, we need to be just as situationally aware in our everyday lives.

In the course of one week, Laura and I had three very close calls with motor vehicles. Two in the same day. We were heading north and was stopped at a stoplight. There was a larger SUV in the left-turn lane that I could not see over. When my light turned green, just before I stepped on the accelerator, I gave it a pause. A split second later, an 18-wheeler barreled on through his red light. Had I pressed that accelerator, we would have been toast. Later that day, we were heading north on Highway 81 during a section where it is narrowed down to just two lanes. Off in the distance I saw a line of cars in the opposing lane. Then I saw another 18-wheeler in my lane passing that line of cars. I pressed hard on the brakes and dove into the emergency lane, just as I did the 18-wheeler passed us. It pays to be receptive to the gentle nudging of the Holy Spirit and to be situationally aware.

The next Saturday afternoon, I was driving up to Wichita on the I-35 highway. It usually is a fairly boring two-hour drive. I was traveling in the left lane with no one insight in front of me. For no explainable reason, I changed lanes to the right lane. After completing the lane change, I looked up to find a car barreling down on me in the left lane; he was going the wrong direction! He was close enough when he passed me that I saw the whites of his eyes. As I was changing lanes, this was when he had crested an overpass hill; that was why it seemed like he came out of nowhere. I called 911 to alert them, but for God's grace, he did not hit anyone that day! It pays to be receptive to the gentle nudging of the Holy Spirit and to be situationally aware.

And that leads us up to this one! As I am finalizing the completion of this book and going over some of the finer points with Laura, we were driving toward the country. We were reminded about just how important that we are always aware that we are in the middle of a spiritual battle. We were remembering one of our JCP days of prayer when Laura saw what she thought to be a dog running in a field. As it leaped over a small fence, she realized that it was a deer; she cautioned me to slow. I did press hard on the brakes; the deer ran across our lanes just in front of us, crossed the center divider, and proceeded to be struck by a car on the opposite side. We were situationally aware; the deer and other car were not. As this just happened today, we still have a little pit in our stomachs having witnessed the death of a Bambi. It pays to be receptive to the gentle nudging of the Holy Spirit and to be situationally aware.

Twelve years ago, my son was an aspiring Olympic athlete in the sport of bicycle racing. He had won silver and bronze medals on the velodrome track national championship in 2008. We would train with the local racers out in the rural countryside, just outside of Wichita, Kansas. Yes, we would train together, but I could not hold a candle against my son. A typical training day for this forty-five-year-old was that I was able to hang with the younger faster riders for about fifteen miles or so, but then I would putter out and I would drop back and ride by myself. Each week, I could hang on for a little longer and a little farther with the pack.

On this one day, that happened just like clockwork: I puttered out, I rode for another five to ten miles and then turned back around, figuring that the faster guys would "catch back" up with me on their return trip. I crossed over the railroad tracks and was proceeding to climb this slight incline in the road. The hills were not my friend this day. At about a quarter way into the ascent of the hill, out of the corner of my eye, I saw movement on the porch of this farmhouse. I looked over, and to my surprise there were two young pit bulls. They were just like a middle linebacker who saw that a wide receiver had just caught a pass near the sidelines and he instantaneously did the geometry in his mind to calculate the right pursuit angle to tackle the runner. These two pit bulls had done just that: they lay down a pursuit angle on me. In that instant, I had to make a choice; they call it "fight or flight." Well, even though I had already ridden about twenty-five to thirty miles, this forty-five-year-old chose *flight*! I *put the pedal to the metal*! I was riding that bicycle as fast as these old legs would take me. The two pit bulls were now on me; one was at my side trying to bite my right leg while the other was slightly in front and to the right as he was trying to coral me. These two dogs were working together as a team and were on the hunt, and I was to be their dinner! I was edging myself more away from the right side of the road to almost at the center double yellow divider lines. I looked up to see if there was a truck cresting the hill. It was then that I felt a very sharp but burning pain in my right leg. In the same way that in an instant I chose *flight*, now I chose *fight*! Welling deep inside me was this voice. I do not know where it came from, but within me, but I screamed at these two hunter dogs at the top of my lungs. I do not know what I said, but it worked; both pit bulls went running back to their house with their tails between their legs. I looked down and saw a little blood. Thankfully, the dog did not latch on to my leg, but his fangs only grazed the outer calf muscle resulting in two fairly deep cuts. I pedaled a little farther up the hill and then stopped. Although I was not bleeding profusely, if this dog were to be infected with something, I did not want to be exercising my heart to pump that infection all over my body. I got off the bike and stood there beside the road with my bike being positioned between me and the dogs, just in case they got some courage back. Just then, down the road was the pack of cyclists "catching up" with me. I tried to alert them of the dogs, but they did not understand. One of the riders on the back of the pack stopped to see what was wrong; he agreed that I should not ride. A passing motorist with a small truck gave me a ride back to my car so I could go get the wound taken care of.

> *Be alert and of sober mind. Your enemy the devil prowls around
> like a roaring lion looking for someone to devour. (1 Peter 5:8,
> NIV)*

Like those pit bulls that wanted me for dinner, Satan wants to eat us alive.
He has put a pursuit angle on us; he has his eyes targeted; he has his laser
target on all our weak points and wants to come in for the kill.

> *The thief comes only to steal and kill and destroy. (John 10:10,
> NIV)*

> *For God has not given us the spirit of fear; but of power, and of
> love, and of a sound mind. (2 Timothy 1:7, NKJV)*

We need to be alert to how the enemy operates, and when we are being
attacked, we are forced to make a decision, fight or flight. Are we going
to be scared and tremble in fear? Or are we going to take a stand in faith?
As believers in Christ, we have been given the authority to stand in faith
against any attack from the adversary. Remember in several locations
and translations of the Bible, the word power can be interchanged with
authority. I do not know if it is the case for this 2 Timothy 1:7 scripture. I
believe, for the sake of this message, let's pull in the substitute! For God
has not given us the spirit of fear but of authority and of love and of a sound
mind.

When we are attacked, we have the authority based on our relationship
with Christ in the power of His Word to fend off any attacks. Remember, the
battleground is in the mind.

> *For the weapons of our warfare are not carnal, but mighty
> through God to the pulling down of strong holds; Casting down
> arguments, and every high thing that exalts itself against the
> knowledge of God, and bringing into captivity every thought to the
> obedience of Christ. (2 Corinthians 10:4–5, KJV)*

When attacked—fight or flight, what will it be? Do we cower over in a
corner trembling in fear, or do we take a stand in faith? Operating in the
proper authority as a blood-bought believer in Jesus Christ, taking a stand of
faith. Because...

> *So shall they fear the name of the LORD from the west, and his*

glory from the rising of the sun. When the enemy shall come in, like a flood, the Spirit of the LORD shall lift up a standard against him. (Isaiah 59:19, KJV)

Stand on His Word and He will raise a standard against the enemy. The fight is the Lord's; it is not ours. We just need to fight in and with His authority. Let's not operate in fear but operate in faith.

So let God work his will in you. Yell a loud no to the Devil and watch him scamper. Say a quiet yes to God and he'll be there in no time. Quit dabbling in sin. Purify your inner life. Quit playing the field. Hit bottom, and cry your eyes out. The fun and games are over. Get serious, really serious. Get down on your knees before the Master; it's the only way you'll get on your feet. (James 1:7–10, MSG)

So then, surrender to God. Stand up to the devil and resist him and he will turn and run away from you. Move your heart closer and closer to God, and he will come even closer to you. But make sure you cleanse your life, you sinners, and keep your heart pure and stop doubting. Feel the pain of your sin, be sorrowful and weep! Let your joking around be turned into mourning and your joy into deep humiliation. Be willing to be made low before the Lord and he will exalt you! (TPT)

We take a stand against the adversary, not just when we are under attack but on a daily basis, moment by moment as we lift up our glorious Heavenly Father in praise for all that He has done and is doing in our lives.

But if serving the LORD seems undesirable to you, then choose for yourselves this day whom you will serve, whether the gods your ancestors served beyond the Euphrates, or the gods of the Amorites, in whose land you are living. But as for me and my household, we will serve the LORD. [Emphasis added.] (Joshua 24:15, NIV)

It pays to be receptive to the gentle nudging of the Holy Spirit and to be situationally aware.

CHAPTER 4
PRAYER | KEY THREE

Remember, our Commander in Chief, Jesus Christ, commanded us to go into Judea, Jerusalem, Samaria, and to the ends of the earth; our prayers need to be directed to all those areas. Your Judea (family), Jerusalem (friends)... And from there, whether the subject is a onetime event like Open Heaven or an ongoing ministry or praying for revival, prayer is the key! We must start this in prayer; we must pray all during the function of the other keys noted here to make it happen, and at the end of the day, we must pray. Prayer is the plow that turns over the soil to cultivate the field of souls. Oh, and when we have thought we have done enough in prayer, we must pray some more. Prayer is where the battle will be won or lost in the spiritual realms. When we consider this battle, we also must consider what is at our disposal to aid us in this battle. I will call you to consider the following scripture several times in this reading.

And if anyone longs to be wise, ask God for wisdom and he will give it! He won't see your lack of wisdom as an opportunity to scold you over your failures but he will overwhelm your failures with his generous grace. Just make sure you ask empowered by confident faith without doubting that you will receive. For the ambivalent person believes one minute and doubts the next. Being undecided makes you become like the rough seas driven and tossed by the wind. You're up one minute and tossed down the next. When you are half-hearted and wavering it leaves you unstable. Can you really expect to receive anything from the Lord when you're in that condition? (James 1:5–8, TPT)

For though we walk (live) in the flesh, we are not carrying on our warfare according to the flesh and using mere human weapons. For the weapons of our warfare are not physical [weapons of flesh and blood], but they are mighty before God for the overthrow and destruction of strongholds, [Inasmuch as we] refute arguments and theories and reasonings and every proud and lofty thing that sets itself up against the [true] knowledge of God; and we lead every thought and purpose away captive into the obedience of Christ (the Messiah, the Anointed One), Being in readiness to punish every [insubordinate for his] disobedience, when your own submission and obedience [as a church] are fully secured and complete. (2 Corinthians 10:3–6, AMPC)

The world is unprincipled. It's dog-eat-dog out there! The world doesn't fight fair. But we don't live or fight our battles that way—never have and never will. The tools of our trade aren't for marketing or manipulation, but they are for demolishing that entire massively corrupt culture. We use our powerful God-tools for smashing warped philosophies, tearing down barriers erected against the truth of God, fitting every loose thought and emotion and impulse into the structure of life shaped by Christ. Our tools are ready at hand for clearing the ground of every obstruction and building lives of obedience into maturity. (MSG)

For although we live in the natural realm, we don't wage a military campaign employing human weapons, using manipulation to achieve our aims. Instead, our spiritual weapons are energized with divine power to effectively dismantle the defenses behind which people hide. We can demolish every deceptive fantasy that opposes God and break through every arrogant attitude that is raised up in defiance of the true knowledge of God. We capture, like prisoners of war, every thought and insist that it bow in obedience to the Anointed One. Since we are armed with such dynamic weaponry, we stand ready to punish any trace of rebellion, as soon as you choose complete obedience. (TPT)

Now when He had taken the scroll, the four living creatures and the twenty-four elders fell down before the Lamb, each having a harp, and golden bowls full of incense, which are the prayers of the saints. (Revelation 5:8, NKJV)

Think on this little fact: For every hour of flight, the FA-18 E/F requires fifteen hours of maintenance, or $24,400 per hour to fly. Just like there is a ratio of maintenance hours to flying hours, there needs to be similar prayer time to ministry time ratio. Is it 15:1? I don't know, that is between you and your Father God. But if you do not make time pray, you are planning to fail in whatever you do in your life. Your life, your ministry, your success and failure all are dependent on your prayer life. I know that sounds harsh, but it is plainly and simply the truth.

Before we embark on any major effort, we need to count the costs.

*And whoever does not carry his cross and follow Me cannot
be My disciple. Suppose one of you wants to build a tower. Won't
you first sit down and estimate the cost to see if you have enough
money to complete it? For if you lay the foundation and are not
able to finish it, everyone who sees it will ridicule you, saying,
"this person began to build and wasn't able to finish." Or suppose
a king is about to go to war against another king. Won't he first
sit down and consider whether he is able with ten thousand men
to oppose the one coming against him with twenty thousand? If
he is not able, he will send a delegation while the other is still
a long way off and will ask for terms of peace. In the same way,
those of you who do not give up everything you have cannot be my
disciples. (Luke 14:27–33, NIV)*

We are in the middle of a spiritual war that is fought on our knees. Is it
that prayer time to ministry time ratio 15:1 ratio? Again, I am not the one
to determine that, but I will say it is clearly not a 1:1 ratio. Jesus Himself
spent much time in prayer before and after His ministry times. The Bible
records Jesus praying twenty-five times. I happen to think that this is just
what was recorded and that He spent much more time in prayer while the
disciples were sleeping. Prayer can be done from any bodily position; the
Bible lists five specific postures: sitting, standing, kneeling, prostrate (face
to the ground), and with hands lifted up. The Bible lists at least nine main
types of prayer: prayer of faith, prayer of agreement, prayer of request
(petition or supplication), prayer of thanksgiving, prayer of worship, prayer
of consecration (also known as dedication), prayer of intercession, prayer of
imprecation, and praying in the spirit.

We know that it was Joshua that sent spies into Jericho and then later was
led by God to march around the walled city of Jericho for six days and on
the seventh day to march seven times then, after that, blow the rams' horns.
The walls fell, and the Israelite army of God rushed in. Yes, that is a very
Reader's Digest version of what is accounted in the book of Joshua in the
Bible. I strongly encourage you to read story in Joshua chapters 1 through
7. I am very excited to put pen to paper on this portion of the story—well,
finger to keyboard, that is…

Close to three years ago is when God gave me a drive to develop this prayer concept. And now with the writing of this, He has caused me to revisit that prayer concept, and while I am at it, He is nudging me to go even deeper. Well, what is accounted in the next pages details that nudge.

To better understand all this, you must also understand some of the giftings that God has blessed me with. I am a very visual person. In my role as an aircraft design engineer, the gift to visualize a concept and then to transfer that concept in the form of a drawing was very vital. Today we do not use drawings on paper drawn with a pencil; today we use the computer. We take what was internally visualized and using design software make a virtual part of what we have conceived. This part is called a solid. We can assign certain attributes to the virtual part and perform analysis to determine if the part is structurally sound and if it would perform as designed. Think of the movies like Avatar; that entire world was conceived by the movie artist, and they use a similar form of software to generate this world in all its elements. Well, that is how we do it for aircraft design as well as about 99 percent of the manufactured products you consume today.

So now that you have had the opportunity to get inside my head a little, scary, is it not? I am excited to share what God has been birthing in my spirit concerning Joshua and the wall of Jericho. For about two weeks now, since I have been revisiting this prayer concept, I have been envisioning certain aspects of the Jericho story. We recently purchased The Message Bible (MSG), and so last night I studied the story of Jericho as told by MSG, AMPC, NIV, NKJV, and a few other translations that seem to allude my memory at the moment. But I ramble. Back to my excitement! I was very happy that what I had envisioned was not heretical in nature but could very well have happened as I have visualized. So I warn you, I am about to take a little (*little*) artistic license in the retelling of the Jericho. So please do not establish any new doctrine out of my illustrations of the siege of Jericho.

To visit Jericho and the significance of some of the elements of the story, one must turn back time even a little farther and revisit Abraham and the Abrahamic Covenant to appreciate some of the finer points of Jericho. The Abrahamic Covenant is where God made the everlasting agreement with Abram. We see this in Genesis chapter 12. We see that the land of Canaan would be given to Abram by God.

I will make you into a great nation, and I will bless you; I will make your name great, and you will be a blessing. I will bless

*those who bless you, and whoever curses you I will curse; and all
peoples on earth will be blessed through you. (Genesis 12:2–3,
NIV)*

"All peoples on earth will be blessed through you" is one of the
foretelling promises of the coming of Christ. We see again God entering into
a covenant with Abram, that Abram and Sarai would have a son and through
that son, Abram would be the father of many nations. God signed this
covenant in blood. This is detailed in Genesis 15. And when I say "blood,"
wow, there was a lot of it. A heifer, goat, and ram were sacrificed and cut in
two and laid on the ground, each half opposing the other. In Genesis 15:17
(NIV), "When the sun had set and darkness had fallen, a smoking firepot
with a blazing torch appeared and passed between the pieces." The Spirit of
the Living God passed between the halves—again demonstrating that God
is a fire-and-smoke kind of a God! Now God did His part of sealing this in
blood now it was Abram's turn. Abram then circumcised his foreskin; we
see this in Genesis 17.

> *This is my covenant, which you shall keep, between me and
> you and your descendants after you; Every male child among
> you shall be circumcised. And you shall circumcise the flesh of
> your foreskins; and it shall be a sign of the covenant between
> me and you. And he that is eight days old shall be circumcised
> among you, every male child in your generations, he that is born
> in the house, or bought with money of any foreigner, who is not
> of your descendants. He that is born in your house, and he that
> is bought with your money, must needs be circumcised: and my
> covenant shall be in your flesh for an everlasting covenant. And
> the uncircumcised male child whose flesh of his foreskin is not
> circumcised, that soul shall be cut off from his people; he has
> broken my covenant. And God said unto Abraham, As for Sarai
> your wife, you shall not call her name Sarai, but Sarah shall her
> name be. And I will bless her and give thee a son also of her; yea,
> I will bless her, and she shall be a mother of Gentiles; kings of
> peoples shall be of her. (Genesis 17:10–16, NKJV)*

Can you imagine that conversation Abraham must have had with all the
males that were in his company? "Uh, yeah, so I had this meeting with God,
and…ahh, yeah, and He said that I was going to be a father through my

wife, Sarah. Yeah, you heard that right. And then there is this other thing... Hmmm, yeah, so to seal the deal...I had to get circumcised. Oh, and not only that, we all must get circumcised. Oh, yeah, what does it mean to get circumcised you ask? Well, yeah, here is the thing, we must cut the foreskin of our..." I can imagine what went through some of the men's minds: *You want to do what?* Now I know the text does not record this conversation. But I could definitely see it happen in my mind's eye. I know it would be difficult to break the news to the guys. They knew him to be a man of integrity and that God has already blessed him in the past, and in doing so, they have been blessed, so they accepted.

> *On that very day Abraham took his son Ishmael and all those born in his household or bought with his money, every male in his household, and circumcised them, as God told him. Abraham was ninety-nine years old when he was circumcised, and his son Ishmael was thirteen; Abraham and his son Ishmael were both circumcised on that very day. And every male in Abraham's household, including those born in his household or bought from a foreigner, was circumcised with him. (Genesis 17:23–26, NIV)*

The God that I know is very particular about the order of things. The text we just read seems to indicate that Abraham was the first to be circumcised followed by his son and then the rest of Abraham's crew. A true leader would lead by example. The text does not indicate that there was any dissention in the camp with regard to this procedure. I firmly believe that Abraham's men believed him to be a man of integrity, drive, and purpose. They had already witnessed God blessing Abraham, and His blessings gave credence in validating the necessity of this procedure. Either way, it must have been one bloody and loud night!

These are the three main tenets of the Abrahamic Covenant:

1. The promised land of Canaan (Gen. 12:1) (Gen. 15:7)

2. The promise of numerous offspring (Gen. 15:4–6) (Gen. 17:6–8)

3. The promise of blessings unto the world (Gen. 12:3)

Now fast-forward to Joshua and the Battle of Jericho. Again, I encourage you to read the text in the Bible, Joshua chapters 1–7. A quick note, just in the first chapter of Joshua alone is four admonitions to be strong and courageous. I know that in those cases that I wanted my children to learn a valuable lesion. I would repeat myself several times, until I had a reasonable feeling that they caught whatever the lesson I was attempting to convey. Our Heavenly Father tends to repeat Himself very often in the holy scriptures.

God speaking to Joshua after the death of Moses, He reiterates His promises to Joshua and to the nation of Israel. God makes sure that Joshua knows that the torch is now passed on to him from Moses.

> *Be strong and very courageous. Be careful to obey all the law my servant Moses gave you; do not turn from it to the right or to the left, that you may be successful wherever you go. Keep this Book of the Law always on your lips; meditate on it day and night, so that you may be careful to do everything written in it. Then you will be prosperous and successful. Have I not commanded you? Be strong and courageous. Do not be afraid; do not be discouraged, for the Lord your God will be with you wherever you go. (Joshua 1:7–9, NIV)*

The second chapter indicates that the king of Jericho was very aware of the close proximity of the Israelite encampment, just on the other side of the Jordan River. Of course, it is kind of difficult to hide an encampment that is housing between 2.5 to 3 million people. There is no doubt that the king of Jericho as well as the other leaders in the land of Canaan had prior knowledge of the God of the Israelites. They had heard of the parting of the Red Sea by Moses. They heard about this God Who crushed the entire army of the Egyptians just forty years prior. Yes, they were very aware of the Israel encampment, and that is why they wanted to find the spies.

As detailed in Joshua 2:8–11, people were in fear of the God of the Israelites. And I am just blown away by the following found in Joshua:

> *They said to Joshua, "The LORD has surely given the whole land into our hands; all the people are melting in fear because of us." (Joshua 2:24, NIV)*

I started to ponder about what it meant to melt in fear. A term for fear and cowardice used in old westerns was yellow belly. So I pondered yellow belly and was wondering how that term even got coined. Could it be that yellow belly was coined when someone peed their pants in fear? Okay, now, back to the *melting in fear*. Different translations describe it as "terrified," "overthrown with fear," "panicking," "cringing," "deathly afraid," "trembling," and "fainting." I am looking at these words, and several of them involve outward bodily manifestations of this inward fear. So I could easily see that melting in fear could be understood as peeing oneself in fear—again, not enough to form doctrine but just an interesting thought.

God told Joshua to reinstate the Abrahamic Covenant, first by consecrating themselves before Jehovah God and then celebrating the Passover—again telling Joshua, as leader of this nation, to follow the Law of Moses.

> The LORD told Joshua, "It was a disgrace for my people to be slaves in Egypt, but now I have taken away that disgrace." So the Israelites named the place Gilgal, and it still has that name." (Joshua 5:9, CEV)

The next day the manna from heaven stopped. Abba Father is transitioning them away from being wanderers to inhabitants of the land. *The promised land*! If you really pause to think about it, their biochemistry had grown accustomed to this manna from heaven. The entire nation was now going into a transitionary period of their biology adjusting to new foods, and their bodies had to adjust their distribution of the necessary enzymes for proper digestion of said new foods. The text does not indicate that God intervened in the biology of the Israelites, so it could be safe to assume that this transition probably had its own internal challenges!

The crossing of the Jordan River by the Jews, this is when the entire nation of Israel passed on dry ground, much like Moses with the Red Sea. This new event did not go unnoticed by the king of Jericho; his watchmen were keenly spying on every movement of the Israelites. When you move close to three million people, their belongings and livestock, you kind of leave a well-worn path to and from wherever you are going, and a cloud of dust follows.

The priests who were leading this procession into the promised land were carrying the Ark of the Covenant. The two priests who were in the front of the procession, when their feet touched the water, the water rushed away to the right and to the left. As they did this, the Holy Spirit of God rushed in like the sound of a mighty rushing wind from a hot furnace that blew the mud and transformed it into dry ground instantly! With the crossing of the Jordan, I envision each of the men of fighting age that were in the Israelite army walking across on dry land. I envision that as they looked down in amazement, with each step as their sandal strikes the dry ground, they saw billows of dry dust wisp out from under their feet and create little Eddie swirls of rotating small dust clouds. With each step on the dry ground, seeing those clouds of dust swirl, these men in the army of God, the God of the Israelites, each step their faith increased. With each step, they looked to the left and then to the right; they saw the waters being held back forming a wall of water on each side. Each step, fear subsided. Each step, courage grew. Each step, the army of God grew stronger. Faith grew with each step.

The crossing of the Jordan by the Israelite nation did not go unnoticed by the peoples of Jericho. They witnessed with their own eyes the parting of the Jordan River. They saw the large dust cloud that trailed the nation of Israel as they were marching toward Jericho. Now the people of Jericho realized that it was not a mere rumor of the parting of the Red Sea because now God was giving an encore performance right before their very eyes. The number of Jericho watchmen on the walls were increased to monitor the Israelite movements. No detail of the goings-on in the Israeli encampment was to go unnoticed! This is a code red situation for the people of Jericho; tensions could not have been higher within the city. Joshua 5:1, "Their hearts melted in fear and they no longer had the courage to face the Israelites."

Apparently, all the wandering in the desert for forty years contributed a significant number of Israelites not following the Abrahamic Covenant. The fathers had not passed on the heritage of their forefathers in the cutting of the foreskin. The right, ritual, and obedience of circumcision had been lost in the desert. If the Israelites were anything like the modern church of today where you only have about 10 percent doing 100 percent of the work, if this was the case; then of the 600,000 men of fighting age, only about 60,000 were circumcised. So on the eve of the fall of Jericho and Israel entering the promised land, God wanted to reinstate the Abrahamic Covenant with His people. He is keeping His promises, and so He wanted His people to have the very personal sign of the covenant that He is their God and they are His chosen people. Every man of fighting age that was not circumcised (approximately 540,000) was put under the knife. I am sure that this did not go unnoticed by the watchmen on the wall of Jericho. There must have been some amount of noise that had been made by these grown men being circumcised—I mean, really, no Tylenol? Maybe wine was used to help minimize the pain, I do not know; it is not in the text. I know that God allows for endorphins to be released on the eighth day after birth so that a male child can endure the circumcision with less pain, thanks be to God for that grace… But these circumcisions were done to make up for the disobedience of the earthly fathers; my gut says that God probably did not provide the same grace for those grown men. I don't know. What do you think? The place became known as "Gibeath-haaraloth," or "the Hill of Foreskins." God's people were now in full compliance with His decrees.

God allowed them to heal before marching on Jericho. Did He speed up the healing process? I do not know; it is definitely within His power. This is not known from the text. With modern medicine, it takes anywhere between four to six weeks for an adult to heal from circumcision. The Israelites celebrated the Passover, thus consecrating themselves before the Lord.

I envision from the observance of Passover and the circumcision, including the healing, to be spanning at around forty-three days. Now, given that it was a seven-day march around the walls, this would mark the walls coming down fifty days from the Passover. Could it be a precursor to the Pentecost? Could it be? I think it is something to ponder, don't you think?

> And it came to pass, when Joshua was by Jericho, that he lifted
> up his eyes and looked, and, behold, there stood a man opposite
> him with his sword drawn in his hand: and Joshua went unto
> him, and said unto him, are you for us, or for our adversaries?
> "Neither," he replied, "but as commander of the army of the
> LORD I have now come." Then Joshua fell facedown to the ground
> in reverence, and asked him, "What message does my Lord have
> for his servant?" The commander of the LORD's army replied,
> "Take off your sandals, for the place where you are standing is
> holy." And Joshua did so. (Joshua 5:13–16, NKJV)

This Man was the Son of God, the Eternal Word, and He had His battle gear on! I want Him on my side as I go into battle!

Joshua relayed the battle plan to his leaders. He relayed the Word of the Lord, "Be strong and courageous." The plan was simple, but at the same time, it had to have been a faith-building exercise, to march around the wall once for six days. A plan that, from all accounts from all outside appearance, a worldly person would not have the ability to understand. Joshua had commanded the army, "Do not give a war cry, do not raise your voices, do not say a word until the day I tell you to shout. Then shout!" But for a man of faith like Joshua, he put his trust in the Lord; this man his men could trust and follow.

Recent examination of the archaeological findings of Jericho reveals this:

The mound of Jericho was surrounded by a massive earthen embankment. This embankment had a retaining stone wall standing 15 feet tall at its base. On the top of this retaining wall stood a mud brick wall that was 6 feet thick and stood up to 25 feet tall. As the elevation of the embankment increased, at its crest was the second mud brick wall. If one was at the base of the first retaining wall looking up at the second mudbrick wall, that base of the second wall would be some 46 feet higher than where you are standing. This second wall was, again, 6 feet thick and about 15 feet tall. So if standing at the base, the top of the second wall was some 61 feet tall. The city of Jericho was a towering projection of power that from a human perspective, considered impossible to penetrate this impregnable bastion. Within this fortified, walled system was 9 acres of inhabitable land. Archaeologists consider that the upper city had a population of approximately 1,200. Recent excavations have uncovered people living on the embankment between the upper and lower city walls. The population could have been upward to 3,000 to 4,000 people inhabiting the city of Jericho.

Now we know that the city was 525 feet wide by 1497 feet long and shaped more like a pumpkin seed; that being said, it was not a perfect square, but for the sake of simplicity, the following numbers are considered as if it were square. To keep the numbers simple to understand, although most sources put the outer wall as containing 9 acres within, let us round it out to 10 acres. Ten acres is 435,600 square feet. To get the length each side of a square city we take the square root of the 435,600 and get 660 feet—660 feet times 4 gets us the perimeter length of 2,640 feet, or half a mile. Each lap around the city of Jericho was approximately one half mile. This is less than a Sabbath day's journey of two-thirds of a mile. I feel that given the promise that God gave to Joshua, "Shout, for I have given you the city!" is indicating that since God is promising to do all the battle work, this was no violation of the Sabbath law.

This is what I envision each lap looking like: picture a halftime show at a college football game. When the marching band comes out and performs the precision maneuvers. Picture, if you will, how when an entire column rotates, the band member at the center barely moves, as the column is rotating around him. And although his movements are slight, they in sync with the team, and now if you look at the member at the other end of the column, he is walking in double time to keep the column straight and in sync. What I envision is the priestly precession leading the Ark of the Covenant to the gates of Jericho. Once at the gates, they did a "left face" and start marching around at a slow pace of one mile an hour. They were followed by the twelve tribes, each tribe individually represented. Leading each tribe were their bannermen and trumpeters. As each row of leading tribesmen comes to the front of the gate, all, in unison, did a "left face," and as they marched around this pumpkin-seed shape of a wall, as the columns fanned out, the outer columns of men would speed up or slow as the curvature of the wall dictated. Inner men closest to the wall were walking a constant one mile an hour while the outer men in that column were walking speeds up to approximately three miles an hour. All in precision, and by the time that the twelfth tribe had started the lap, the priestly procession leading the Ark of the Covenant was just finishing their lap. Each individual lap would take approximately thirty minutes per tribe, but collectively each lap would take approximately an hour.

In considering what kind of operation this was, let us allot 50 feet for the armed guard and the Ark of the Covenant as they were marching before the army. I am basing the units of measure between the fighting men while marching on how the United States Marine Drill and Ceremonies Manual dictate. All things being equal, which they usually are not, assume that each of the tribes of Israel are fielding an equal amount of men, based on this, at the base of the wall; they have two linear rows of 20 armed men from each tribe. From those 2 rows of 20, then radiating out beyond each of the individual in those 2 rows of 20 are columns of men marching in unison. This is an entire sea of men, 1,250 men deep, spanning 5,625 feet, which is over a mile in the distance. When all tribes were marching on the wall, you had almost a 360-degree coverage of a wall of men over one mile deep. The only holes were the separation between the tribes where the bannermen were holding the tribal banners.

The day was now finally here to start the siege on the city of Jericho. Joshua, like any good leader, spoke to his commanders and repeated the battle plans and repeated the instruction that each man was to remain silent. Above all, he repeated what God had told him about Jericho, "Be strong and courageous, for I have given you the city."

The army of Jericho is quaking in their sandals, seeing the army of God advancing on them and there is nowhere to hide! So on this, the first day with the army of Jericho seeing the Israelite army advancing, some 600,000 strong as they were marching around the wall, it must have been puzzling. They were marching with the Arch of the Covenant going before them. Just as before, while walking on dry ground through the Jordan River, I envision the same thing. With each step the men took, their faith was built up. Each step they saw the dust clouds swirling, and they looked to their right and saw not a wall of water but a wall of stone, the stone walls of the city fortress of Jericho. On this day, it was a fighting day; there was more of a sense of urgency. The dust cloud that followed the marching army was thick, so thick, and the men tasted the dust. An ever-present reminder of the seriousness of the event was the knowledge that they had been circumcised.

Now, I have not been circumcised as an adult; that occurred as a child for me. But I do remember vividly of having a vasectomy—I know, not the same, but in the same area of sensitivity. Mine had complications; it felt like my insides were being ripped out from that small incision. I remember that for several months, I was very guarded when a sudden motion was directed to that area. I would wince and throw my hands and arms in defensive protection, like when the dog jumps up on my lap, well, you get the picture.

These men in the army of God were about to do battle for Him and were suited up for this battle. I imagine that they did not have nice, comfortable cotton briefs or Under Armour, but some sort of wool undergarment. Wool is probably not the most comfortable fabric to wear after having had a circumcision. As they marched on the city, every now and then, they would be reminded of the Covenant that they and God made, and it reminded them of His promises. They remained silent, but with each step, they said to themselves, "Be strong and courageous, for the battle is the Lord's." Each step, faith was built. Each step, courage was built. Each step, the army of God grew stronger in determination. Each step, the full manifest presence of God was with them in the Ark of the Covenant, and He was with them *each step*! The trumpeters were blaring the trumpets of rams' horns.

They finished the first lap around the wall with not a single offensive shot fired from any man-made weapon within the Israelite army of God. Joshua communicated with his commanders to relay to the men in the army of God, that he was proud of the conduct and that the plan is going on as scheduled.

The people of Jericho sat in bewilderment. The watchmen on the wall and their commanders and on up to the generals then to the king himself—they were all scratching their heads in confusion as to what they just witnessed.

On day 2, like day 1, Joshua spoke to his commanders and repeated the battle plans and repeated the instruction that each man was to remain silent. Above all, he repeated what God had told him about Jericho, "Be strong and courageous, for I have given you the city."

The army of Jericho was on the wall; they were peering down on the advancing army of God. They were confused by day 1. They expected an attack, but none came. They were still apprehensive about the army of God advancing on them. The trumpeters were blaring the trumpets of rams' horns. Normal activities were starting to fall by the wayside because of the fear within the city. The disposal of food had stopped, and the smell of rotten food was starting to permeate out into the streets. As with the day before, with each step the army of God became stronger. They remained silent, but with each step, they said to themselves, "Be strong and courageous, for the battle is the Lord's." Their resolve became fiercer. When the day 2 lap was finished and the men were back at the camp, Joshua again gave his army praise for honoring God in what they were doing.

Day 3 rolled around, and as before, Joshua spoke to his commanders and repeated the battle plans and repeated the instruction that each man was to remain silent. Above all, he repeated what God had told him about Jericho, "Be strong and courageous, for I have given you the city."

The army of Jericho was on the wall, and they were peering down on the advancing army of God. Two days and not a single attack, the army of God just continued to silently march. The trumpeters were blaring of the trumpets of rams' horns. They were now finishing day 3 lap when some of the men of the army of Jericho started to feel emboldened by the lack of attack; they started to hurl insults at the army of God. It did not matter; the army of God were reminded of the Abrahamic Covenant when God said, "I will bless those who bless you, and whoever curses you I will curse." They continued marching, and they remained silent, but with each step, they said to themselves, "Be strong and courageous, for the battle is the Lord's." Upon completion of the lap and the return to the camp, Joshua again praised the men in his army for their conduct and faithfulness.

Now we are on day 4, and this is game day, and you must put your game face on, so Joshua spoke to his commanders and repeated the battle plans and repeated the instruction that each man was to remain silent. Above all, he repeated what God had told him about Jericho, "Be strong and courageous, for I have given you the city."

Most of the Jericho army was still apprehensive when seeing the army of God yet again advancing on their city. They had never encountered an army conducting such a strategy. In fact, there were several generals from the ranks that still did not trust what they had seen in the previous three days. They tried to squash any additional taunting of the army of God, but those who were successful the previous day in hurling insults were even bolder this day.

The Ark of the Covenant went before the army of God (as in previous days), and the entire Israeli attack party continued to remain silent. The trumpeters were blaring of the trumpets of rams' horns. Those Jericho men who were insulting the army of God started to grow in numbers. This did not detour the men in the army of God; it only continued to embolden them in their resolve to see God take the city, remembering the covenant they each had with the God of Abraham. Again, each step they took, they grew stronger, had more faith and courage. The God of the Israelites is faithful and is going before them into battle. They continued marching, and they remained silent, but with each step, they said to themselves, "Be strong and courageous, for the battle is the Lord's." They finished the march around the walls of Jericho, and then they returned back to the encampment to hear the encouraging words from their commander, Joshua, "Well done, my warriors."

Time to put your game face on for day 5. Joshua spoke to his commanders and repeated the battle plans and repeated the instruction that each man was to remain silent. Above all, he repeated what God had told him about Jericho, "Be strong and courageous, for I have given you the city." The trumpeters were blaring of the trumpets of rams' horns. With day 5, the men of Jericho have had yet another night to think this over, or maybe they had a night of drinking liquid courage. Either way, now many more were feeling emboldened by the lack of attack from the army of God. With this newfound courage, the men of Jericho decided to amp up their assault on the army of God. When the army of God advanced from their camp with the Ark leading the way, the men of Jericho saw them coming.

As the army of God started marching their lap that day, the men of Jericho started throwing rotten food at them along with their vile insults. These Jericho men had already seen these same columns of men in the army of God and figured who they wanted to target with their verbal assault or assault of a rotten tomato. No matter to the men in the army of God. They stiffened their jaw; they stood tall with their chest pushed out, and they pressed into the march with stronger resolve. They continued marching, and they remained silent, but with each step, they said to themselves, "Be strong and courageous, for the battle is the Lord's." The trumpeters were blaring of the trumpets of rams' horns. Day 5 came and went, with not a shot fired by the men in the army of God. Joshua again praised his men for how they conducted themselves and for their faithfulness.

As before, Joshua spoke to his commanders and repeated the battle plans and repeated the instruction that each man was to remain silent. Above all, he repeated what God had told him about Jericho, "Be strong and courageous, for I have given you the city."

Well, day 6 was now here; the men of Jericho were now getting pretty raucous. They did not realize that those who mocked the Israelites were mocking God. God's anger was building, and His wrath would soon be poured out on the city of Jericho and its inhabitants. By now, the men of Jericho had their favorite targets from which to hurl insults, rotten food, and now rocks. These little attacks meant nothing to the men of the army of God. The trumpeters were blaring of the trumpets of rams' horns. The men of the army of God were persistent with courage, strength, and faith in God that He would deliver the city. They continued marching, and they remained silent, but with each step, they said to themselves, "Be strong and courageous, for the battle is the Lord's." They were confident that God was with them as the Ark of the Covenant still went before them. Again, not a single offensive attack from the army of God; they remained faithful to the plan.

Day 7 of the siege on the city of Jericho, Joshua spoke to his commanders and gave them the final portions of the battle plans and repeated the instruction that each man was to remain silent until the sound of the trumpets of rams' horns went silent and when Joshua commanded them to shout! Above all, he repeated what God had told him about Jericho, "Be strong and courageous, for I have given you the city."

Now almost every man of fighting age in the city of Jericho was now in on these attacks hurled toward the army of God. By now, the men of Jericho held nothing back, although they did not attack with weapons of war; they just continued with the verbal assaults and hurling rotten food plus rocks down at the army of God. The men of Jericho grew complacent about not receiving a single reaction back and no response in anger whatsoever. Their testosterone was on overdrive with this confidence; they felt like "big man on campus" picking on the army of God. What is the saying—"Pride leads before a fall." The men of Jericho fully expected the army of God to finish this lap and go back to their encampment with their tail between their legs. It was then that they saw the Ark of the Covenant continue as it passed the gates and started a second lap. The men of Jericho immediately took notice of this new development. Some were still doing their assault on the Israelite army, but then, one by one the rocks fell from the hands, and one by one the mouths were silenced.

By the completion of the second lap, there was silence in the land of Jericho. Fear started to set over the city of Jericho. It was as though fear hung like a dark storm cloud over the city. There was not the hustle and bustle of commerce through the streets. Everyone was gripped with utter fear, fear of what would happen next—fear for their lives. There were only a few predominant sounds coming from the area: the sound of the army of God marching around the city, the echoing sound of dogs barking, and the hushed whispers of the men of Jericho. The city was dumbfounded with confusion. The men of the army of God continued to meditate on what God had said, "Be strong and courageous, for I have given you the city."

Seventh day with lap 2 now finishing, the utter fear coming from within the city was growing darker and darker. The haunting sounds of the army of God marching around the city grew more ominous as each minute passed by. Oh, now they were doing a third lap, and no one could understand the what, why, and how of all this happening. And yet, the army of God remains silent. By the middle of lap 3, the sounds of babies crying started filling the streets; the mothers' own fears had overtaken them, and they refused comfort even their own children. The babies did not know what was happening, but they could feel the stress levels of their loved ones rising, and the only thing they could do was to cry. The men of the army of God continued to meditate on what God had said, "Be strong and courageous, for I have given you the city."

Lap 4 was upon the city. Was it their imagination, or was the sound of the army of God marching, step by step, growing louder? Were the blaring of the trumpets of rams' horns getting louder? No one was in the streets of the city. The women and children were desperately trying to find any small location to hide inside. Still, the sound of the marching continues to play on the minds of the inhabitants of the city of Jericho. Tempers were starting to flare within the city walls. Arguments were breaking out; old feuds were being relived with fatal outcomes. The men of the army of God continued to meditate on what God had said, "Be strong and courageous, for I have given you the city."

Lap 5 was upon the city, and the men on the wall were slowly leaving their posts. But where could they go? Where could they hide? Yet still, not a sound from the army of God; the only sounds coming from them were the echoing sound of the footsteps as they continued to march on and the blaring of the trumpets of rams' horns. This pounding sound of the marching was becoming torturous to the inhabitants; they knew that life as they knew it was about to end, but the hard part was the not knowing when it was to come. The men of the army of God continued to meditate on what God had said, "Be strong and courageous, for I have given you the city."

Lap 6 was upon the city. The army of God was still quiet, but the tension within the city was so thick; random fights were flaring up all over the city. The rumble of chaos was now growing as terror had taken a tight grip on all those living within the city. The evil in the hearts of men had now taken over, and the infighting was at a fever pitch. Contrast that with the look on the faces of the men in the army of God, almost a peaceful look because these men were filled with faith and power. They had faith in God that God had this! As they continued to meditate on what God had said, "Be strong and courageous, for I have given you the city."

Lap seven was now upon the city, and the dogs, roosters, and other animals within the city were starting to act very strange, as if they were starting to sense a change in the atmosphere. Dogs were howling, and the other animals were stirring and making noises in distress. They also know that dread was about to come their way. The sound of the marching of the army of God was now almost deafening as it drones on. And all at once, the blaring of the trumpets of rams' horns and the marching stopped with the completion of lap 7. With the deafening drone of marching now stopped, the look of panic spread throughout the land as the people of Jericho were frozen in fear. A call to the army of God came out, "Right face!" Now the army of God were face-to-face to the wall of Jericho. Those watchmen of the wall who remained, as they peered down to the army of God, they saw eye to eye with those whom they had been tormenting, low, these last several days. As they looked deep into the eyes of those in the army of God, they saw no fear, only confidence. A strong, resilient spirit looking back at them. Then the inhabitants of the city heard, at the top of his lungs, Joshua was heard to scream, "Shout! For the Lord has given you the city!" The army of God shouted as loud as they could, singing praises to the God of Abraham, Isaac, and Jacob, and the walls came tumbling down! The army of God rushed in and cleansed the city. As the Lord instructed, all the gold, silver, and bronze was collected to be devoted to the Lord, for it was sacred to the Lord and must go into His treasury.

I firmly believe that as the army of God was marching around the city, each step they took was also a step in the spirit realm. As they meditated on God's Word and His promises, they were casting those inward meditative words into the battle in the heavenlies. At the base, the very foundation of the walls, they were circling. They were doing battle in the spirit realm and basically dispatching the heavenly army of warring angels to start doing damage in the unseen world to the foundation of the wall by battling the demonic spirits that controlled the city. With the increased activity in the spiritual realm, the inhabitants were left to their own debase devices, and this was one of the main reasons for the chaos within the walls. I believe this is a visual of what might be happening in the unseen world as we do battle on our knees before an Almighty God in His throne room of grace as we pray. Oh, one might say that there is power in the Word and they are speaking God's Word in prayer. To that I give you Psalm 139.

Lord, you have examined me and know all about me. You know when I sit down and when I get up. You know my thoughts before I think them. You know where I go and where I lie down. You know everything I do. Lord, even before I say a word, you already know it. (Psalm 139 (NCV)

Many believe that God used an earthquake to bring Jericho's wall down, and if this was the case, it was a prime example of Him using a natural phenomenon to accomplish His will. We know that when Isaac

Newton discovered the law of gravity, God was like totally surprised and said, "Now, why didn't I think of that?" Obviously, I am kidding. God completely understands all the laws of physics and the nature of the universe. He is, after all, the Creator of everything. He created gravity, magnetic fields, and others like the law of thermodynamics. Interesting, if any scientist is honest with themselves, the law of thermodynamics proves the theory of the big bang wrong. Well, let us get back to the wall and its falling. May I interject another possibility of how our Father God may have brought the walls down? God spoke this entire universe into existence; the power of His Word is infinite. The spoken Word involves sound, and sound travels as wavelengths. Wavelengths involve a frequency. Every object in the universe has its own unique frequency. Example, take a wine glass, when you pair it up with an opera singer… When that singer sings and hits the proper notes at the proper frequency, the wine glass shatters.

On a much grander scale, let us look at the Tacoma Narrows bridge collapse from 1940. The bridge was a suspension bridge over the Puget Sound in Washington State. It was opened for traffic on July 1, 1940, and dramatically collapsed on November 7, 1940. (I am giving an extreme Readers Digest description here.) The collapse was captured on video. This collapse helped increase the overall understanding of elementary forced resonance. Engineering and science were forever changed as a result. Research into bridge aerodynamics and aeroelastics was increased considerably because of this collapse. The designs of every bridge since this event have been affected by this event. If you have opportunity to look at the video on YouTube, please do; it will explain a lot. Why do I bring this up? Each structure has a natural frequency. The wind was flowing over the bridge at forty-two miles an hour. As the wind flowed over the bridge, it created vortices. When the frequency of the vortices match the natural frequency of the structure, it will begin to resonate, and the structure's movement is self-sustaining and destruction is eminent.

So with this limited understanding, what was the effect that seven days of six hundred thousand men marching around the perimeter of the walls have? Well, now consider adding to this the rams' horns trumpeting. Could the combined noise and vibration frequency match up with the natural frequency of the wall, causing the mud mortar between to stone in the wall to start breaking down? Could the sustained seventh day with its three and a half hours of continuous marching and trumpeting have weakened the joint structure of the walls that when all the armies of God did a "right face" and shouted at the top of their lungs, could such a violent battle cry have been like a final sledgehammer blow that the walls just shattered, much like the wine glass? This is just a proposal, again, nothing to stand on and make doctrine about. I am sure there is some physicist out there that is more than willing do to the math to prove this hypothesis right or wrong. The one thing I do know is God is a God of wonders, marvels, and extraordinary manifestations. He could have caused the walls to fall with just His pinky finger, but He chose to use the army of God to march on the wall for seven days. He is famous for confounding the wise with the simple.

As an aside, I do find it quite interesting the similarities in the series of events surrounding Feast of Pesach (Passover). Rabbis have determined that the Feast of Shavuot coincides with God giving His Torah (the Law) to Moses on Mt. Sinai. The Feast of Shavuot is one of the three great pilgrim feasts that God instructed the Israelite people to observe and celebrate (Deuteronomy 16:16); it occurs fifty days after the Feast of Pesach (Passover). When this occurred, there was a rebellion against Moses and the Law that resulted in three thousand men being killed because of their idolatry (Exodus 32:25–28). With Joshua and God fulfilling His promise to the Israelites of giving them the promised land, He had them reinstitute the Abrahamic Covenant with the observance of the Passover. With that, the Israelites gave back to God their first fruits in the gold, silver, and bronze. Now with Christ, He ate the Passover, was killed, buried, and rose from the dead. He then promised that the Helper would come and to wait until the Comforter came. The disciples fasted and prayed for ten days, and then on the day of the Feast of Shavuot, we see the Holy Spirit fall on the believers, and they were filled with the Holy Spirit and with fire in the second chapter of Acts. That day, three thousand believers were added. God in His redemptive spirit is consistent, three thousand for three thousand. But this three thousand were the first fruits post-resurrection and post-ascension. The law of sowing and reaping.

We see that in this, the first city that God delivered into the hands of the Israelites was to be considered as "first fruits," as accounted for in the Law of Moses. This is a prime example of how God wants us to honor Him with our tithe. The first fruits of our labor are to go to Him; this in turn will consecrate the rest of the harvest. This is a great example of the principle of sowing and reaping.

As I stated earlier, this illustration is how God gave it to me in my mind's eye. Did it happen similar to what I have enunciated here? We will only know once we make it to heaven. I, like many people, am a student of human behavior. I believe what I have illustrated with the men of Jericho is pretty consistent within the norms of human behavior. Given that this was a godless city, what I enumerated is probably very conservative. I actually imagined much worse, but I endeavor to keep this PG-rated. But again, I will give the disclaimer: Do not form doctrine with my illustration of the Jericho miracle; please base yours on the scripture.

I firmly believe that God demonstrated a key principle at Jericho. With the appearance of Jesus bearing His sword before Joshua, we need to sit up and take note! Much like the men of Jericho were watching the army of God, we need to examine this principle in more detail with a keen eye like that of a spy.

What does this all have to do with prayer, you might ask? Well, I am glad you asked. Please read on.

This is the Jericho principle that we are basing the following prayer exercise on. We are praying for the walls to fall and the kingdom of God to rush in. We read in Mark:

> But no one can go into a strong man's house and ransack his household goods right and left and seize them as plunder unless he first binds the strong man; then indeed he may [thoroughly] plunder his house. (Mark 3:27, AMPC)

> Jesus said to them, "Listen. No one is able to break into a mighty man's house and steal his property unless he first overpowers the mighty man and ties him up. Then his entire house can be plundered and his possessions taken." (TPT)

We are binding the strong man (demon) that is assigned over a region and or subject matter. And we are coming into agreement with our prayers as we read of Jesus saying in the following verse:

> Truly I tell you, whatever you bind on earth will be bound in heaven, and whatever you loose on earth will be loosed in heaven. Again, truly I tell you that if two of you on earth agree about anything they ask for, it will be done for them by my Father in heaven. (Mathew 18:18–19, NIV)

This is a time that we must force a paradigm shift in our thinking. We must get away from thinking just with our natural mind and start considering what is really happening in the realms of the spirit. I will call you to consider the following scripture several times in this reading.

> For though we walk (live) in the flesh, we are not carrying on our warfare according to the flesh and using mere human weapons. For the weapons of our warfare are not physical [weapons of flesh and blood], but they are mighty before God for the overthrow and destruction of strongholds, [Inasmuch as we] refute arguments and theories and reasonings and every proud and lofty thing that sets itself up against the [true] knowledge of God; and we lead every thought and purpose away captive into the obedience of Christ (the Messiah, the Anointed One), Being in readiness to punish every [insubordinate for his] disobedience, when your own submission and obedience [as a church] are fully secured and complete. (2 Corinthians 10:3–6, AMPC)

> The world is unprincipled. It's dog-eat-dog out there! The world doesn't fight fair. But we don't live or fight our battles that way—never have and never will. The tools of our trade aren't for marketing or manipulation, but they are for demolishing that entire massively corrupt culture. We use our powerful God-tools for smashing warped philosophies, tearing down barriers erected against the truth of God, fitting every loose thought and emotion and impulse into the structure of life shaped by Christ. Our tools are ready at hand for clearing the ground of every obstruction and building lives of obedience into maturity. (MSG)

> For although we live in the natural realm, we don't wage a military campaign employing human weapons, using manipulation to achieve our aims. Instead, our spiritual weapons are energized with divine power to effectively dismantle the defenses behind which people hide. We can demolish every deceptive fantasy that opposes God and break through every arrogant attitude that is raised up in defiance of the true knowledge of God. We capture, like prisoners of war, every thought and insist that it bow in obedience to the Anointed One. Since we are armed with such dynamic weaponry, we stand ready to punish any trace of

rebellion, as soon as you choose complete obedience. (TPT)

The following demonstrates the providence of God, in the spring of 2016. I felt lead to develop a prayer time that I eventually started calling the Jericho Cross Prayer (JCP). These are very targeted prayers with scripture to back up each prayer. It was later in early summer of 2016 that I was asked to lead the prayer effort for Open Heaven (OH). God was already bathing the region in prayer for a solid year prior to the actual Open Heaven event and several months before I even knew of the existence of the OH. God is so good to be cultivating the region in prayer that way, using this prayer to plow the soil of souls.

Before I get into the meat of explaining this revolutionary prayer concept based on the Jericho principle, I would add, on the day before conduction the JCP, one critical thing takes place… Just as with the nation of Israel partook in the celebration of the Passover prior to going into the promised land and then reinstituted the right and ritual of circumcision in adherence to the Abrahamic Covenant, in like manner, we consecrate ourselves by partaking in Communion. We conduct Communion using a special prayer that was constructed by Wanda Walker. This prayer is a unique and very powerful prayer and confession of faith. You will find this prayer in the reference section at the end of the book.

Enid has one major north/south and one major east/west streets and four perimeter streets that encircle the city. During the JCP, we drive those streets in the car while we pray, much like the army of God as they marched on Jericho to see the walls fall.

We start with the Cross portion of the prayer on the west side of town. When we pray the Cross portion, we are praying for our pastor in thirty different subjects of prayer, as we drive in the symbol of the cross. (I am about to describe the path that we drive; you may want to get out a map of Enid and follow along as you read the following.)

We start on the west side of town at Garland and Highway 412. We drive on Highway 412 east to Highway 81 and turn south. On 81 we drive to Southgate and flip a U-turn. North on 81 back to 412 and turn east. On 412 to Thirtieth Street and flip a U-turn. We then turn north on 81. We then take 81 up to north Enid but don't do a U-turn. We take a little detour and head over to our pastor's house. At our pastor's house, we pull into the driveway and stop and pray. We do this as a point of contact. Jesus commanded us to pray and lay hands on the sick. As we are praying and driving, the vehicle is an instrument of that prayer, so it is a point of contact between the tires and the driveway. This might sound silly, but I am totally serious. Now back to the 81 and south to the 412. West on the 412, and when we are finishing up at Garland, we then speak out and name each Christian church that resides in Enid as well as others that we have close contact with. So as we are praying for our pastor, by proxy we are also praying for each of those churches' pastors and church leadership. That is twenty-two miles and approximately thirty-five minutes. But wait, there is more. As the TV commercials state, given that we are praying over our pastors in thirty different categories of prayer, one can use this portion of the JCP manual to also pray one prayer a day for your pastor!

Now for the Jericho portion of the prayer, which starts at the west side of Enid. We go north on Garland to Willow, east on Willow to Thirtieth street. South on Thirtieth Street to Southgate, west on Southgate to Garland and then north. We have now done one lap around the city. We continue until we finish seven laps. Each lap we are praying for a different combination of subjects, binding the demonic forces involved and loosening God's angelic army to fight. Each lap is approximately twenty miles and thirty minutes.

This is the list of what we pray about on each lap:

- *Jericho Lap 1*—family: husbands, wives, ex-husbands, ex-wives, children, children of divorce, grandparents, great-grandparents, and child abuse
- *Jericho Lap 2*—City of Enid, Garfield County, and the State of Oklahoma
- *Jericho Lap 3*—United States of America
- *Jericho Lap 4*—sexual sin (lust), the Jezebel spirit, addiction to porn, sexual assault, human trafficking, and abortion
- *Jericho Lap 5*—alcohol addiction and drug addiction
- *Jericho Lap 6*—discouragement, despair, depression, anxiety, and suicide
- *Jericho Lap 7*—Satan and his demons

Once we have finished all this praying, it looks like this: over 160 miles driven and 4 1/2 hours of prayer.

We do take potty breaks and have water bottles to keep hydrated. What have we accomplished? Our prayers dispatched God's heavenly army of angels on our behalf. He dispatched warring angels to do battle in the spirit realm, protecting those for whom we prayed. He dispatched ministering angels to minister those for whom we prayed. We effectively prayed Matthew 6:10 over the city and region. "Your kingdom come. Your will be done in earth, as it is in heaven." We were praying against the dominion of darkness and advancing the kingdom of light through Jesus Christ.

When I was led to develop this JCP, I was just being obedient to what I believe God was telling me to do for that specific time. Then I saw this as a critical tool in preparation for preparing the region for Open Heaven. I did not question it or even examine it in detail until the time of this writing. When God created the heavens and the earth and placed man in the garden, He gave Adam dominion over the earth and its contents. Sadly, when Adam fell, Satan now was given dominion over the earth. We know that Satan had dominion over the earth from the time of the temptation of Christ.

Again, the devil took him to a very high mountain and showed him all the kingdoms of the world and their splendor. "All this I will give you," he said, "if you will bow down and worship me." Jesus said to him, "Away from me, Satan! For it is written: 'Worship the Lord your God, and serve him only.'" (Matthew 4:8–9, NIV)

Notice that Jesus did not correct Satan and say that Satan did not have dominion over the earth. If Satan did not have dominion, it would not have been his to give to Jesus. We know that Christ brought the kingdom of heaven back to earth when He died on the cross, was buried, and raised from the dead. Now it is our responsibility as believers in Christ to advance His kingdom on earth. In Revelation, we read Jesus saying,

I am the Living One; I was dead, and now look, I am alive forever and ever! And I hold the keys of death and Hades. (Revelation 1:18, NIV)

Let us take a look at Joshua 5:13–6:27. Note that each time the army marched around the city of Jericho, they marched with the Ark of the Covenant. The Ark of the Covenant was the manifestation of God's physical presence on earth. By marching around the city, I believe, God was claiming the city for himself, and when the walls fell, we see in the natural what was the by-product of the battle that was waged in the spiritual realm. As believers in Christ, we are now the Temple of the Holy Spirit; like the Ark, we are the manifestation of God's physical presence on earth. By performing the JCP, we are casting down the principalities, the princes of darkness that have dominion over a region and claiming the kingdom of God having dominion over that region.

As I am writing this, I am getting deeper revelation as to exactly how powerful this JCP really is. One time while doing the Cross portion of the JCP, I was driving. I believe that God allowed me a glimpse to see into the spirit realm what was actually happening while we were praying. If you google a photo of the FA-18 Shock Wave, what you are seeing is when they are going transonic; there is a pressure wave that is very visible. The shock wave is compressing the air molecules as they are being pushed out of the way. It is also called a vapor cone. Now in those photos, you will see that the vehicle is ahead of the vapor cone; what I was seeing was that the manifest presence of the warring angels as they were going ahead of us. They were being dispatched by God to do His bidding.

> *Then he dispatched horses and chariots, an impressive fighting force. They came by night and surrounded the city. Early in the morning a servant of the Holy Man got up and went out. Surprise! Horses and chariots surrounding the city! The young man exclaimed, "Oh, master! What shall we do?" He said, "Don't worry about it—there are more on our side than on their side." Then Elisha prayed, "O GOD, open his eyes and let him see." The eyes of the young man were opened and he saw. A wonder! The whole mountainside full of horses and chariots of fire surrounding Elisha!" (2 Kings 6:14–17 (MSG)*

A LITTLE MORE DETAIL ON THE JERICHO PRINCIPLE

I am reminded of when I first started working at Rocketdyne on the space shuttle main engine. I was at the copier machine to make a copy of a picture that was drawn by a brother in the Lord. He drew this picture before I was privileged of God to lead him to Christ. The picture depicted Satan on his throne. In his hand was his scepter with his arm extended. On his throne were symbols: the cross, the Star of David, and surrounding the cross and star were circles drawn. As I was at the copy machine, I met a man who spied on the picture. He informed me that he had been a member of the

Hell's Angels gang. As I was conversing with him, I was not fearful, but my spirit man was sensing what was happening in the spiritual realms. A battle was waging; he sensed it as well. He asked me how long I had been practicing. I passed on answering that question; I did not let on to him what my real background was. I just continued to probe his understanding of the picture. He told me that the circles around the cross and star is used in black magic to cast a dominion spell over people. He thought I was one who practiced white magic, and this was what he thought he was sensing. What he was sensing was the Holy Spirit living with in me, but from his understanding, black magic and white magic were in opposition to each other, not opposite sides of the same coin. The enemy uses any tool that he can to wield his power; he even misuses the Word of God. We read that in Luke 4:1–13.

I believe Satan uses the Jericho principle to have his followers cast the spells and, as such, to dispatch his demons. I strongly believe it is incumbent on all believers to utilize the Jericho principle, the proper way in our prayer life to tap into God's principles for spiritual warfare!

> *When the enemy shall come in, like a flood the Spirit of the LORD shall lift up a standard against him. (Isaiah 59:19, NKJV)*

This is true spiritual warfare; we are calling on God to raise a standard against the enemy on the behalf of those who we are in intersession for. We are boldly entering into the throne room of grace and pleading the cause for those we are making intersession for.

> *For the weapons of our warfare are not carnal but mighty in God for pulling down strongholds, casting down arguments and every high thing that exalts itself against the knowledge of God, bringing every thought into captivity to the obedience of Christ. (2 Corinthians 10:4–5, NKJV)*

> *Finally, be strong in the Lord and in his mighty power. Put on the full armor of God, so that you can take your stand against the devil's schemes. For our struggle is not against flesh and blood, but against the rulers, against the authorities, against the powers of this dark world and against the spiritual forces of evil in the heavenly realms. Therefore put on the full armor of God, so that when the day of evil comes, you may be able to stand your ground, and after you have done everything, to stand. Stand firm then, with*

the belt of truth buckled around your waist, with the breastplate of righteousness in place, and with your feet fitted with the readiness that comes from the gospel of peace. In addition to all this, take up the shield of faith, with which you can extinguish all the flaming arrows of the evil one. Take the helmet of salvation and the sword of the Spirit, which is the word of God. And pray in the Spirit on all occasions with all kinds of prayers and requests. With this in mind, be alert and always keep on praying for all the Lord's people. (Ephesians 6:10–18, NIV)

Just like the military where you see rankings demonstrated by the stripes on the shoulder—private, corporal, sergeant, and so on—in the spiritual realms we see it as well. God's angels have rankings; this is why Michael and Gabriel are considered archangels. When the angel Lucifer fell and took one-third of the angels with him, I firmly believe that they continued with the ranking's hierarchy. This is demonstrated in Daniel 10:12–13. "Then he continued, 'Do not be afraid, Daniel. Since the first day that you set your mind to gain understanding and to humble yourself before your God, your words were heard, and I have come in response to them. But the prince of the Persian kingdom resisted me twenty-one days. Then Michael, one of the chief princes, came to help me, because I was detained there with the king of Persia.'"

The Bible says in the following verse,

For we wrestle not against flesh and blood, but against principalities, against powers, against the rulers of the darkness of this world, against spiritual wickedness in heavenly places. (Ephesians 6:12, KJV)

I firmly believe that these are separated out for a specific reason; they deal with rankings and responsibilities in the spiritual realms. These are separated in four distinct rankings and authorities. Against principalities. Against powers. Against the rulers of the darkness. Against spiritual wickedness in heavenly places. And as such, this is how we should target our prayers against them. This is the reason why this JCP prayer was conceived. To do battle against these four areas of dominion and their strongholds. The principalities, powers, and rulers of darkness are earthly bound demonic while the spiritual wickedness is those demonic in the heavenlies.

How you are fallen from heaven, O Day Star, son of Dawn! How
you are cut down to the ground, you who laid the nations low! You
said in your heart, 'I will ascend to heaven; above the stars of God
I will set my throne on high; I will sit on the mount of assembly in
the far reaches of the north; I will ascend above the heights of the
clouds; I will make myself like the Most High. (Isaiah 14:12–14,
ESV)

His tail swept down a third of the stars of heaven and cast them
to the earth... (Revelation 12:14, ESV)

At first read, this JCP might sound like a daunting task, in and of itself,
but it truly is not. Don't let the size and scope of this discourage you before
you even start! Start out small, and then allow it to grow. I usually have a
worship CD in the car, and as the spirit leads, we play a song. We enter into
His presence in praise and worship, and God truly meets us while we do
this. His manifest presence becomes very thick. Yes, four and a half hours of
prayer sounds like it would be difficult, but it really is not when God shows
up. And the beauty of being able to use your prayer language is awesome, in
that you do not need to know the particulars of a given subject that you are
interceding for. As you pray in tongues, you are praying the perfect will of
God over that situation. During JCP, I am driving while Laura is saying the
prayer as called out in the JCP manual. I am praying in tongues while she is
praying in English. At times she will also break into her prayer language as
the spirit leads. As I have been writing this, I have been led to modify how
we do the JCP, in that historically, we do the Cross portion and then seven
laps. Now we are going to do the Cross portion with one lap for six days,
and then the seventh, we will do the Cross portion and seven laps.

The JCP prayer can be adapted to whatever city or town you live in. If
one lived in Wichita, Kansas, this is how I would adapt JCP for it: The
Cross portion would be using Highway 54 east/west, Highway 135 north/
south, and for the Jericho portion, I would go into the center of the city
and do a nice ten-mile lap around city hall while following the prayer
guidelines. This I would do six laps, then for the seventh lap, I would
expand it to the entire city by going to Highway 235 north, K96 east, to
I-35 south back to the 235. The final lap would be approximately thirty-five
miles.

In Los Angeles, the symbol of the cross could be on First Street and

Broadway. And for Jericho, I would do six-to ten-mile laps around city hall followed by one large lap would go east on the 110 to the I-5, down to the I-10 back to the 110 for final one lap.

In Las Vegas, the symbol of the cross could be Flamingo Road and the Las Vegas Strip with the small laps around city hall and the large lap taking the Highway 515 south to the Highway 215 west to the Bruce Woodbury Beltway up to the Summerlin Parkway back east to the Highway 515.

One other suggestion, if the reader is incarcerated in a Department of Corrections facility, totally take this JCP into action and declare God's kingdom and dominion over the yard and over the city from which the DOC facility is located. The JCP manual is adaptable to any and all cities. A fellow believer in Christ at a DOC facility can pair up with another brother or sister (whichever the case may be). Once you get your chaplain's approval and, if necessary, the warden as well, you can walk the yard while praying the JCP. The power of agreement in action!

One key aspect (if performing in a car) is to have a prayer navigator who is directing the prayer from the JCP manual while the driver is paying attention to the road. DISCLAIMER—do not perform the JCP while driving alone! Operate in wisdom! You cannot read the JCP manual and drive at the same time. Always, always have a JCP prayer navigator.

If this entire JCP scares you, please do not be. You can start off small and do five-mile laps around city hall and do the Cross portion smaller as well. As you are faithful in the smaller, gradually grow it larger. God will show up in your car; you will be empowered by the Holy Spirit. You will not be drained of energy; quite the contrary, you will be energized, and I know I am very energized every time after finishing a JCP. Another option for incorporating the JCP would be to drive the symbol of the cross as stated earlier, but now when it comes to the Jericho, you can get out of the car and walk around city hall.

At Open Heaven, each Saturday for a month leading up to the event, I walked around the event center seven times praying. The day of the event, I walked up and down every aisle praying and laying hands on every seat. This was just an extension of what Laura and I do each Sunday morning before church services: we pray and lay hands on every seat, praying for those who will be occupying each chair. We even did that on a Sunday while on a cruise ship. I prayed over each lounge chair on the lido deck.

And later in the day, we were able to witness to several people.

As of this writing, we have embarked on a new aspect of ministry. In March we started going into a local prison twice a week. It is a two-year commitment resulting in those students who participate will receive an AA degree in ministry. The prison is in a rural area. Our plan is to construct a specialized JCP manual for this small town that also includes the prison. We will do an abbreviated version of the JCP specifically for this outreach of ours. It will be very specific so we can laser-target our prayers. We are to take dominion back for God; the adversary does not like it when we do, so he will try to get under our skin to thwart the move of God. Read on for just such an instance.

In the fall, the plan is for me to join two other ministries on a missionary trip to Uganda. At the time of this writing, I really do not know the details of which villages we are going to go and minister at. These will be villages that Anita, Rex, and Wilma have gone to in the past. Our primary mission is to support the pastors in those villages. We will be conducting camp meetings where the Gospel will be preached with the expectation that God will confirm His Word with signs and wonders and the workings of miracles. We will be flying into Kampala and then traveling about a hundred miles a day to visit each village. Since I do not know what villages we will be ministering at, I am selecting Katera, Bukwiri, Kitoba, Kitanyata, Kimbangya, Nakasongola, and Wobulezi. I am applying the JCP prayer for these villages. They form a big loop around the central portions of Uganda. The next JCP that I conduct, I will also be applying it to the nation of Uganda and these regions that have these villages as well. I do not know which villages, but our Father in Heaven does know which ones. Prayer makes things happen; I really do not need to know at this time, but God will transfer those prayers for the actual villages and actual people we will encounter. At the same time, since I am naming off targeted villages, I know that there will be a work of God in those named villages as well as His Word will not go out and come back null and void, but it will accomplish the task that it set out to do. Either way, it is a win-win situation.

By laying a good foundation of prayer, we can be prepared for whatever the adversary could want to throw our way. God answers prayer, and the following is a prime example of being under the protective wings of our Heavenly Father. Laura says, "Faith and fear cannot coexist!"

A little background. For most of Laura's life, she has had different varying fears—heights, bridges, and such. It has only been in the last four years that God has given her victory over these fears. Since learning what her authority is as a believer in Christ, she has learned to operate in that authority. She likes to say, "Fear and faith cannot coexist." You either operate in fear or you operate in faith—can't have both.

When we indicated that we wanted to have communion on Maundy Thursday, the students were elated. When we arrived at 5:25 p.m., I was told that I could not enter the facility with camo pants on. Laura and I looked at each other, and she asked if we should cancel the evening. I said I did not want to cancel; the students were so looking forward to it. I asked if she would be willing to go in by herself while I went to get something at the Dollar Store. She said she no problem, entering the yard by herself. Each evening in the past when we went in, we had two of our volunteers meet us, just inside the yard, and they escorted us to the chapel. Upon exiting the guard building, I encountered Drew Drawbridge as he was about to enter the guard building. He informed me that the session on the minimum side was canceled for some reason. We conversed for a little, and I proceeded to walk to the parking lot. As I did, I noticed that there was not the usual sight of orange inmate apparel on the yard. I gave pause. I started scanning for Laura—oh, there she was, but wait, she was walking alone! I knew something was up. I just did not know what. I cautiously drove away, wondering if I should go back to get her. As I was diving down that long, twelve-mile road to the 412, fear started to grip my heart. I was her husband; it was my mandate to protect her, and what was I doing driving away from her while she might be in danger? The adversary was on my shoulder speaking words of fear and lies in my ear. I was now in a fight-or-flight moment. I chose to fight. I started praying in the spirit and quoting scripture. Faith started to grow, forcing the fear out. These are the scriptures that I was quoting and standing on.

> For God did not give us a spirit of timidity (of cowardice, of craven and cringing and fawning fear), but [He has given us a spirit] of power and of love and of calm and well-balanced mind and discipline and self-control. (2 Timothy 1:7, AMPC)

> For God will never give you the spirit of fear, but the Holy Spirit who gives you mighty power, love, and self-control. (TPT)

Here is no fear in love [dread does not exist], but full-grown (complete, perfect) love turns fear out of doors and expels every trace of terror! For fear brings with it the thought of punishment, and [so] he who is afraid has not reached the full maturity of love [is not yet grown into love's complete perfection]. (1 John 4:18, AMPC)

God is love. When we take up permanent residence in a life of love, we live in God and God lives in us. This way, love has the run of the house, becomes at home and mature in us, so that we're free of worry on Judgment Day—our standing in the world is identical with Christ's. There is no room in love for fear. Well-formed love banishes fear. Since fear is crippling, a fearful life—fear of death, fear of judgment—is one not yet fully formed in love. (MSG)

By living in God, love has been brought to its full expression in us so that we may fearlessly face the day of judgment, because all that Jesus now is, so are we in this world. Love never brings fear, for fear is always related to punishment. But love's perfection drives the fear of punishment far from our hearts. Whoever walks constantly afraid of punishment has not reached love's perfection. In this [union and communion with Him] love is brought to completion and attains perfection with us, that we may have confidence for the day of judgment [with assurance and boldness to face Him], because as He is, so are we in this world. (TPT)

I got some sweats at the Dollar Store and got back to the prison facility. My entry was delayed until after the six-thirty movement. When I got to the chapel, the students were there, and so was Laura. She had the Communion elements set up. We immediately went into program. We prayed and had a sweet moment of worship with all of us singing "Amazing Grace." All these men singing a capella in the chapel was just so beautiful! We conducted Communion, and the atmosphere was so sweet. We conducted the class with the videos.

Between the videos, I spoke. I was honest in letting our students know what my experience was on the road to the Dollar Store. That for a brief moment, I allowed the voices of the adversary instill fear, but then I exercised my authority and walked in faith. I told them that I was just being transparent and this was a practical example of turning the tide and trusting

God for her protection. I indicated that I was not worried about our students in the chapel, just the guys in the yard that I didn't know. One student said to not worry, that they had our back.

The cause—an incident happened that they were on some form of lockdown, and Laura should not have been allowed in the yard. When Laura arrived at the chapel, she went in and set up the Communion elements and then went into prayer and worship. She indicated that she had no fear about walking the yard by herself and that God would have His warring angels to protect her.

The adversary tried to make a bad situation, but God stepped in, and Jesus gets the glory!

CHAPTER 5
PLANNING | KEY FOUR

On planning, there is a famous saying about that; it is called, "The 5 p's of success—proper planning prevents poor performance."

For I know the plans I have for you," declares the LORD, "plans to prosper you and not to harm you, plans to give you hope and a future." (Jeremiah 29:11, NIV)

God has plans for us! If God is a planner, then so should we be planners! The challenge for us is to make sure our plans line up with those of our Heavenly Father's plans. Above all, ask the Creator of the Universe to guide you in the planning process.

Write the vision And make it plain on tablets, That he may run who reads it. For the vision is yet for an appointed time; But at the end it will speak, and it will not lie. Though it tarries, wait for it; Because it will surely come, It will not tarry. (Habakkuk 2:2–3, NKJV)

Your word is a lamp for my feet, a light on my path. (Psalms 119:105, NIV)

Our prayer must be that our planning is illuminated by the light of His Word. We must remove selfish pride and motives and continually ask God for guidance.

As a trained engineer, I roll over and play dead on command. No really... In all seriousness, I have been trained to design aerospace systems and structure. Obviously, we design an item to perform a very specific function. When I am set to design something, one goal is to try to anticipate as many failure modes as possible and then design those failures out of the system. We establish safeguards in place and create redundancy within the system to prevent failures. These redundancies help prevent single-point failures within the system that could result in catastrophic and fatal consequences.

That is all and good, but where does one start?

What was will be again, what happened will happen again. There's nothing new on this earth. Year after year it's the same old thing. (Ecclesiastes 1:9, MSG)

Whatever it is that you are called of God to do, something similar probably has been done before. Why reinvent the wheel? Find a role model, examine the successes, and more importantly, try to find out what the failures were. When possible, contact the role model and ask. Ask if there were anything they would do differently. Ask them what some of the greatest successes were. Ask them what some of the greatest failures were. Ask how often they pray.

I just finished an e-mail where I am practicing exactly what I just enumerated in the paragraph above. Our pastor has a vision of streaming our services into the local correctional facility much like Pastor Morris does at Gateway Church with the Coffield and Sanders Estes facilities. Now, our approach will not be a cookie-cutter duplicate of what they are doing; through much prayer and discernment we will use whatever helpful information and allow God to work through our unique opportunities to bring Him glory. However it is manifested at this facility, the Gospel of Jesus Christ will be proclaimed and lives will be changed.

God gave us His best in Jesus; we need to give Him our best. If you read in the Law, God established very precise dimensions of the Ark of the Covenant, Tabernacle, and Temple. He established the bill of materials for everything that went into building the Ark of the Covenant, Tabernacle, and Temple. He was very detail-oriented about all aspects of their construction. He has a great attention to detail; as we plan our life's successes, we need to plan it with that attention to detail as well. Physical lives are at risk if I do not do my job well as a design engineer. Spiritual lives are at risk if I do not do my job well as a minister of the Gospel. Proper planning under the guidance of the Holy Spirit will bring whatever endeavor great success in the natural, but it must be done in the spirit first before it is manifested in the natural. Pray for guidance at each step of the way.

If your ministry requires you to go before city representatives, make a PowerPoint presentation; be as professional as you know to be. Pray over every word that is in that presentation. Pray over your verbal presentation to be led and guided by the Holy Spirit. Like I stated earlier, plan out the failures. Use the demographics you found to target your presentation. Try to anticipate every question and have an answer to that question. Expect opposition to your proposal, and have an answer combating that opposition. This is the point where praying for your city representatives will come in handy; you are allowing God to give your insight into areas that in the natural, you would not necessarily know the answer, but God gave you the insight. And God will be working favor on your behalf in the eyes of the officials.

With Open Heaven, one of the challenges in working with different churches was dealing with differing hierarchy within those churches. Oftentimes, speaking with the church receptionist was a challenge, in that there seemed to be a suspicion built into the conversation. Why would we want to work as one church, one body of Christ? Once the goals and objectives were communicated, those suspicions subsided.

A lot of churches did not have a designated prayer person or team, and as a result, getting the word out to pray for a given subject matter about OH was difficult. One church was offended that during the planning stages, they were not consulted about it being on a Saturday evening, and they felt they could not promote this night, as it would interfere with their ongoing scheduled Saturday evening services. In hindsight, praying the JCP prayer and spying out the land more effectively early on in the planning would probably have averted this misunderstanding.

> To the weak I became as weak, that I might win the weak. I have become all things to all men, that I might by all means save some. (1 Corinthians 9:22, NKJV)

What does this mean to me? We must think outside the box when planning for ministry. One of my gifts in the natural is that of being a chameleon. It really comes to me so very naturally. In high school, at lunchtime, I would spend time with the following groups: the jocks (played football), the surfers (which also were the stoners, but I did not get stoned), the nerds (still am a nerd), and a few other groups that don't really have a label. I could pop in and out of these groups quite fluidly. I have an uncanny ability to blend in and function in almost any group. I have the ability to find common ground and relate in many situations. Paul, with all his knowledge as an elite Jew, shed his bias against the Gentiles and became a missionary to the Gentiles.

Whatever we are in the natural, whatever gifts we have been given, we also need to pursue that of being a chameleon so that some may be saved. Yes, it can be uncomfortable to think about, but Christ left the comforts of heaven to bring heaven to earth and establish His kingdom. We need to get out of our comfort zones and push ourselves into situations and allow God to stretch us. What does this have to do with planning? Planning is intentional, and stepping out of your comfort zone is intentional; you need to plan ahead to be an intentional chameleon for the sake of Christ. Make plans to intentionally put yourself into a situation to share Christ. The more you do, the more natural it will come. We must be intentional Christians in our daily lives. Race your strengths; train your weakness.

CHAPTER 6
PERSISTENCE | KEY FIVE

Persistence wears down resistance.

They say that good things come to those who wait; I believe good things come to those who persist patiently (author unknown).

PERSISTENT TEENAGER

June, summer of 1977, I was fourteen years old and very bored with nothing to do in the early afternoons. High school football practice was only once a day in the mornings, so what to do? We only had one television in the house, and I could only stomach about one hour of soap operas with mom. Yes, I must admit, I got into One Life to Live. Oftentimes, after the soap, I would retire to my bedroom listening to the radio. My AM station of choice was KHJ Radio playing the top 40 hits (this was before FM radio gained popularity). They held call-in contests, and that I would attempt to win. It seems that I was quite proficient at winning those contests—even with the disadvantage those days of having a dial phone! Yes, those antiques that you occasionally see in a museum or on TV. I would speed-dial, forcing the dial rotation back before dialing the next number. They were 930 on the AM dial, so they were always looking for caller number 9, so often I would dial and be like the third caller. Eventually I got the timing right for the call-ins, and so over the course of June and July, I won several times. I won several consumer products, but the items that stand out are a year's supply of Panama Red Shampoo (could they smell me from Downey?), an AM/FM boom box portable stereo, and two tickets to the Led Zeppelin concert at the Forum. I think these three prizes stick out in my brain some forty-two years later is for peculiar reasons: the oddity of the name of shampoo; my mom gave the boom box to my grandfather, "Pappy"; and she gave the tickets to my brother Chris, who took Cousin Bobby. It would seem that I still have the touch, as while living in Wichita, I was known to also win several of the contests there with B98 FM and Light 99 FM. Thinking back, I am probably one of the reasons that radio stations now put in the restriction that only one win per household per month, because I was so persistently winning. In hindsight, as a parent now, I can understand why my mom would not want me to attend a Led Zeppelin concert at age fourteen.

By now, you must be pondering how this has anything to do with keys to the kingdom? Well, this has all things to do with persistence! I was very focused on winning—in fact, one might say that I was obsessed with winning. It really did not matter what it was that I was competing to win; the thrill was in the chase. I was very persistent in paying attention to detail about the questions they were asking. I was persistent in dialing. I was persistent in learning how to time the call-ins to the station. In this case, I was knocking and kept on knocking. I was dialing and kept on dialing I was seeking and kept on seeking until I was given the prizes they were offering. Now, unlike the radio station, when we dial God, He always picks up; we never get a busy signal! We never need to be the right number of caller. He does not screen His calls, and your call will never go directly to voice mail. He does not put conditions on hearing our prayers—oh, but one condition, we must first forgive, and it shall be forgiven to us.

And on further examination of these events, I really was unknowingly practicing the Jericho principle. Just like there are natural laws, there are spiritual laws that come into effect. The law of sowing and reaping is in effect for the believer and the unbeliever alike. In much the same way, the Jericho principle was applied. When you dial a local number, how many are there? Seven numbers are used. Old-school phones, you used your fingers to dial in circles, much like the army of God encircled the city of Jericho seven times. Some might say that I am over spiritualizing this, which is okay; you have that prerogative. Either way you look at it, my persistence paid off. I won several times. And I believe God taught me a good lesson while He was at it!

An example of a man interceding for another is found in the parable Jesus told in Luke 11:5–13. But with this parable, Jesus makes it quite personal and interjects you into the story. You woke up a friend in the middle of the night and asked for assistance so that you can help out a third friend. Your second friend does not want to help, but you persist. We see in the Luke 11:8–9 the results of the persistence, and I believe that this is how God wants us pray.

> *I tell YOU, although he will not get up and supply him anything because he is his friend, yet because of his shameless persistence and insistence he will get up and give him as much as he needs. So I say to YOU, Ask and keep on asking and it shall be given YOU;*

seek and keep on seeking and YOU shall find; knock and keep on knocking and the door shall be opened to YOU. (Emphasis added.) (Luke 11:8–9, AMPC)

Moses went to Pharaoh several times requesting to let God's people go. Moses asked and kept on asking until Pharaoh let them go.

Therefore, confess your sins to one another [your false steps, your offenses], and pray for one another, that you may be healed and restored. The heartfelt and persistent prayer of a righteous man (believer) can accomplish much [when put into action and made effective by God—it is dynamic and can have tremendous power]. (James 5:16, AMP)

Back to performing the JCP, being fervent and passionate in our prayers. God is steadfast; He does not change, and we should live our lives likewise. He was consistent and persistent in pursuing us; we need to be consistent and persistent in pursuing Him in our prayers to bring heaven down to earth.

In Matthew 15:22–28, the woman was pleading with Jesus to heal her daughter of demon possession. She was a Canaanite woman, not a daughter of David. She was persistent, so persistent was she that she was annoying the disciples. I can just see it: His disciples were trying to push her away. There was this natural love/hate relationship with the Israelites and the Canaanites, actually more hate than love. Jesus kind of demonstrated this relationship when He said, "I was sent only to the lost sheep of Israel." Her reply both demonstrated her love for her child but also a subservient attitude to the Christ when she knelt before Him and said, "Lord, help me!" Yet again Jesus replied, "It is not right to take the children's bread and toss it to the dogs." She persisted even more and replied, "Yes it is, Lord, even the dogs eat the crumbs that fall from their master's table." And in this He exclaimed, "Woman, you have great faith! Your request is granted." At first glance, one might think that her stubborn faith turned Jesus's heart toward her child and He granted the woman's request and the child was healed. But I firmly believed that this situation along with others like it were used to teach a point. She was consistent and persistent with her requests to Jesus. We need to be consistent and persistent with our requests and petitions to Jesus.

Again, Jesus told a story of a widow who was persistent in her petition to an unjust judge. Her relentless pleadings caused the judge to rule in her favor. Now we all know that Jesus is not an unjust judge. We find this story in Luke 18:1–5 where the judge is annoyed with the widow, and to shut her up, he granted her request! . She was consistent and persistent with her requests to the unjust judge. We need to be consistent and persistent with our requests and petitions to Jesus.

> *Crushed in soul, Hannah prayed to God and cried and cried—inconsolably... Hannah was praying in her heart, silently. Her lips moved, but no sound was heard. (1 Samuel 1:11,13 (MSG)*

Hannah was persistent in her petitions to have a child; her persistence was answered by God giving her a son, Samuel, who would be the voice of God to the first king over the nation of Israel, Saul.

SNAPPING TURTLE

Let us look at the snapping turtle; once it grasps your finger, it will not let go until sundown. Now, this I cannot personally attest to. I have only heard this happening, and believe me, I will not put it to the test. Once a snapping turtle was crossing a street, this street had a relatively low traffic flow as it was leading into a neighborhood development. We were concerned for the turtle's safety. Laura and I were attempting to handle it and to move it to safety. As we were trying to do this, we noticed that it was very quick and violent when he would whip his head around to latch on to a member of our body. We used a stick and a hubcap to move it over to safety. Yes, we relocated it but were very concerned while we were doing it! And no, we did not ask why the snapping turtle crossed the road.

Like that snapping turtle who once he latches onto something, he will not let go until sundown, we, too, need to have a prayer life like the snapping turtle; we lay hold of God's promises and not let go until the Son returns. First I told you to be a chameleon and now a snapping turtle. No, I do not have a particular fondness to reptiles, and they are just good word pictures to demonstrate the idea.

This is an endurance race, not a sprint.

> *Therefore, since we are surrounded by such a great cloud of witnesses, let us throw off everything that hinders and the sin that so easily entangles. And let us run with perseverance the race marked out for us. (Hebrews 12:1, NIV)*

So let us not be like the hare but the turtle and run the race well.

BULLDOG

Now I am going to encourage you to be as tenacious as a bulldog. There once was this evangelist who loved to hunt. He tells of a story of getting two top-tier bird-dog-setter pups. They were his pride and joy; he spent hours each day training them in his backyard. As each week passed by, he was getting excited that the pups were progressing in their training quite well. One day, a vicious-looking bulldog came sauntering down the back alley behind the evangelist's house. The bulldog snorted loudly and made his presence known. When he saw the two setter pups in the backyard; he found a spot in the fence that he could squeeze under. The evangelist wanted to protect the pups and considered taking them to the basement, but he then thought that it was two against one, so he just sat back and observed. The pups and this bulldog went at it, attack after attack. The bulldog took on each one, but when he got tired, he went back under the fence, snorting and licking his wounds. The next day, the bulldog pranced back down the alley, snorting as he came. Again, he squeezed under the fence and was ready for round two of this epic dogfight battle. As before, when he got tired, he left licking his wounds. Each day at around the same time, that bulldog showed up for a fight. The evangelist had to leave for a few weeks for a revival. When he returned, he asked his wife how the pups were doing. She said that the bulldog continued coming each day for the fight. Now, when the bulldog is heard snorting and sauntering down the alley, the pups start whining and running down to the basement. That little bulldog squeezes through the fence and struts around the yard as if he owns it. He helps himself to the two bowls of food intended for the pups. Persistence wears down resistance. This little bulldog wore down the pups because of his perseverance. We need the tenacity of that little bulldog in our prayers. Oh, and by the way, I am not encouraging you to be a bully to others like this bulldog. Just have tenacity like him in your prayers to Almighty God.

Let us not become weary in doing good, for at the proper time we will reap a harvest if we do not give up. (Galatians 6:9, NIV)

Consider it pure joy, my brothers and sisters, whenever you face trials of many kinds, because you know that the testing of your faith produces perseverance. Let perseverance finish its work so that you may be mature and complete, not lacking anything. (James 1:2–4, NIV)

Blessed is the one who perseveres under trial because, having stood the test, that person will receive the crown of life that the Lord has promised to those who love him. (James 1:12, NIV)

So let us seize and hold fast and retain without wavering the hope we cherish and confess and our acknowledgement of it, for He Who promised is reliable (sure) and faithful to His word. (Hebrews 10:12, AMPC)

Not only so, but we also glory in our sufferings, because we know that suffering produces perseverance; perseverance, character; and character, hope. And hope does not put us to shame, because God's love has been poured out into our hearts through the Holy Spirit, who has been given to us. (Romans 5:3–5, NIV)

Men, do you find it odd that the examples given of fervent, relentless prayer warriors are mostly women? This should not be! We need to step up to the plate and start swinging. We need to set down the remote, step away from the TV, and get in our prayer closet! We need to rush into this spiritual battle on our knees. We are directly responsible for the state of this nation because we have not taken prayer seriously.

TWO SQUIRRELS

A tale of two squirrels—no, not those squirrels, Chip and Dale that is—or should it be, a tail of two squirrels? Can you be the judge, please?

When we moved to Oklahoma, we rented a house that just happened to be built the same year we were born; that is kind of cool. In the front yard was this very dominant and intimidating tree. This oak tree had at its base a trunk approximately 3.5 to 4 feet in diameter. I would estimate that the tree had a height in excess of forty feet. During the summer and early fall, this tree, or rather the inhabitants of this tree, became a source of entertainment and amusement for Laura and I. The tree was inhabited by two little squirrels. We would spend early evenings out on the front lawn, sitting on folding chairs just watching these little squirrels scamper about as they were collecting the acorns as we sipped on an ice-cold glass of lemonade. All summer long, they did not rest; they would gather these acorns and bury them for future consumption. The tree had some limbs that were close to the house; we would see them leap to the roof of the house, acorn in mouth! I assume that they were going to the backyard to hide their acorn. One time when one was leaping back to the tree, he missed the limb and fell some twenty feet to the ground! He lay there on the ground, seemingly lifeless or stunned. He regained consciousness, shook his head, then ran back to the tree. These high-energy entertainers were in motion constantly; the only time they seemed to rest was when they paused to eat one these acorns. Even then, they did not leisurely kick back and slowly enjoy their meal. They ate their meal in ravishing manner, like firefighters just as they were being called to a fire.

At other times we would see these two squirrels get into an argument over something; in their tiny, squeaky voice they yell at each other, and then one would chase the other literally around the tree and jump from branch to branch. All summer long and into the fall, these two industrious little squirrels kept Laura and I entertained. To be honest, we were kind of sad to see winter come as we would be without our little friends putting on a show for us. Little did we know how accurate that would be. Sometime in the late winter, one of our little friends were trying to cross the street—yes, you guessed it, he was hit by a car. We had to give him a formal burial. His companion, well, was nowhere to be found by the springtime. Did his companion move to Florida for better weather or die of a broken heart? One will never know.

By the next summer, we had noticed that our tree did not take up new tenets. Maybe our landlord needed to put an advertisement out about this vacant tree in need of two squirrels. We actually were quite sad to find out that our friends that we grew so fond of were nowhere to be found.

Fall rolled around; we started noticing acorns starting to collect at the base and around the perimeter of the tree. Given that the landlord had a lawn service, we paid little attention to the lawn care of the house. But these acorns, they were starting to really grow in numbers all around the perimeter. The numbers seemed to be growing exponentially, to the point that we were growing tired of hearing the acorns drop and hit the top of our cars. So prolific the number of these acorns that when we walked out to the car, if we were not careful, they were like ball bearings and you would slip on them like ice. This was now becoming a health hazard. If someone were to slip and fall on these acorns, the landlord could be sued. We started raking them up and putting them into the trash container. We had the standard municipal trash collection containers that the city provides. I believe they are between seventy to eighty-gallon capacities. Well, at the end of the day, once we finished collecting about 95 percent of the fallen acorns, we filled up one and a half of those trash containers. Literally millions of acorns!

Persistence wears down resistance. I believe we need to be like these squirrels. From the time that the first acorn drops up until the last one drops from the tree; these two little squirrels were at work. After all, they knew that winter is coming. They were persistent and did not tire from the work. They did eat and sleep, but other than that, they knew the seasons and acted accordingly. They knew each location where they hid the acorns, and by the end of spring, surprisingly, we had very few newly sprouted trees. We need to be like these squirrels, diligently working the work that God has called us to do. We need to be going about the Father's business. We also need to be better than these squirrels, in that we need to be aware that we have an adversary that wants to squash us like that car did one of our friends. These are the end-times, and like the squirrels, we need to know that winter is coming; this must be a driving force in us to witness for Christ.

I believe this also illustrates another key principle, the power of agreement. These two working as a team in agreement with each other— were they male and female mates? Only God knows that. The power of the two in agreement going about doing the Father's business can accomplish seemingly impossible tasks. But with God, nothing is impossible.

> *Though one may be overpowered, two can defend themselves.*
> *A cord of three strands is not quickly broken. (Ecclesiastes 4:12,*
> *NIV)*

Let us be inspired by these two little squirrels! They, with their limited intelligence, are able to do the seemingly impossible. How much more you and I, believers in Jesus Christ, filled with the Holy Spirit—how much more can we do? I believe that is why Christ said that we would do greater works because He would be leaving to join the Father.

> *And if the Spirit of him who raised Jesus from the dead is living*
> *in you... (Romans 8:11, NIV)*

And now for one of my favorite scriptures, purely because of my background as a runner, but also it does speak to my very core as a believer:

Do you see what this means—all these pioneers who blazed the way, all these veterans cheering us on? It means we'd better get on with it. Strip down, start running—and never quit! No extra spiritual fat, no parasitic sins. Keep your eyes on Jesus, who both began and finished this race we're in. Study how he did it. Because he never lost sight of where he was headed—that exhilarating finish in and with God—he could put up with anything along the way: Cross, shame, whatever. And now he's there, in the place of honor, right alongside God. When you find yourselves flagging in your faith, go over that story again, item by item, that long litany of hostility he plowed through. That will shoot adrenaline into your souls! (Hebrews 12:2–3, MSG)

One final thought on persistence—*faith* and fear *cannot* coexist.

An intense battle waged last night.

For most of my life, the phrase "I can't" was just something that was not in my vocabulary very often. Even the times I told my brother "I can't" when he wanted me to play some baseball because I was suffering with a bout of bronchial asthma… I ended up playing. I relented only because if I had not, he would have continued to punch me in the arm… LOL. But seriously, I learned from my Pappy how to dream, plan, and build whatever he had a desire to build. So when I was given a task and a challenge in my profession, "I can't" was just not in my vocabulary. Design the nose section of an airplane—I had never done it, but now I can say, "Done." Design the rudder of an airplane—had not done that before, but now I can say, "Done." Put on a bicycle race… Now I have done over twenty-five. Write a book? Well, no one ever really posed that question directly. On January 21, 2019, I was asked by a friend to write an article. He gave me a title: "Keys to Building Strategic Partnerships for Unlocking a Region: Release the Kingdom in Your Community." Within two weeks I had written thirty-two pages. He then said that he was only expecting about five hundred words. So writing a book, well, that is not a process that I was familiar with, until now.

Growing up, fear was a daily reality for me. I would have a hard time going to sleep each night as fear would grip me. I would be frozen in fear as this torment wrapped around me like a boa constrictor that squeezes the life out of its prey, snapping the victim's bones like twigs as the lungs begin to collapse. What was I fearful of? In sixth grade, I was molested by a friend of the family. It only happened the one time, but there was the ever-present danger of it occurring again as he was a weekly visitor over at the house. He stood over six feet tall and was probably over three hundred pounds. I was no match to resist. This fear and high anxiety lasted until I was delivered from it by our Lord Jesus Christ. I had not experienced this gripping fear and anxiety for some thirty-four years now. Well, until last night.

A strong thunderstorm rolled through the entire state of Oklahoma last night, dropping up to four inches of rain in some locations. I am not one who cowers over in a corner when a thunderstorm hits the area. I usually watch the radar so as to see if we need to hit the basement, as the May 3, 1999, Haysville, Kansas, tornado ran in front of my home some 150 yards away. So as a result, yes, I monitor storms, but I am not afraid of them.

So with a flash of intense white light that illuminated the entire house, followed by an extremely loud boom of thunder, I was violently awakened. Okay, so it's a thunderstorm, big deal. But it was then that like a ton of bricks just seemed to drop on top of me. I was gripped in fear and anxiety. Off in the distance was the rolling thunder that just continued to rumble for over a minute and half. My mind tried to rationalize the situation and understand why I am frozen in the grips of fear. Not a single muscle could move. My mind raced to the thought that a window might be open and I needed to check them all to ensure we have no water intrusion, but "I couldn't." I was frozen in the grips of fear. And now another continuous round of rumbling, rolling thunder. I was frozen, and yet my face was sweating. As I lay there, trying to come out from under this pile of bricks and get unwrapped by this torment that had wrapped around me like a boa constrictor, nothing that was in my mind could figure out how to get me out of this situation.

Nothing but God. As I lay there in silence, I did not quote scripture in my mind. A perfect one would have been *2 Timothy 1:7 (NKJV), "For God has not given us a spirit of fear, but of power and of love and of a sound mind."* That is a scripture that I advise fearful people to memorize." But no, I was not quoting this, or any other scripture for that matter. I just started silently praying to the Lord, saying things like, "Thank You, Jesus" or "Praise You, Jesus." I went to the Lord with thanksgiving in my heart and continued to praise our Father. Slowly over the course of what seemed like about an hour and half, the pressure began lifting off my body, layer by layer the boa constrictor torment that had wrapped around me was unwrapping. I continued an attitude of thanksgiving and praise in my heart. I was free from the grip of fear and anxiety and torment. Praise His holy name!

I proceeded to check the windows; none were opened. In the natural, I just could not reason why this fear and anxiety came in like a flood. But when it did, I cried out to my God, and He raised a standard against him. The adversary comes to kill, steal, and destroy, but Christ came to give us life and life abundant. Christ, my rock and my salvation, delivered me; it is only in Him that I can trust. He alone is worthy to be praised. He alone is worthy to be worshipped.

It was then, as I was silent in this attitude of thanksgiving, praise, and worship, that I remembered what I was doing the previous day... I was rewriting the lap 6 of Jericho cross prayer. Lap 6 targets prayer dealing with discouragement, despair, depression, anxiety, and suicide. The adversary does not want this message to go out, and he will use whatever tool is in his toolbox. That tool has been in his toolbox, lying there, unused for over thirty-four years, until last night. I believe our wise and loving Father allowed this to happen so that He could nudge me to rewrite those prayers from yesterday to include not only an attitude of thanksgiving but also an attitude of praise.

The battle is really between our ears. Satan wants to put an idea in our heads. He knows we are very proficient at making mountains out of molehills. Instead of taking that idea and chucking it in the trash bin, we put that idea into the spin cycle and ramp it up to greater than an F-5 tornado between our ears. I firmly believe that it is these mountains that we have spun up from molehills that we are strongly encouraged to pray, and God will move the mountain and chuck them into the sea! Therefore, we need to control our thought life.

> *For though we walk in the flesh, we do not war according to the flesh. For the weapons of our warfare are not carnal but mighty in God for pulling down strongholds, casting down arguments and every high thing that exalts itself against the knowledge of God, bringing every thought into captivity to the obedience of Christ. (2 Corinthians 10:3–5, NKJV)*

Yes, this is that book, and as of right now—not bad for a mustard seed of expectation of five hundred words.

All the negative voices that I heard over the years—"You will never amount to anything," "Scrawny Ronnie," "You're stupid," "You are worthless," "You're an accident waiting to happen," and the list goes on— these voices internally did communicate "I can't." At pivotal moments of my life, the adversary likes to plant those words between my ears. At several points in the writing of this, he tried to use those words several times. I counter those words with the following:

> I can do all things [which He has called me to do] through Him who strengthens and empowers me [to fulfill His purpose—I am self-sufficient in Christ's sufficiency; I am ready for anything and equal to anything through Him who infuses me with inner strength and confident peace]. (Philippians 4:13, AMP)

> I have strength for all things in Christ Who empowers me [I am ready for anything and equal to anything through Him Who infuses inner strength into me; I am self-sufficient in Christ's sufficiency]. (AMPC)

> I can do all things through Christ who strengthens me. (NKJV)

> And I find that the strength of Christ's explosive power infuses me to conquer every difficulty. (TPT)

I no longer, consciously or unconsciously, operate in "I can't"; I operate in *"I can!"*

In summary, in this chapter on persistence, I have encouraged you to be like a snapping turtle, a bulldog, and a squirrel in your consistent and persistent attitude in prayer to our Father.

CHAPTER 7
POSITIVITY | KEY SIX

Disclaimer—this is not a name it–and–claim it message. I am, however, going to encourage you to have a paradigm shift on how you pray. A smile is a very contagious thing, so pass it along. Yes, that sounds very cliché, but it really works. The passion that was spoken of earlier, through being very positive, will be contagious. Okay, so I have encouraged you to be a chameleon, a snapping turtle, and a bulldog, so what is next, you might ask? A loveable golden retriever. A goldie, you might ask? Well, we have all had one of those dogs. As soon as they hear you driving into your driveway, they cannot contain their joy. Don't even stand near their tail; they will beat your shin silly with that tail wagging so violently. Oh, and when you step in the door, they want to jump into your lap. Grab your hand towel; you will need it to wipe your face from your dog licking it so profusely. Our love for God and all that Jesus did for us, we should be like the goldie, expressing our love for a merciful God in like manner. This is the joy of the Lord that is our strength.

> *You have enlarged the nation and increased their joy; they rejoice before you as people rejoice at the harvest, as warriors rejoice when dividing the plunder. (Isaiah 9:3, NIV)*

> *Though you have not seen him, you love him; and even though you do not see him now, you believe in him and are filled with an inexpressible and glorious joy, for you are receiving the end result of your faith, the salvation of your souls. (1 Peter 1:8–9, NIV)*

> *For everyone born of God is victorious and overcomes the world; and this is the victory that has conquered and overcome the world—our [continuing, persistent] faith [in Jesus the Son of God]. (1 John 5:4–5, AMP)*

> *But let all who take refuge in you rejoice; let them sing joyful praises forever. Spread your protection over them, that all who love your name may be filled with joy. (Psalm 5:11, NLT)*

When we sit back and really ponder what this mystery is and how we have been saved from ourselves, how can we not be joyful? We must allow ourselves to be joyful. Sometimes we allow the enemy to lie to us and say that we are unqualified because of our sin. He wants to condemn us for our past; just remember, when he does that, all we have to do is remind him of his future!

> But the fruit of the Spirit is love, joy, peace, patience, kindness, goodness, faithfulness, gentleness, self-control; against such things there is no law. (Galatians 5:22–23, NASB)

The more joyful that you are, the more positive you will be; the more positive you are, the more that people will want to be on your team and give you favor in your endeavor.

Now for a shift on how you pray, rather than a prayer of petition asking God's favor on this, that, or the other thing. If you are confident that what you are praying is within God's will, then thank Him for it! Praise Him that the answer is already on its way! Praise Him! In the following pages, we will be looking at different names for praising God. Please use this time to allow God to shift your paradigm away from petition-style praying to one of praising through it and praising God for already answering your prayers. We need to stop thinking of only in the three-dimensional world and start transforming our mind into the mind of Christ Who transcends time and space into the fifth dimension, into the mysteries of God. The method, the catalyst, and the conduit resides in a simple yet complex six-letter word, praise! Follow with me as we learn more about *praise*!

The garment industry makes billions of dollars each year convincing the public that we must have the latest styles to be relevant in other people's eyes. There is one garment that you can put on that will never go out of style, one that you will always look brilliant, dazzling, beautiful, handsome, and most of all, you are not being set up to fail. This is one garment that you will always be relevant in.

> The Spirit of the Sovereign LORD is on me, because the LORD has anointed me to proclaim good news to the poor. He has sent me to bind up the brokenhearted, to proclaim freedom for the captives and release from darkness for the prisoners, to proclaim the year of the LORD's favor and the day of vengeance of our God, to comfort all who mourn, and provide for those who grieve in Zion— to bestow on them a crown of beauty instead of ashes, the oil of joy instead of mourning, and a garment of praise instead of a spirit of despair. They will be called oaks of righteousness, a planting of the

LORD for the display of his splendor." (Emphasis added.) (Isaiah 61:1–3, NKJV)

I want to encourage you to fuel your spirit man by practicing abiding in His presence by continually praying, praising, and worshipping while meditating on God's holy Word. For the next eight days, I want to encourage you to start a practice of putting on the garment of praise. I firmly believe that praise is key to abiding in His presence. Praise ushers in the presence of the Almighty. Yes, the following is kind of presented as an eight-day daily devotional. If it helps you to think of it that way, then great! I would encourage you to conduct this in conjunction with the JCP (your mission, if you choose to accept it). Throughout the day practice one of the following types of praise in your walk. I envision it looking like this: One week out from doing the full JCP seven-lap prayer march, on that Saturday prior, you start this praise practice. Then on Sunday, continue to do Sunday's praise practice throughout the day in culmination with the JCP for the first lap, and then Monday and so on, leading up to the final, full Saturday seven-lap JCP.

There are eight Hebrew words for praise that we need to know. These words are as follows: *Yadah, Barak, Tehillah, Zamar, Shabach, Hallah, Todah,* and *Hallelujah.*

SATURDAY

It is Saturday—no, that does not mean it is satire Saturday… Saturday is traditionally the Sabbath, the day of rest. So let us praise His holy name. Praising God changes the atmosphere. This might be a refresher course; if it is, then it is good to revisit this from time to time… Today we look at *Yadah. Yadah* means to worship with extended hands.

Lift up your hands in the sanctuary, And bless the LORD. (Psalm 134:2, NKJV)

Why are you down in the dumps, dear soul? Why are you crying the blues? Fix my eyes on God soon I'll be praising again. He puts a smile on my face. He's my God. (Psalm 43:1–5, MSG)

Ezra opened the book. Every eye was on him (he was standing on the raised platform) and as he opened the book everyone stood. Then Ezra praised God, the great God, and all the people responded, "Oh Yes! Yes!" with hands raised high. And then they

*fell to their knees in worship of God, their faces to the ground.
(Nehemiah 8:5–6, MSG)*

*Since prayer is at the bottom of all this, what I want mostly is for
men to pray - not shaking angry fists at enemies but raising holy
hands to God. (1 Timothy 2:8, MSG)*

*Therefore I want the men everywhere to pray, lifting up holy
hands without anger or disputing. (1 Timothy 2:8, NIV)*

Yadah often is translated as "to give thanks." *Yadah* can be considered a
cry for help. *Yadah* praise is used when we are in the middle of the storm.
This is when we are in need of the Lord to deliver us to unto victory. *Yadah*
pictures a young child running in fear toward their daddy with hands raised
high, screaming and crying out, "Hold me, Daddy, hold me!" Raising the
hands is one of the sincerest, deepest, most meaningful, and most explosive
expressions of praise. Raising the hands is also the international sign of
surrender. A worshipper who raises their hands in total adoration signifies a
complete surrender to God.

May today be a day of praises with lifted hands for His deliverance of
us, especially while we are still in the storm. Praise Him with a heart of
thanksgiving, knowing that He is faithful and will deliver you from the
raging storm.

SUNDAY

It is Sunday—the day that most evangelicals have established as the day
of worship. I believe we need to shift that paradigm; we need an attitude
of worship every day, and every moment of every day we should be
worshipping our Father God.

*God is Spirit, and those who worship Him must worship in spirit
and truth. (John 4:24, NKJV)*

When Jesus said this, he was speaking to the Samaritan woman; she
posed the question as to the location of worship, which was His response.
With the tearing of the veil at the Holiest of Holy, God's Holy Spirit is now
released so we can worship Him whenever and wherever we are! Because,
after all, we are now the temple of the Holy Spirit; the spirit that raised
Christ from the dead lives and dwells in our hearts! Praising God changes
the atmosphere.

Today we look at *Barak*. *Barak* is used to denote blessing.

> *On that day Deborah and Barak son of Abinoam sang this song: "When the princes in Israel take the lead, when the people willingly offer themselves-- praise the LORD!" (Judges 5:1–2, NIV)*

> *Long may he live! May gold from Sheba be given him. May people ever pray for him and bless him all day long. (Psalm 72:15, NIV)*

We all seek the blessings from our earthly fathers and mothers. When we get it, we love it; we love the praises from our parents, so why would we think God to be any different? He enjoys the praises of His people. *Barak* suggests the transcendent honor and privilege of blessing the Lord as we surrender completely to His Word and will for our lives. May today be a day of praising Him in humility and in surrender for the privilege of being able to bless Him in every way we can. Everything we do, say should bring Him a blessing.

MONDAY

It is Monday—yes, it is Monday, the day that most of us go back to work from a weekend. Praising God changes the atmosphere, and on most Mondays, we can really use a change in the atmosphere.

Today we look at *Tehillah*. *Tehillah* means "to sing." It is pronounced similar to *tequila*, and some may sing loud while drinking it, but no, not *tequila* but *Tehillah*.

> *Yet you are enthroned as the Holy One; you are the one Israel praises. (Psalm 22:3, NIV)*

> *God is my strength, God is my song, and, yes! God is my salvation. This is the kind of God I have and I'm telling the world! This is the God of my father - I'm spreading the news far and wide! (Exodus 15:2, MSG)*

> *To care for the needs of all who mourn in Zion, give them bouquets of roses instead of ashes, Messages of joy instead of news of doom, a praising heart instead of a languid spirit. Rename them "Oaks of Righteousness" planted by God to display his glory." (Isaiah 61:3, MSG)*

He's your praise! He's your God! He did all these tremendous, these staggering things that you saw with your own eyes. (Deuteronomy 10:21, MSG)

Tehillah involves mostly singing but can be accompanied with music. Singing is vital to the worship of God. We are mandated to sing over three hundred times in the Word of God. Tehillah suggests that God Himself is, in fact, a song of praise. And another way to say it is, "God is our song."

If you are like me, I can't carry a tune in a bucket, but praise His holy name, to Him my singing is a joyful noise in His ears! May today be a day of singing praises to Him, making melody in our hearts. Make a point today to spend time singing His praises. Whether it is putting in your favorite praise and worship CD or if you are gifted to be musically inclined, then sing to His heart's content!

TUESDAY

It is Tuesday—yes, it may be taco Tuesday, but that is not our subject… Praising God changes the atmosphere.

Today we look at *Zamar*. *Zamar* means "to pluck the strings of an instrument." *Zamar* is translated into the New Testament as "*Psallo*."

David, the servant of the Lord, he sang to the Lord the words of this song when the Lord delivered him from the hand of all his enemies and from the hand of Saul. David was a musician who played the harp. He was so skilled at playing the harp that King Saul had him play to help keep the demonic spirits away.

The Lord is my rock, my fortress and my deliverer; my God is my rock, in whom I take refuge… I called to the Lord, who is worthy of praise, and I have been saved from my enemies. (Psalm 18:1–3, NIV)

God! Arise with awesome power, and every one of your enemies will scatter in fear! Chase them away—all these God-haters, Blow them away as a puff of smoke. Melt them away like wax in the fire. One good look at you and the wicked vanish. But let all your godly lovers be glad! Yes, let them all rejoice in your presence and be carried away with gladness. Let them laugh and be radiant with joy! Let them sing their celebration-songs for the coming of the cloud rider whose name is Yah! (Psalm 68:1–4, TPT)

Also see more songs of praise that David wrote to our God Who saves us from the grasp of our adversaries in Psalm 46–50.

> He continued, "Go home and prepare a feast, holiday food and drink; and share it with those who don't have anything: This day is holy to God. Don't feel bad. The joy of God is your strength!" (Nehemiah 8:10, MSG)

There is much rejoicing when *Zamar* is used; *Zamar* involves a very joyful and explosive expression of song and music. It involves using every available instrument capable of making harmonious music before the Lord. Like David with his harp, *Zamar* means to touch the strings and to sing praises. It is God's will that we be joyful. Use *Zamar* when you are rejoicing after God has done something great for you in your life or in the lives of those around you. You might want to go to YouTube to find some instrumentals of your favorite praise songs to help meditate on as you praise His holy name.

> Don't drink too much wine. That cheapens your life. Drink the Spirit of God, huge draughts of him. Sing hymns instead of drinking songs! Sing songs from your heart to Christ. Sing praises over everything, any excuse for a song to God the Father in the name of our Master, Jesus Christ. (Ephesians 5:19–20, MSG)

> And your hearts will overflow with a joyful song to the Lord Jehovah. Keep speaking to each other with words of Scripture, singing the Psalms with praises and spontaneous songs given by the Spirit! Always give thanks to Father God for every person he brings into your life in the name of our Lord Jesus Christ. (TPT)

I do not know how to play a musical instrument, but I can sing (vocal chords are a stringed instrument), I clap my hands (percussion), and so I guess you can say, I do know an instrument or two. May today be a day of singing praises to Him, making melody in our hearts. Although—another disclaimer—if you are around me when I sing His praises, you might want earplugs; I make a joyful noise (emphasis on noise).

WEDNESDAY

It is Wednesday—yes, the world calls it hump day… When I think of a camel, I visualize them kneeling as in an attitude of worship. For me, it is wonderful Wednesday, and praising God changes the atmosphere.

Today we look at *Shabach*. *Shabach* also means "to shout or to exclaim in a loud tone." The pagan king of Babylon, Nebuchadnezzar, because of his pride, God struck him with insanity. Seven years later, when God restored his sanity, Nebuchadnezzar shouted words of *Shabbach* in praise to the King of Heaven:

> *Now I, Nebuchadnezzar, praise and exalt and glorify the King of heaven, because everything he does is right and all his ways are just. And those who walk in pride he is able to humble. (Daniel 4:37, NIV)*

May today be a day of loudly singing praises to Him and shout to the mountains His glory in all the heavens! Be like King Nebuchadnezzar, and shout your praises of our Savior, Jesus Christ, for all that He has brought you through. Praise Him for the chains of bondage He saved you from. Praise Him for His mercy. Praise Him for His healing you and washing you from all your sins.

THURSDAY

It is Thursday, which means it is thankful Thursday. Today we look at *Hallah*. The most common word for praise—*Hallah*. This word in its simplest form is "to brag, boast, rant (positive rant), or rave about God." This is extravagant boasting and raving to the point of appearing foolish. In a former life, I had season tickets for UCLA football. After moving to Wichita, I started becoming a fan of WSU Shocker basketball. One could easily say that I was a super Shocker fan! Well, we do not have to think hard to picture what a true fanatic looks like—think of how some football fans dress up in outrageous costumes and painted faces at the Super Bowl.

It is a very sad commentary that if we shout and scream and brag on God, we are almost considered lunatics and that we should be locked up. Why is it acceptable to be a fanatic about a sports team and not a fanatic about a merciful Heavenly Father? A Father that sent His Son to die for all mankind?

> *Because your love is better than life, my lips will glorify you. I will praise you as long as I live... (Psalm 63:3–4, NIV)*

May today be a day of boasting, bragging, and raving about God's mercy and grace that He has bestowed on us. May Christ illuminate your mind with all the small blessings that He gives you throughout the day so you can exclaim in a shout, "Praise God for _____ this blessing!"

FRIDAY

It is Friday—which means it is fan-flipping-tastic Friday; what does that mean? Well, you do not have to be a gymnast to have a fan-fipping-tastic day as long as you are praising His name. Praising God changes the atmosphere. I do recall how King David was praising God so hard that his clothes fell off; maybe he was doing some leaping for joy and some radical flips. I firmly believe that it is okay to look the fool for Christ when we praise His holy name! We should put down any pretenses and not care what we look like before the hearts of men; we should only be concerned with how God the Father looks at us. His Word illustrates that He likes to see us and hear us praising His name.

Today we look at *Todah*. *Todah* means "to shout and to exclaim in a loud voice." It is an attitude of gratitude for God's promised deliverance. Note that the deliverance is promised, not currently realized in the natural, so the attitude of gratitude is operating in faith that God will deliver on His promise. This type of praise also refers to lifting of the hands in inviting God's help. *Todah* praise is now, having the faith and assurance even before the victory is actually come about. This is a praise operating in faith. It is a now kind of praise because it is a now faith, knowing that God is faithful to fulfill His promise.

For example, David is trapped by the Philistines in Gath. He gives thanks and offers *Todah* praise even before God delivers him.

> *Lord, show me your kindness and mercy, for these men oppose and oppress me all day long. Not a day goes by but that somebody harasses me. So many in their pride trample me under their feet. But in the day that I'm afraid, I lay all my fears before you and trust in you with all my heart. What harm could a man bring to me? With God on my side I will not be afraid of what comes. The roaring praises of God fill my heart, and I will always triumph as I trust his promises. (Psalm 56:1–4, TPT)*

Offer *Todah* praise and trust that God will deliver. May today be a day of shouting our praises for His deliverance of us, even while we are still in the storm. Shout your praises to out God in the middle of the storm; shout your victory in Jesus through the storm.

SATURDAY

Today we look at *Hallelujah*. The premier word for praise in the Bible is *Hallelujah*. *Hallelujah* transcends the languages of the world. It is not a mere translation—no, it is transliteration. Hallelujah is the combination of two words: *Hallel* and *Yah*.

Hallel means "to boast or to brag on, to make a show, even to the point of looking ridiculously foolish," as spoken of earlier.

Jah is the short form of the name for God. Most understand it to be the shortened version of *Yahweh*.

Hallelujah is a spontaneous outcry of a follower of Yahweh who is excited by what God is doing! We find that it is used twenty-four times between Psalm 104 and 150 and that it is reserved for times of extreme praise and exultation to the Most High God. We need to raise a *Hallelujah*!

> *Praise the Lord. Praise God in his sanctuary; praise him in his mighty heavens. Praise him for his acts of power; praise him for his surpassing greatness. Praise him with the sounding of the trumpet, praise him with the harp and lyre, praise him with timbrel and dancing, praise him with the strings and pipe, praise him with the clash of cymbals, praise him with resounding cymbals. Let everything that has breath praise the Lord. Praise the Lord. (Psalm 150, NIV)*

The word hallelujah is used only four times in the New Testament, and all of them are found in Revelation 19:1–7:

> *Hallelujah! Salvation and glory and power belong to our God.*

> *Hallelujah! Revenge on the Harlot: God is just after all.*

> *Hallelujah! God is still on his throne even though the world is destroyed.*

> *Hallelujah! For our Lord God Almighty reigns. Let us rejoice and be glad and give him glory! For the wedding of the Lamb has come, and his bride has made herself ready.*

On this day, the final day of the JCP, we can sing a Hallelujah, for the Lord is mighty and He reigns forever! He is faithful to bring the walls down and usher in victory for His people. Praising His name, praising God, changes the atmosphere. Praising God makes us more positive. Let us be consistent and persistent in praising our Heavenly Father!

CHAPTER 8
PEOPLE | KEY SEVEN

We see in Habakkuk 2:2 where the plans and goals need to be effectively communicated with those whom you are working with. Whether it is your family expressing the goals of the family or it is your ministry team. We see in Habakkuk 2:2 where we are admonished to share the vision—write it down! Let us look at several translations to get a deeper understanding of this vital scripture:

> *Then the Lord answered me and said: "Write the vision And make it plain on tablets, That he may run who reads it. For the vision is yet for an appointed time; But at the end it will speak, and it will not lie. Though it tarries, wait for it; Because it will surely come, It will not tarry. (Habakkuk 2:2, NKJV)*

> *And the Lord answered me and said, Write the vision and engrave it so plainly upon tablets that everyone who passes may [be able to] read [it easily and quickly] as he hastens by." For the vision is yet for an appointed time and it hastens to the end [fulfillment]; it will not deceive or disappoint. Though it tarry, wait [earnestly] for it, because it will surely come; it will not be behindhand on its appointed day. (AMPC)*

> *And then God answered: "Write this. Write what you see. Write it out in big block letters so that it can be read on the run." This vision-message is a witness pointing to what's coming. It aches for the coming—it can hardly wait! And it doesn't lie. If it seems slow in coming, wait. It's on its way. It will come right on time." (MSG)*

Okay, this is a deep statement. You are called to do ministry; just because you are called, do not step into that calling until you are sent—that is, until you have the anointing from on high. A prime example is Moses; he knew he had a call on his life; he tried to operate in that calling by defending a fellow Jew against an Egyptian taskmaster. He killed that taskmaster but found that since he was operating within his power and not in the power of the Almighty Jehovah God, he did not have the blessing. Thus he had to flee to the desert. We all know that he was humbled before God for forty years. And at the right time, God made His voice known in the burning bush.

Again, God expressing His nature and being inside fire and smoke!

Ministry is all about the people. Whether it is a one-night event like the Open Heaven or an ongoing outreach into an elder-care facility or a traveling evangelist and even a prison ministry, we need people. Both to give and receive this message that God has entrusted us with, we all need people. As we follow these seven keys, we will be more effective at spreading the Gospel in a method and means for the hearers to hear the message.

Moses had Joshua and Aaron; Jesus had his three with the twelve. We need people to help us spread the Good News of the Gospel of Jesus Christ!

If you are called to be a traveling evangelist, you cannot be a lone wolf; you need to be in a pack. Again with the animal comparisons, truly, I am not doing it intentionally. It really is how the spirit is flowing.

Let us take a quick look at how a wolf pack operates to see if we can learn a little more from the animal kingdom. When a pack of wolves are migrating from one hunting ground to the next, they migrate in a specific line of succession. At the head of the pack are the elderly and sickly or weaker members of the pack; this way, they set the pace of the migration and do not get left behind. They are followed by five or six of the stronger wolves to defend the weaker from a frontal attack. Following them are the main body of the pack. Immediately after the main body, again four or five of the strongest wolves to protect the main body. Finally, the alpha male leader of the pack is protecting the rear. From this vantage point, he can scan the entire path and respond to any attack from any direction. Whether you are an evangelist that travels to small-town churches, off of the highways and byways, or you are like Greg Laurie—we all need people to assist in this, and that is why we are the body of Christ. No matter the level of ministry that we have, we must be in a system of accountability. Today, like never before, men and women of God are falling left and right because of this lone-wolf mentality. We the body of Christ are interdependent with one another. I know I just singled out the evangelist, but in reality, this analogy applies to any believer who may only go to church on Christmas or Easter and can apply to the pew-sitter, who is not really involved in the ministry but just sits and checks the box of attending.

A popular GOT quote these days is, "The lone wolf dies, the pack survives." It holds a lot of truth to it.

ANATOMY AND PHYSIOLOGY
AND THE BODY OF CHRIST 101

I have been learning a few things about my body lately since last year the doctor gave me a diagnosis of type 2 diabetes. Practically everything that we consume for food these days has added processed sugars. These foods are causing us to be addicted to sugar. The more of it that we eat, the more we overload our pancreas as it is processing our food and regulating our blood sugar levels. This is not a situation of, "So you have elevated blood sugar, oh, aren't you so sweet?" Well, after years of my body growing an addictive dependency on sugary foods, my pancreas has basically thrown up its hands and said, "Stop the train, I want to get off!" Please see that the body needs all systems and organs to function properly… Otherwise, chain reactive events can take place. Think of your blood like the oil in your car's engine. My Honda Pilot's owner's manual indicates that 5W-20 oil is the proper weight to put in the engine. (Enter the big debate of high mileage engines should use a thicker oil.) As an engineer, I say, use the factory-recommended oil. Internally, the engine has passageways for the oil to flow through; thicker oil will not flow as easily through those passageways. Now you are asking, How does this relate to my blood? Well, if your pancreas is not regulating your blood sugar, then you will have much thicker blood. What does this mean? It is harder for the thicker blood to flow into the capillaries to places like your eyes, toes, fingers, and last but not surely least, your nerves. It starts to develop a condition called neuropathy; without the blood, the nerves start to misfire. Think of the tingling sensation when your hand falls asleep. But instead of just an annoying tingle, add a sharp/hot pain that pulses. On a scale of 1 to 10, about a 7 or an 8, and it will come without warning, just boom! It is this lack of blood circulation that can result in many other complications like the eyes going blind and amputations, starting with the toes, then the foot, then on up the legs.

Jonah was called to preach to the peoples of Nineveh and warn them of their coming destruction. But we know that he ran from God; after enduring much adversity, he finally relented and gave this message to the Ninevites. They heard it and took it to heart and then fasted and repented. What if he had not relented? What if he continued to be stiff-necked against the will of the Father? Well, more than 120,000 people would have perished as a result of the wrath of God because their evil was so great. He was obedient to the call of God on his life, and over 120,000 lives were spared. For over thirty-five years, like Jonah, I ran from the call of God on my life. Who are the people that I was divinely ordained to minister to and lead to Christ during that time frame? Was I meant to be someone's last hope of hearing the Gospel, but since I was running from God, I was not there to convey the message? How many more souls would be included in the body of Christ, had I answered the call? Are there some who would not have walked away from the faith, had I been there available to encourage them in their hour of need? One will never know on this side of heaven.

I remember, back in 1984, after having just returned from doing summer missionary work with campus crusade for Christ in Lake Tahoe. On two occasions, after completing a long-distance bicycle ride with a friend, we were relaxing in his front yard. One of Brad's friends rolled up on a motorcycle. He got off the bike and sat with us, relaxing in the Indian summer shade of a tree. They were catching up, chatting about this and that, while his friend smoked a cigarette. All the while that he was with us, I was feeling the prompting of the Holy Spirit to witness about Christ to this young man. The adversary gave me doubt and fear; he made me think that Brad would be offended if I started to witness to his friend, like as if I thought that Brad was not doing a good-enough job as being a witness. Well, on both occasions, the opportunity to witness came and went, and I remained silent. Just two weeks after the last encounter with this motorcyclist, he was traveling on the freeway and another vehicle collided with him, and he died. Did he ever receive Christ? I will never know on this side of heaven. If I were the pancreas, then I was not supplying the blood to the eyes to enable the body to have vision; I was not supplying the toes the blood, and they needed amputation causing the body to not walk straight. Wherever my place is in the body, for over thirty-five years, the body suffered because I was running away from my God. What has God called us to do in the body that we are not doing, and how is the body suffering?

SPIRITUAL BUTTERFLY EFFECT

Divine appointments, when they happen, we look back in awe of how God orchestrated the events leading up to this appointment; we are humbled, and yet our flesh can also be dumbfounded by it all. In the end, we can just sit back and praise His name!

Jesus commands us to go. It should be the exception if we stay. (Keith Green)

We are all called to be a witness for Christ, but what happens when we choose to not obey His calling and not operate in the giftings that He has given us? What happens to those who God had called us to witness to? He had ordained a divine appointment, but because we were avoiding our calling and not sensitive to the voice of the Holy Spirit, so we turned left instead of right. What if we were the last person that could have reached this one soul, but we refused to answer the call? Do you hear that, that phone ringing? It is God calling.

From 1980 to 2001, the US Army had a recruitment advertising slogan, "Be all that you can be." We as Christians in God's holy army need to be all that we can be and answer His call in our lives. We need to obey His Word.

It would seem to me that there are three kinds of Christian:

1. Professes to be Christian, but not into "organized church"

2. Christian that does go to church, checks the box on Sunday, but is checked out, not checked in and involved

3. Christian who loves Jesus and, out of this love, is motivated to serve others.

If you count yourself as a Christian, we, the other members of the body of Christ, need you! We need your God-given talents, gifts, and abilities. We are not complete without you! Where in the body do you fit in? Are you an eye, a finger, or a kidney? Just like in the natural, if you are a pancreas, the toes and eyes depend on you; without your gifting's functioning, what amputations will be required? Will the body go blind because the eyes are not getting the blood in the small capillaries? As I write this, my feet are on fire because of the neuropathy. My body is in open rebellion within itself in rebellion to the Word of God! Not good! In Jesus's name, body, align yourself to the Word of God!

All these gifts have a common origin, but are handed out one by one by the one Spirit of God. He decides who gets what, and when.

You can easily enough see how this kind of thing works by looking no further than your own body. Your body has many parts—limbs, organs, cells—but no matter how many parts you can name, you're still one body. It's exactly the same with Christ. By means of his one Spirit, we all said good-bye to our partial and piecemeal lives. We each used to independently call our own shots, but then we entered into a large and integrated life in which he has the final say in everything. (This is what we proclaimed in word and action when we were baptized.) Each of us is now a part of his resurrection body, refreshed and sustained at one fountain—his Spirit—where we all come to drink. The old labels we once used to identify ourselves—labels like Jew or Greek, slave or free—are no longer useful. We need something larger, more comprehensive.

I want you to think about how all this makes you more significant, not less. A body isn't just a single part blown up into something huge. It's all the different-but-similar parts arranged and functioning together. If Foot said, "I'm not elegant like Hand, embellished with rings; I guess I don't belong to this body," would that make it so? If Ear said, "I'm not beautiful like Eye, limpid and expressive; I don't deserve a place on the head," would you want to remove it from the body? If the body was all eye, how could it hear? If all ear, how could it smell? As it is, we see that God has carefully placed each part of the body right where he wanted it.

But I also want you to think about how this keeps your significance from getting blown up into self-importance. For no matter how significant you are, it is only because of what you are a part of. An enormous eye or a gigantic hand wouldn't be a body, but a monster. What we have is one body with many parts, each its proper size and in its proper place. No part is important on its own. Can you imagine Eye telling Hand, "Get lost; I don't need you"? Or, Head telling Foot, "You're fired; your job has been phased out"? As a matter of fact, in practice it works the other way—the "lower" the part, the more basic, and therefore necessary. You can live without an eye, for instance, but not without a stomach. When it's a part of your own body you are concerned with, it makes no difference whether the part is visible or clothed, higher or lower. You give it dignity and honor just as it is, without comparisons. If anything, you have more concern for the lower parts than the higher. If you had to choose, wouldn't you prefer good digestion to full-bodied hair?

The way God designed our bodies is a model for understanding our lives together as a church: every part dependent on every other part, the parts we mention and the parts we don't, the parts we see and the parts we don't. If one part hurts, every other part is involved in the hurt, and in the healing. If one part flourishes, every other part enters into the exuberance.

You are Christ's body—that's who you are! You must never forget this. Only as you accept your part of that body does your "part" mean anything. You're familiar with some of the parts that God has formed in his church, which is his "body": Apostles, prophets, teachers, miracle workers, healers, helpers, organizers, those who pray in tongues. But it's obvious by now, isn't it, that Christ's church is a complete Body and not a gigantic, unidimensional Part? It's not all Apostle, not all Prophet, not all Miracle Worker, not all Healer, not all Prayer in Tongues, not all Interpreter of Tongues. And yet some of you keep competing for so-called "important" parts. But now I want to lay out a far better way for you."

The time is now, now like never before for everyone in the Body of Christ to step up and do what God has called us to do! He has given us all unique gifts that we bring to the table. We need to be doers of the word and not just hearers of the word. God did not call us to be pew sitters. Christ raised Lazarus from the dead; He calls you to rise from your pew and to join in the labor for a lost and dying world. (1 Corinthians 12:12–27, MSG)

I mentioned that I had been a bicycle race promoter in the city of Wichita, Kansas. Bicycle racing, unlike baseball or basketball, does not afford many opportunities to race. On any summer day in any city, you can find a pickup game in those sports, but in competitive cycling in the Midwest, races are few and far in between. In 2004 I started a juniors' team and would travel in a three-hour radius for my team to compete. Wichita only had one race a year, and that promoter moved out in 2005. If someone did not step up and fill the gap, my team of kids would not be able to perform in front of hometown family and friends. Although I had never promoted a race, the first year I put on a three-day event. All told, while in Wichita, I put on twenty-three races over the years. These would not have happened if I had not stepped up and filled in the gap. Spiritually, what is not happening in the spiritual realms because we are not living up to our full potential in what God has gifted us with? And what are the results of our not living up to the call on our lives?

According to a recent study, the current business model for the church is failing for so many ministries. We read in The New York Times (August 1, 2010), "Members of the clergy now suffer from obesity, hypertension and depression at rates higher than most Americans. In the last decade, their use of antidepressants has risen, while their life expectancy has fallen. Many would change jobs if they could."

- 13 percent of active pastors are divorced.

- 23 percent have been fired or pressured to resign at least once in their careers.

- 25 percent don't know where to turn when they have a family or personal conflict or issue.

- 25 percent of pastors' wives see their husband's work schedule as a source of conflict.

- 33 percent felt burned out within their first five years of ministry.

- 33 percent say that being in ministry is an outright hazard to their family.

- 40 percent of pastors and 47 percent of spouses are suffering from burnout, frantic schedules, and/or unrealistic expectations.

- 45 percent of pastors' wives say the greatest danger to them and their family is physical, emotional, mental, and spiritual burnout.

- Though I can find no specific statistics (I'm sure they are out there), the pastorate is seeing a significant rise in the number of female pastors.

- 45 percent of pastors say that they've experienced depression or burnout to the extent that they needed to take a leave of absence from ministry.

- 50 percent feel unable to meet the needs of the job.

- 52 percent of pastors say they and their spouses believe that being in pastoral ministry is hazardous to their family's well-being and health.

- 56 percent of pastors' wives say that they have no close friends.

- 57 percent would leave the pastorate if they had somewhere else to go or some other vocation they could do.

- 70 percent say they don't have any close friends.

- 75 percent report severe stress causing anguish, worry, bewilderment, anger, depression, fear, and alienation.

- 80 percent of pastors say they have insufficient time with their spouse.

- 80 percent believe that pastoral ministry affects their families negatively.

- 90 percent feel unqualified or poorly prepared for ministry.

- 90 percent work more than fifty hours a week.

- 94 percent feel under pressure to have a perfect family.

- 1,500 pastors leave their ministries each month due to burnout, conflict, or moral failure.

Now, you will not find me quoting The New York Times very often. I find them to be far too anti-Christian for my taste. I just hope these numbers are not true—please do not let them be that bad. I hope The New York Times may be slighting the report to make it look more dire than true. Based on the bias against the church that The New York Times have demonstrated, it could be so as to bring more discouragement to the body of Christ. With that said, the numbers are what the numbers are. Church, we cannot allow this to continue! As the body of Christ, we need to set down the remote, step away from the TV, and live up to God's calling on our lives. We need not be keeping up with the Kardashians and more like keeping up with Paul the apostle of Christ.

Imitate me, just as I also imitate Christ. (1 Corinthians 11:1, NKJV)

Jesus had His three closest disciples, Peter, James, and John, and then He had the rest of the twelve. Along with them He also had Martha, Mary, and a team of other women helping in the ministry. It is also made mention that He sent out the seventy. We know that with five loaves and two fish, He fed five thousand besides women and children Many Bible scholars believe the actual number fed that day could have been fifteen to twenty thousand people. Okay, besides the obvious miracle of multiplying the actual food, to distribute that food to the tens of thousands that were present required a small army of workers, far more than the twelve and even the seventy.

The current business model of the church operating in the three primary functions, pastors, teachers, and evangelists is failing. The pastors are afforded breaks from time to time, letting the evangelists come in for a few weekends a year. That is all fine and good; we all need a vacation from time to time, but the numbers stated above seem to indicate that it is just not enough.

SQUARE PEGS

Back in 1983, there was this situational comedy on TV called *Square Pegs*, about a group of nerds trying to fit in at their high school. One week, they were filming at the college I attended. I was able to be used as an extra in one episode. A little while later in 1984 when I was exploring the questions of life and career, I considered becoming an LA County sheriff. I took the written, psychological, physical agility, and phase one of the medical physical tests and passing them all. I was in the middle of the background investigation when I received a call about going to a short-term mission's trip for the summer with Campus Crusade for Christ. I prayed about it and felt called to go on the mission's trip. In hindsight, becoming an LA County sheriff would have been akin to a square peg trying to fit into a round hole.

My wife and I were eating brunch at 580 Coffee shop. The 580 shop used the proceeds to support Forgotten Ministries homeless outreach. While consuming our meal, we could not help but overheard the conversation between two men next to us. It would appear to have been a first meet and greet between the men as they were giving each other their personal history. Both had gone to seminary and graduated. Both indicated that they did not feel called to pastor a church. One indicated that he continued to law school and became a lawyer while the other became a police officer. Their spiritual background was with a mainline denomination. They both continued to talk about financial successes in the market, almost from a boastful expression.

Later, as we were driving home, I felt my spirit grieving for these men. These men, at one point in their lives, felt the tug of the Holy Spirit to pursue vocational ministry, but somewhere along the way, they realized that being a square peg, they could not fit into the round hole of being a pastor. I firmly believe this is a prime example of why the paradigm of pastor centric ministry model is flawed. If you hear the calling of God on your life but do not fit into the role of an evangelist, pastor, or teacher, what are your choices?

Think of the old childhood toy that taught of the different shapes—square, octagon, star, round, and triangle—each being a different color. The fivefold ministry is likened to these shapes. Square being the apostle, octagon being the prophet, star being the evangelist, round being the pastor, and triangle being the teacher.

Could it be that the lawyer and police officer were called to be a prophet? Their giftings in the natural could lend them to be either a prophet or apostle. They both indicated that they could not fit into the pastor position. They obviously felt a call on their lives; sadly, the pastor-centric paradigm failed to facilitate them in answering their call.

Do you hear the phone ringing? It is God on the line, and He is calling you to the ministry. Are you a square, octagon, star, round, or triangle? Answer the call please. The body of Christ needs you operating within your calling.

> *The Lord is my Shepherd [to feed, to guide and to shield me], I shall not want. He lets me lie down in green pastures; He leads me beside the still and quiet waters. He refreshes and restores my soul (life); He leads me in the paths of righteousness for His name's sake. (Psalm 23:1–3, MSG)*

In the King James Version, in verse 2, it states that He makes me lie down in green pastures. I believe the numbers above about the overstressed, overworked, and soon-to-be burned out pastor feels he cannot just rest in the Lord because he is too busy doing the work of the ministry.

We need to do something else! What does the Word of God say about equipping the saints? Have we all come in the unity of the faith? No. Have we been transformed into the perfect man? *No.* Unto the measure of the stature of the fullness of Christ? No. What does the Word of God say about equipping the saints?

I firmly believe that every believer is called to function at times in all five ministries of the fivefold ministry in some capacity or form. What is the fivefold ministry, you might ask? Come with me to the book of Ephesians.

> *But to each one of us grace was given according to the measure of Christ's gift. Therefore He says: "When He ascended on high,*

131

He led captivity captive, And gave gifts to men." (Now this, "He ascended"—what does it mean but that He also first descended into the lower parts of the earth? He who descended is also the One who ascended far above all the heavens, that He might fill all things.) And He Himself gave some to be apostles, some prophets, some evangelists, and some pastors and teachers, for the equipping of the saints for the work of ministry, for the edifying of the body of Christ, till we all come to the unity of the faith and of the knowledge of the Son of God, to a perfect man, to the measure of the stature of the fullness of Christ; that we should no longer be children, tossed to and fro and carried about with every wind of doctrine, by the trickery of men, in the cunning craftiness of deceitful plotting, but, speaking the truth in love, may grow up in all things into Him who is the head–Christ–from whom the whole body, joined and knit together by what every joint supplies, according to the effective working by which every part does its share, causes growth of the body for the edifying of itself in love. (Ephesians 4:7–16, NKJV)

We are all called to do the work of the ministry, but we need to be taught how to do the work of the ministry, and a local body must have all five offices functioning for the body to function properly.

Yet again, the reference to the body of Christ and defining some of the functions of the individual elements of the body that are knit together, and each part doing its share of the workload. We know from scripture that our God is a God that never changes and His promises are true and everlasting. We know that the gifts and callings of God are without repentance. He gave us the fivefold ministry for the equipping of the saints for the work of the ministry. We as a church have abandoned the fivefold ministry and become lazy, allowing evangelists, pastors, and teachers to do all the work. Some would say that the office of the apostles died with the apostles when they finished writing the Bible. I believe that this is a lie straight from the pit, as I do not see an expiration date on this gift or any other promise and gift from God. They would say that the Bible has been written and the apostles and prophets laid the foundation for the church. But later Paul implores us in Hebrews to go beyond those very foundations that the traditionalists state is the reason for the fivefold ministry to be obsolete. Paul is imploring us to grow to maturity:

Therefore leaving the principles of the doctrine of Christ, let us go on unto maturity; not laying again the foundation of repentance from dead works, and of faith toward God, Of the doctrine of baptisms, and of laying on of hands, and of resurrection of the dead, and of eternal judgment. And this will we do, if God permits. (Hebrews 6:1–3, NKJV)

Some of the same traditionalists who feel that the fivefold is obsolete are not practicing in the basic elements listed above. They are not teaching of the three baptisms (blood, water, and spirit); they are not practicing the laying on of hands for healing and, sadly, not raising many from the dead. The gifts are not dead. God works the same today as He did with the first-century church. Our left-brain logic has gotten in the way of God working His signs and wonders in the Western church. Yet we see again the in Corinthians:

And God has placed in the church first of all apostles, second prophets, third teachers, then miracles, then gifts of healing, of helping, of guidance, and of different kinds of tongues. (1 Corinthians 12:28, NIV)

There is no way to entirely alleviate the stress and pressures that pastors face on a daily basis. However, the pressures, stress, and strain is significantly compounded when the fivefold ministry gifts are not fully operating in churches today. I firmly believe that it is not God's intention for pastors being the lone ranger or lone wolf in attempting to equip and build up the body of Christ. I have not found a single scripture that even comes close to suggesting that one senior shepherd has been given every necessary gifting to perfect a particular local body of believers. I mean, come on, no one person can multitask that efficiently! A local body of believers should have fivefold ministers that are meant to cooperate within their special giftings and abilities—these working together to help disciple, govern, guide, and guard God's people in everyday life.

We are to be God's hands and feet of this ministry of reconciliation.

Therefore humble yourselves under the mighty hand of God, that he may exalt you in due time. (1 Peter 5:6, ASV)

When Christ ascended, He took His entire ministry mantle and gave it to his disciples and said,

All authority in heaven and on earth has been given to me. Therefore go and make disciples of all nations, baptizing them in the name of the Father and of the Son and of the Holy Spirit, and teaching them to obey everything I have commanded you. And surely I am with you always, to the very end of the age. (Matthew 28:18–20, NIV)

He gave his ministry anointing to us as we read in John:

Believe me: I am in my Father and my Father is in me. If you can't believe that, believe what you see—these works. The person who trusts me will not only do what I'm doing but even greater things, because I, on my way to the Father, am giving you the same work to do that I've been doing. You can count on it. From now on, whatever you request along the lines of who I am and what I am doing, I'll do it. That's how the Father will be seen for who he is in the Son. I mean it. Whatever you request in this way, I'll do. (John 14:11–17, MSG)

I tell you this timeless truth: The person who follows me in faith, believing in me, will do the same mighty miracles that I do—even greater miracles than these because I go to be with my Father! For I will do whatever you ask me to do when you ask me in my name. And that is how the Son will show what the Father is really like and bring glory to him. Ask me anything in my name, and I will do it for you! (TPT)

He took His ministry mantle (anointing), multiplied, and gave it in five parts to men and women alike as He is no respecter of persons. All five are needed to perfect, mature, and equip the saints. These gifts are sometimes called the equipping or ascension gifts; they are to function together work harmoniously to the glory of Christ. One way to better understand them is through the analogy of how a physical hand functions. So quickly look at your hand, flex the fingers, like playing the piano or typing on the keyboard; they can work independently or together as a team as the task dictates. We will look at the fivefold ministries as a hand but also consider each function and correlate them with other body parts as well.

THE APOSTLE IS THE THUMB

The thumb may look like it is in opposition to the other fingers, but it is not. The thumb is not in opposition or competition to nor is it to lord over the fingers. This fact is unique to mankind, in that we are the only inhabitants on the face of the earth with an opposing thumb! The thumb is designed to complete the full function and power of the hand. The thumb is the digit that enables us to grip a tool or a weapon. The apostle's function in the administration of working together with prophets to lay the foundation with the proper doctrinal and spiritual structure within the local body. The apostle is much like the heart revealing compassion and strategy for advancing the kingdom. Apostles move primarily in the gifts of healing, gifts of faith, the working of miracles, words of wisdom, discerning of spirits, and sometimes prophecy. In more traditional churches, there may be individuals functioning with in the office of the apostle, without actually knowing that they are, in fact, performing that function. It is God that is the giver of the gifts, and it is His desire to move and work, regardless of challenges that our mind wants to put in His way. In a more denominational setting, those functioning in the office (unknowingly) by laying the foundation of proper doctrinal and spiritual structure within the local body, while not necessarily operation in the other spiritual giftings normally associated with the office of apostle.

In a modern church setting, the apostle would oversee building a strong foundation and the development and the sending of apostolic teams for workings of miracle ministries. The apostle also activates, imparts, and demonstrates the apostolic anointing to other bodies of believers. Today we more commonly call them "church planters" in that they would participate in going to other regions and nations to establish new churches. Brother Rex, mentioned in the first of this book, was a missionary, and he fully operated in his office of apostle. Apostles also assist local pastors in a region to restore order and unity in existing congregations.

THE PROPHET IS THE FOREFINGER

The office of the prophet is different than the gift of prophecy; the office is often confused with prophesying; they are not one in the same. The forefinger is often called the pointer finger. The prophet functions in revelation and points the way for believers. The prophet is like the mouth communicating guidance correction and love. The office of prophet carries a governing authority. The prophet's role comes with higher responsibility and, thus, higher accountability. The prophet flows in those areas of guidance, instruction, rebuke, judgment, and revelation. They function in whatever Christ through His Holy Spirit chooses to speak for the purification and perfection of His bride, the church. The gift of prophecy, however, is for the edification, exhortation, and comfort.

Prophets have the special ability to recognize God's gifts and callings on other individuals. It is their responsibility to be the conduit of the Holy Spirit in activating people's giftings through the laying of hands in prayer. Not everyone who prophesies is a prophet (just as not everyone who moves in miracles is an apostle). We see this written by Paul to Timothy.

> *I'm writing to encourage you to fan into a flame and rekindle the fire of the spiritual gift God imparted to you when I laid my hands upon you. For God will never give you the spirit of fear, but the Holy Spirit who gives you mighty power, love, and self-control. So never be ashamed of the testimony of our Lord, nor be embarrassed over my imprisonment, but overcome every evil by the revelation of the power of God. (2 Timothy 1:6–8, TPT)*

In a modern church of today, prophets would oversee the development of qualified prophetic teams. These teams are able to give accurate and timely personal prophetic words. They form a prophetic group of ministers and elders for the purpose of ministering prophetically to individuals or the church body at large. Not everyone who says "Thus says the Lord" is a prophet; it is vitally important that the local body operates in discernment before labeling someone as a prophet. They can wield too much power over a congregation, so this needs to be under His guidance.

THE EVANGELIST IS THE MIDDLE FINGER

The middle finger extends the furthest on the hand. The middle finger represents the outreach ministry extended to evangelize the world. Think of Jerusalem, Judea, Samaria, and then the ends-of-the-earth statement—well, the evangelist is reaching all those and more. The evangelists are the hands that are always reaching out to souls with the love and grace and forgiveness of our Heavenly Father.

An evangelist in today's church would oversee evangelism teams and outreach. They assist the pastors in maintaining the passion and vision for winning souls to Jesus. They are impassioned in the training of prophetic evangelists. Evangelists are given the unique ability by the Holy Spirit to clearly and effectively communicate the Gospel of Jesus Christ to others. They have the gifting to take some of the obscure mysteries of God and put them plainly for the average person to understand. I believe they can be likened to the chameleon; in that they have the innate gifting to connect the dots and find common ground with the hearers of the message. Like Paul writes to the Corinthians,

To the weak became I as weak, that I might gain the weak: I am made all things to all men, that I might by all means save some. (1 Corinthians 9:22, NIV)

The evangelist is burdened in their hearts for the lost and will go out of their way to share the truth with them. As the spirit leads, they might be going one way at the airport, but yet the Holy Spirit directs them to make a U-turn to minister to just one. Likened to Jesus leaving the ninety-nine for the one.

THE PASTOR IS THE RING FINGER

The ring finger is the wedding ring finger. For the pastor it symbolizes the pastor's commitment to his flock. Prophets, apostles, and evangelists might come and go, but the pastor is in a covenant relationship with the local saints within his flock. He is in a shepherding relationship, one of tender love. Another way to look at it is that the pastors are the feet leading the sheep to pasture and the paths of righteousness. The pastor's rod and staff comfort the sheep with his protection. The pastor is the one who most gets his/her hands dirty. Dealing with the day-to-day stresses and pressures of his local flock. He is the one who hears on the daily basis about the adultery, drug abuse, child abuse, alcohol abuse, and many more of the challenges of life that present a flock. He is at the forefront of bearing the burden of his flock. Whether it is a flock of fifty or of fifty thousand, it is his/her shoulders that these burdens are laid upon. If he/she is being led by the spirit, he/she casts the burden on the Lord, for the Lord will sustain them. The pastor is oftentimes on the front lines of all these battles, and unless he/she takes the advice of Moses's father in law Jethro about delegation, all that was detailed in the above *New York Times* study can befall on that pastor.

Those in the pastoral care of a local body would oversee discipleship leaders; they assist the senior pastor in duties, such as performing funerals and weddings, conducting hospital visitations, prayer and counseling, and other ministerial capacities which may include prison visitations.

THE TEACHER IS THE LITTLE FINGER

Although it's the smallest finger, never, never—I say not to ever—discount the little finger! It is essential in providing balance. The teacher is the one who is grounding the church in the foundational truths through very concise and detailed instruction. The teacher is able to break down the prophetic enunciations from the apostle and prophet; they break them down to bite-size servings to make the complex simple to understand. It is their instruction in the primary principles of the Word of God—just like a bricklayer, brick by brick, layer by layer establishing the foundation. The teacher lays the good foundation through methodically teaching verse by verse, line by line. The teacher has the mind of Christ to bring wisdom and understanding.

The teacher in a today's modern church would oversee the educational and training ministries of the adult and children's Sunday school and midweek service settings. The teacher writes and develops new curriculum. They may review other curriculum for appropriateness for the local body for said classes. In all this, the teacher is impassioned to performing teaching duties to the body. It clearly is a gifting from God.

I do not know if you have ever broken a finger, when one is broken, the entire hand suffers, as it is the hand working in unison that is required to complete a task. Last year, I broke my little finger. It was very surprising how much I depended on it just to function. Even buttoning my shirt became a great task to undertake. The body needs all five fingers working together to compete the task of equipping the saints for the work of the ministry.

We do not call or appoint ourselves to any of the fivefold ministries. It is a gift and call of Christ Himself. Sometimes it is confirmed by other believers before we realize it in ourselves. But it is up to us to answer the call! It is up to us to be open and available to God to teach us in the full operation of those giftings and to take the steps of faith when we choose to operate in them.

In general, a fivefold minister usually has one primary calling and divine enablement to fully manifest that one equipping gift. That being said, they may also have a secondary leaning in another fivefold area. But just like the nine spiritual gifts, the most important gift to operate in is the one needed right now to minister to an individual so we may be called to manifest other fivefold gifts at various times. As long as we continue to stay diligent sharing this Good News, there will be new converts and there will still be people who need to be trained and equipped.

I firmly believe that every believer is called to function at times in any and all the five ministries of the fivefold ministry in some capacity or form. Here is an example for you. Every believer is called to prayer and a minister of the word. Every believer is called to the ministry of reconciliation. Every believer is called to a ministry of working miracles, signs, and wonders.

Mark 16:17–18 expressly states this. Every believer is called to fight for sound doctrine and "go into all the world." Every believer has been sent into the world. And yet, not all are apostles.

Every believer is capable of hearing God's voice, John 6:44–45 and 10:27, yet not all are prophets. In 1 Corinthians 14:31, Paul writes, "You may all prophesy…" So yet again, not all are prophets, but you may all prophesy!

No one is ever allowed to say, "Sorry, I'm not an evangelist, I work in hospitality [or whatever excuse] at our church, so I don't need to evangelize."

Jesus commanded us to go; it should be the exception when we stay; to put it bluntly, evangelism is every believer's mission and mandate. Paul told Timothy (who was either a pastor or an apostle) to "do the work of an evangelist." In the same way, not all are teachers, but every believer is called to teach in some capacity. Paul writes in Colossians 3:16, "Teach and admonish one another with all wisdom."

A pastor has a shepherd's heart to care for the sheep, the flock of the church. It is the pastor's responsibility to spend his or her life for the sheep's well-being. The pastor is to "bear one another's burdens…" The pastor is to be devoted to one another in love. The pastor is to honor one another above themselves and "serve one another humbly in love." We as individuals are all expected to "do the work of" a pastor as we live this walk of faith. But we are not all pastors.

And you guessed it—we are all to teach, but not all are called to be teachers. Paul writes in Romans:

> *I myself am convinced, my brothers and sisters, that you yourselves are full of goodness, filled with knowledge and*

competent to instruct one another. (Romans 15:14, NIV)

Again Paul admonished us in Colossians:

> *Let the message of Christ dwell among you richly as you teach*
> *and admonish one another with all wisdom through psalms, hymns,*
> *and songs from the Spirit, singing to God with gratitude in your*
> *hearts. (Colossians 3:16, NIV)*

Not all are teachers, but every believer is called to teach in some capacity. In the same way, every believer is capable of "doing the work of" all five ministries. But not all are called and gifted in those individual offices.

Fivefold ministry is for this present age. A small three-letter word makes this argument for the fivefold ministry still so relevant, the word until in the Ephesians 4 passage. Until we have "all" reached "unity in the faith. Until we have reached the knowledge of the Son of God. Until we all become mature, attaining to the whole measure of the fullness of Christ. I know I have not attained these virtues, and if you scan the nightly news, so many have not as well. If you are honest with yourself, you might also come to the same conclusion: we all have not "arrived" as believers to the fullness of what God has to offer but God! We strive on to the higher calling of God in Christ Jesus! Yes, we are the redeemed of the Lord; we are sons and daughters of the Most High God. We are the righteousness of God in Christ Jesus. We have His Word to live by and His Holy Spirit to lead and guide us in all truth. That being said, we still need each other in the body of Christ to contribute our talents and giftings from God for the edification of all the saints.

Just as there is an overwhelming need to evangelize the world, just as we need to continue to teach and believers need to be shepherded, we still need to have the offices of apostle and prophet full in operation. Without them, we have what we have, burnt-out pastors.

Just think of it, in heaven, we will have no need for the apostle. Everyone will have already been transformed in the blink of an eye and experiencing the fullness of the kingdom! All truth will be revealed, and all will understand the mysteries of God. Until then, we need apostles!

In heaven, everyone will be with God face-to-face in loving worship and adoration of our Heavenly Father. There will be nothing to get in the way of perfect communication with Abba Father. This is why Paul said, "Prophecy will cease." But until we get to heaven, we still need prophets.

Everyone will already be saved in heaven! We would have no need for anyone to equip God's people to evangelize. Until then, we need evangelists!

Yes, you are getting my drift, in heaven we will not need pastors (shepherds). After all, the true Shepherd is on hand, and we can say in all faith and worship, "The Lord is my Shepherd, I shall not want." Pastoral ministry will be a thing of the past. Until then, we need pastors!

And finally, there won't be any teachers in heaven. The Holy Spirit is there, and He will lead us and guide us in all truth. All the wisdom and knowledge of the deep mysteries of God will be available to us quicker than you can google it. The Holy Spirit will be teaching us, so no need to have other teachers. Until then, we need teachers!

To come into Christ's fullness, it takes all five ascension gifts working harmoniously together to accomplish this.

Church, we desperately need to humble ourselves under the mighty hand of God. We the body of Christ need you on fire for God! In closing, please look at the following warning:

> I know your works, that you are neither cold nor hot. I could wish you were cold or hot. So then, because you are lukewarm, and neither [a]cold nor hot, I will vomit you out of My mouth. (Revelation 3:15–16, NKJV)

> I know all that you do, and I know that you are neither frozen in apathy nor fervent with passion. How I wish you were either one or the other! But because you are neither cold nor hot, but lukewarm, I am about to spit you from my mouth. (TPT)

Let's fight this war on our knees, side by side. Will you join me? On the Sunday, prior to the first Saturday of the month, we will be conducting the JCP prayer. From Sunday through Friday, we will be conducting the Cross portion and one lap of the Jericho portion with Saturday being the full-blown JCP prayer session. Can we come into agreement and work together to bring revival to the land? Working together and coming into agreement, one can send a thousand to flight; two can bring ten thousand to flight. Imagine, if you will, several prayer warriors throughout the region praying together the JCP prayer…oh, baby, the walls are gonna come tumbling down! Will you join me on your knees in battle, pushing back the kingdom of darkness and ushering in the kingdom of light in our region? Now, obviously, since we are driving, we are not literally on our knees. Saddle up, let's go!

As I have been fine-tuning this, I came across something pretty interesting: Back when we were conducting the JCP in its early conception, there was this one business that we targeted out prayers to. The owner was extremely notorious for running this nefarious establishment. During the lap that was appropriate for this establishment, we were actually able to do seven laps around this business, using the parking lot. Several weeks later, the owner was arrested on several felony accounts. I do not think that this was a mere coincidence; we were doing battle in the spiritual realms, and God answered our prayers! Praise His name!

The paradigm shifts away from a pastor-centric model and more toward the full operation of the fivefold ministry is what will be required in these end-times.

Two years ago, I got a word from God. It usually happens for me when I am looking at something and God gives specific insight concerning that thing. I told Laura about it, but unfortunately, I kept it to myself at the time. Doubt and fear caused me to not share until much later, well, here it is.

When we see all the big box businesses going out of business, do not be discouraged; this is part of God's plan for the final end-times' harvest of souls. There is going to be such an outpouring of His Holy Spirit that the existing physical buildings of the church will not be able to contain the flock and there will not be time to build new buildings. There just will not be time to get the building committee together in agreement and start a building fund… There must be a paradigm shift in the body of Christ when thinking how "church" needs to look like. The shepherds will now have to think out of the box and start utilizing the vacant big box stores. And soon, those will not be able contain the harvest of souls. Just like Peter, when Christ told him to let down the nets, his boat was not able to contain the catch.

When he had finished speaking, he said to Simon, "Put out into deep water, and let down the nets for a catch." Simon answered, "Master, we've worked hard all night and haven't caught anything. But because you say so, I will let down the nets." When they had done so, they caught such a large number of fish that their nets

142

began to break. (Luke 5:4–6, NASB)

Honor the Lord with your capital and sufficiency [from righteous labors] and with the firstfruits of all your income; So shall your storage places be filled with plenty, and your vats shall be overflowing with new wine. (Proverbs 3:9–10, AMPC)

Glorify God with all your wealth, honoring him with your very best, with every increase that comes to you. Then every dimension of your life will overflow with blessings from an uncontainable source of inner joy! (TPT)

CHAPTER 9
PRINCIPLED PRACTICAL APPLICATION
OF THE JCP

I will detail three opportunities we encountered to apply the JCP in our practical everyday experience. I have made mention on several occasions throughout this writing of the prison ministry outreach as well as the anticipated mission's trip to Uganda. This book was in the editing process while both were occurring. I believe that this writing would not be complete without addressing what has happened in the last few months. I developed two customized JCP manuals for our prison and for Uganda. When we would get into our prayer closet or conduct the JCP, we would dedicate time to lift up these two prayer opportunities.

OPPORTUNITY 1—AN UNPLANNED OPPORTUNITY

On September 11, there was a home invasion in our small city that left a forty-one-year-old mother dead. This happened one week prior to my scheduled departure to Uganda. Still, yet another two more home invasions occurred—one on the day of my departure and one on the twentieth. Laura, now being home alone, took matters in her own hands; she applied the JCP to the situation. After church on Sunday, the twenty-first, she planned on conducting the JCP. While driving home with one of our Glory Care parishioners, Peggy, an eighty-plus-year-old sweetheart saint, Laura told her of the JCP plans. Peggy asked to participate. So with the Honda Pilot full of fuel, these two prayer warriors hit the pavement and set out to exercise their authority in Christ over the principalities, powers, and rulers of darkness over the city. By the end of the day, the last two of the six suspects were arrested. Praise the name of the Lord.

OPPORTUNITY 2

Why do we pray daily for the prison where we minister? Why pray more than we already pray? In the spring of 2019, we started praying about bringing Evangelist comedian Elijah Tindale to come and speak on both the medium- and minimum-security sides of the yard. We applied these concepts detailed in this book to bring about this event. We started praying for the principle human individuals in authority over the facility. We started praying against the spiritual principalities, powers, and rulers of darkness in high places that are over the facility. We did all this leading up to the day that I called Elijah to speak to him about coming.

Unbeknownst to me, a friend of his was now serving time on the minimum side of the yard; this individual felt a burden to pray for Elijah that same day! Elijah was very enthusiastic about coming on out from North Hollywood to be a spokesman for the Gospel of Jesus Christ. We continued to apply the seven keys to the kingdom in planning for this weekend.

We scheduled it for the weekend of September 14/15. I asked the students to apply the concepts in their personal prayer lives as well, incorporating as best as they could with the limited movements required by the facility. Along with our being involved on Wednesday and Thursday evenings, I started going into the prison on Saturdays to facilitate the worship team practices. We planned on utilizing the inmate worship team. These Saturdays also afforded me some one-on-one discipleship time with some of our students, so it was a win-win opportunity.

This is what the plan was: The medium side would have Elijah do two sessions. Session one was a comedy session while the second was his testimony. On the minimum side, Elijah would do just one session with his comedy interwoven into his testimony.

In the weeks leading up to the event, there was some trouble on the yard. For the month of August, we were only able to go in during the week on three occasions. There were lockdowns for this reason and that reason. Notably, August 21, there was a prison fight resulting in two going to the hospital. Close to a dozen others were transferred to other facilities as a result of this altercation. Shanks were used in the fight that measured up to fourteen inches long. Our students felt that although a fight is not a good thing, it did result in some bad apples being relocated, making this yard a little safer.

Helena Christian Church allowed us access to the church and fellowship hall for prayer prior to the event as well as lunch between the two sessions. Laura and I brought our camping trailer for Elijah to use it as his star trailer between sessions. Our team of prayer warriors was interceding for an hour prior to our group heading to security to process through.

Elijah's comedy routine went off very well, and when we returned after lunch, we had a packed house in the auditorium. When the salvation prayer was called, we saw several raise their hands! After the sinner's prayer was said, several more men came up for prayer. All in all, this was a very good day for the kingdom of God!

The worship team started breaking down the equipment, so I figured it would be a good time to visit the men's room. Okay, you have permission to laugh. Well, I guess I took a little too long in the men's room taking care of business. Once I made an exit, I found the auditorium to be empty and dark. I ran to the exit door; it was locked! What do I do? I was locked in prison! Just then, the chaplain and one of our students rushed in. We all had a good laugh. I need to reread this book, the chapter on perspective; having a good sense of situational awareness is a key!

On Sunday, there was one session on the minimum side. The Gospel was presented through His servant, Elijah, to over 350 men in prison this weekend resulting in 112 decisions for Christ! The Holy Spirit had descended on the men in this prison and led the captives free in their hearts! As our team was finishing prayer sending us off, the chaplain informed us that the yard was now on lockdown.

When we returned home, we found out that at the six other prisons throughout Oklahoma on Saturday and Sunday, there had been mini riots. These riots resulted in thirty-six inmates being injured, one ending in death. These fights were among prison racial gangs. This caused the entire Oklahoma DOC to have a statewide lockdown on all facilities. But God! This weekend at our prison, the Holy Spirit had fallen on our yard and protected this move of God! Praise His holy name!

Right on the heels of finishing this outreach, three days later, I was on a plane headed for Uganda.

OPPORTUNITY 3—UGANDA MISSION TRIP

We laid the foundation in prayer for Uganda for the last nine months using the JCP manual customized for the nation. I was to be assisting Wilma Parnell and Anita during this mission's trip that was billed as a memorial trip commemorating the life of Rex. "Papa Rex" who went to dance with Jesus in March. From the time of his passing until the time we arrived in Uganda, the churches that he was responsible for planting grew from nine to twenty-nine churches.

In December of 2018, both Laura and I felt impressed in our spirit that I needed to join Rex and Wilma Parnell and Anita on the mission trip in the next fall. With the passing of Rex, we both just knew I needed to be a Martha to Wilma for this trip. Days after making that decision in March, our pastor asked us to consider. We knew that I had to go; we just did not know how the finances would come about to take me there.

Time flies when you work your forty hours of lifestyle evangelism at your job and then add on to that the twenty to twenty-four hours a week of ministry that we do. Then let's not mention completing this book, June rolled around faster that I thought. I started mailing out ministry fund raiser requests for this mission in June. The basic need was for twenty-five hundred dollars to fully fund the ministry requirements for me being there. I also started selling some of my aerospace collectables and bicycles on eBay and Facebook marketplace. Funds started rolling in; first it was a trickle then something short of a flood. I would describe it as a manifold blessing in that funds came in from several states and all walks of life. Even as I wrote this, I feel an overwhelming sense of gratitude and humility over how God used so many to send me there. Unexpected blessings came in from those who were sowing seeds into this. I am so thankful for each and every one who contributed to this.

We had purchased a lock for the trailer hitch a year prior. It was unwrapped, so we decided to return it for a refund. It would be another $20 for Uganda. When we attempted to return, it was rejected by the retailer as the product was no longer in their system. As we were leaving, a gentleman stated that he could buy it from us. Outside, I told him we would take $10 for it. He went to the ATM. Upon his return, I informed him how thankful we were as it was going to the mission field. He had withdrawn $50; once hearing this, he in turn blessed us with the entire $50. He himself had spent years as a missionary in Mexico. Praise God. After some more time of fellowship, he made another trip to the ATM to bless the mission that much more. This is God's fingerprint in arraigning these types of divine appointments.

A widow's mite—one of our friends who help us in ministry found out that we were selling things on eBay and Facebook and asked if we would be okay with her donating items for sale toward Uganda support. We agreed straightaway to this. She then told some of her friends, who told some others, and we now we were seeing an avalanche of items to sell. From this widow's mite being multiplying several times over of seeds being sown into this effort. Praise God.

The faith of a child—when I was a child, my pastor and I would go do Saturday visitations. While he would speak with the adults, I would speak with the children. Pastor John Ashcroft told my mother that I would someday be an Evangelist. I was seven years old. The faith of a child. One of the other friends from church who was notified that I was selling items for Uganda informed us that their eight-year-old wanted to redecorate her bedroom to be African-themed as she wanted to be a missionary to Africa. When she heard that I was selling stuff to go, she asked if she could donate her old bedroom set as sowing seeds into Africa. I say old bedroom set, but it was in like new condition. Pastor Teddy and April's daughters name is Trinity. Here is one more demonstration of the fingerprint of God. Here this eight-year-old has dreams of going to Africa. I am going to preach to thousands in Africa, and she is sending me. Her name is Trinity. The church I attended as a seven-year-old was Trinity Baptist Church. Praise God. He used an eight-year-old to help fulfill a fifty-year-old prophetic word spoken over a seven-year-old.

The greatest impression that I have taken from my first visit to Uganda is that of the people. Just like beautiful grandeur of the lush green countryside, the people of Uganda are beautiful from the inside out. Their spirits are so full of grace and honor. It has been such a privilege and honor to be a representative of God and the Gospel of Jesus Christ to these beautiful people.

Bishop Kamanzi David is the pastor over the Tower of Faith World Missions headquarters church in Mbarara, Uganda, that Papa Rex and Mama Wilma Parnell planted some fourteen years ago.

I had communicated with David that I knew the song "O Sifuni Mungo" by the group First Call which was an English/Swahili language song of praise. When we were picked up from the airport while driving to Kampala, David played this song on the van radio. He alluded to the possibility of me singing it with the children.

Here is the mission profile for team A:
• conduct three days of teaching and evangelism at a local church;
• pastoral leadership training by team members present;
• then followed by an evening crusade

Team A were consisted of:

- Wilma Parnell;
- Anita Sewell;
- Ron Wade, first two-thirds of the mission;
- Gary Scrogyns, last one-third of the mission;
- Cameron Lauridsen; and
- Noah Jones

National team members were:

- Bp. Kamanzi David;
- Evelyn;
- JR;
- driver, Nakedo Hamis; and
- Kamanzi Moses

Team B went out by themselves and then floated back into team A twice as the mission required. They had scheduled pastoral leadership training but also became quite fluid in ministry as opportunities popped up at schools and other venues. News of them being in a region would spread, and invitations to schools and churches would come about seemingly randomly. Cameron has adopted my favorite saying, "Blessed are the flexible for they are not easily broken." These random speaking opportunities would produce an audience of anywhere from a dozen to twelve hundred students. Both Noah and Cameron just rolled with the punches and delivered a strong right hook of the Gospel of Jesus Christ to whoever was placed before them! Noah was quite skilled at learning the native language. He was able to say very key phrases, and the people enjoyed that he was taking the time to learn.

Team B were consisted of:

- Cameron Lauridsen; and
- Noah Jones

National team members were:

- Kamanzi Moses; and
- driver, Emmy

Team C were consisted of:

- Ron Wade

National team members were:
- national handler, Pius Oule; and
- driver, Garuka Hamisi

Knowing that I would be teaching at least three sessions, one session a day, at a given church followed by the evening of evangelism, at home, I prepared three teaching and three evangelism messages. The teaching messages were the fivefold ministry, spiritual warfare, fear and faith cannot coexist and the centurion faith while the evangelism messages were rich young ruler/Nicodemus, the woman with the issue of blood/the woman caught in adultery, and my personal testimony. The fivefold ministry teaching was taken from the "People" chapter in this book.

On September 20, Wilma Parnell and Anita Sewell taught with power and conviction. As I was called up to the podium, David gave me the mic and cued the music and said sing. He tricked me into singing it in front of the pastors. I cannot carry a tune in a bucket. So I sang the "O Sifuni Mungo" song to pastors. They got a kick out of it.

In the morning session, I taught on the fivefold ministry and the importance of the body of Christ stepping up and doing the work of the ministry. We ended the session by praying over the pastors.

Prior to the crusade, several worship dance teams would get on the stage with native music being played. I started roaming the crowd and started dancing with the little children. I was making sure to make eye contact with them for at least a few seconds before moving on with another in the group. This dancing lasted for some ninety or more minutes. I know that I may look pretty foolish dancing with these kids like I do, but I read the scripture indicating that we are to be all things to all men so that some may come to Christ. I dance as well as I sing, or at lease my version of dancing and singing.

David called me up on stage as well as several of the children. The children and I did the "O Sifuni Mungo" song together. Everyone seemed to enjoy it. This fifty-six-year-old white guy "dancing" must have been quite a sight to behold.

This first crusade had some four hundred or so in attendance. I gave my testimony, and it seemed it was a total success; I had counted thirty decisions for Christ. I was later told that some came later after the formal event because of fear of retaliation from converting from Islam. We saw over eighty-two decisions for Christ! This pattern would be repeated each night.

I then gave testimony and scriptural references to Christ coming to restore the entire man, spirit, soul, and body. Many later came up to be prayed for healings. Some of those testified. I noticed a woman jumping up and down and doing different stretching movements. She came up on the stage, and the woman's back pain from a car accident the previous week was healed with full mobility. She again demonstrated her mobility on stage. Several testified that their malaria joint pain being healed instantly, resulting in full mobility.

Later as the evening was being shut down, Obed, a twenty-year-old young man came up to me. He was stuttering. I was speaking life into his life, giving him fatherly guidance. Then I was led to speak to his curse of stuttering. I commanded that curse to bow at the foot of the cross of Calvary. He was healed of stuttering. I witnessed this right before my eyes. I then spoke a word over him that he will be as Moses, used of God to bring deliverance to set his generation of captives free!

These and many other healings were testified by the thirty or more who came forward that night.

On September 21, Wilma Parnell and Anita Sewell taught very powerful messages. I taught on spiritual warfare. The lessons given by all were well received.

In the evening at the crusade grounds, again I was dancing with the children. David called me up on stage as well as several of the children at the start of the formal portion of the crusade. The children and I did the "O Sifuni Mungo" song together. For the evangelism message, I spoke of the woman with issue of blood and woman caught in adultery resulting in several salvations. I counted eight but would later find out that many more came up later. Again, I spoke of Christ the healer and many healings were testified by the twenty or more who came up.

On September 22, great teachings during the conference were given by all. Wilma Parnell and Anita Sewell taught with the precision of skilled professionals. I taught on fear and faith cannot coexist. At the crusade, the children and I did the "O Sifuni Mungo" song together. My evangelism message was on comparing and contrasting rich young ruler and Nicodemus. We saw close to one hundred salvations this evening with many coming up later for a healing touch from Jesus.

September 23 was a travel day from Kampala to Mbarara, a six-hour trip. I looked for but did not see any exotic African animals on this trip, unfortunately.

On September 24, we continued with the teaching. Cameron and Noah joined up with us. Wilma Parnell and Anita Sewell taught with authority and conviction. I taught on the faith of the centurion which morphed into being a breaker of chains. Many breakthroughs occurred; several being delivered of oppression. The song "Breaker of Chains" was played. This lasted for easily ten minutes. In this setting, I am finding that prepared teaching/ preaching notes become only suggestions when the spirit is flowing.

We conducted a memorial service for Papa Rex at the Tower of Faith Church. It was a day full of reverence to Rex and the God he serves. The evening developed into a more intimate setting of me and Cameron in front of some thirty in the audience. I proceeded to give my testimony with Cameron leading the sinner's prayer. My take on the day was that the needed spiritual move of God occurred earlier with breaking of chains.

On September 25, now don't let the package fool you. Wilma Parnell and Anita Sewell are forces to be reckoned with. They taught powerfully. God moved with all the messages for the pastors. I gave the fivefold ministry teaching and called the pastors, pastor's spouses, and other ministry workers to come up for prayer. We prayed over them. I did not feel lead to conduct the evangelism message for the evening so Cameron and Noah delivered it. We saw between eighty to ninety came to Christ this night.

On September 26, this was the day that the Lord had made let us rejoice and be glad in it. Good morning from Uganda. We had now been in country for almost a full week! I was very excited for what God had already done! In five nights of crusades, we had seen close to three hundred salvations and many healings. Today, we're finished in Mbarara with the pastor's conference teaching sessions, and then the men and women were separated for group question and answer. God is good. His name is glorified. Tomorrow, we would go to the next region for another three days of pastor's conferences. Jesus is Lord!

Each of the teachings I have given have been well received—fivefold ministry, spiritual warfare, fear and faith cannot coexist, faith of the centurion. The fivefold ministry and spiritual warfare messages were much appreciated by the older pastors. I feel really humbled when someone my senior expresses such gratitude. We had the male leadership Q&A session next. I was expecting the gamut of questions from "how to ministry" to the subject of sex.

A father asked for advice with his teenagers. Another man asked if we could start a Bible school. I was able to pray for one guy with a body twisted by scoliosis. God allowed me to see into his spirit and see a strong man of faith. He asked for prayer for a job. Not for healing, but a job. His name is "Somewhere."

A pastor asked how to deal with the aftermath of bringing in a false prophet who took advantage of the congregation and stole money. The congregation was justifiably mad at him.

I told him that he needed to clean up the mess that has been made by:

1. repenting to God;
2. repenting to congregation;
3. surrounding yourself with trusted advisors to pray with you and keep you accountable;
4. only selecting speakers who you know their heart and faithfulness; and
5. making a covenant promise to the congregation to be more selective to who speaks.

In our group session, one man came forward to accept Christ on his own without the prompting of man but of the Holy Spirit.

On September 27, the teachings were in Kashari at the Vine Community Church. The church could hold approximately four hundred. The crusades were held about a mile and half away down as road bordered by a banana plantation on each side.

I felt really impressed in my spirit that the way to the adult's hearts is through their children. The crusade grounds were in a cow pasture on the side of a gentle hill overlooking a valley. Each of the three evenings of crusades, the praise music and worship dancers would be going almost nonstop for close to two hours. What this effectively did was to draw in people in from all throughout the valley. I saw many coming from great distances walking through fields on footpaths.

As before, I started dancing with the kids. Most of the kids were from five to twelve years old. I would also weave in and out of the crowd, and when I came across a two- to five-year-old with a parent, I would coax the child into dancing. The smile on the parent's faces was priceless. Only on three occasions did a small toddler seemed terrified by this white man with silver hair standing before them.

I then started my Jericho March prayer. I marched around the crusade perimeter praying. I was praying against the principalities and powers and rulers of darkness in this region. There were some six to close to seven hundred in attendance with close to two hundred children.

For the crusade, David called me up on stage with several of the children. The children and I did the "O Sifuni Mungo" song together. My evangelism message was on comparing and contrasting the rich young ruler and Nicodemus. I explained that Jesus left His palace in heaven and became a man and walked among us. Just like I have been walking and dancing among them although I am only a man. He is fully God and fully man, and He walked among us. He came and died so that we might live.

Five women that came forward then started exhibiting signs of demonic possession. All five women had congregated on the left side of the stage. The demons threw the women on the ground and causing them to thrash about, flailing their arms and legs in every direction. Several of the local pastors were dispatched to handle these women. The situation was handled. Calmness came back over the area. I called the altar call, and we saw 220 salvations this night!

On September 28, this was another powerful day of ministry. The team teaching the pastoral leadership conference moved mightily this day. Tonight, we saw twice the number of children almost double and nine hundred or more total in attendance between both adults and children.

I continued doing what has been impressed on my heart, dancing with the children during the praise music and dance worship. I spoke on the woman with issue of blood and the woman caught in adultery. I again drew the parallel of Jesus walking among us. When we gave the altar call, we saw God moved in power, bringing in a harvest of 252 souls.

154

On September 29, greetings from Mbarara Uganda! Rejoice in the Lord always and again I say rejoice! For this was the day that the Lord had made. Let us rejoice and be glad in it!

Today we concluded the three days of teachings at a pastoral leadership conference. The Lord had blessed this with such a strong move of His Holy Spirit. Friday and Saturday evenings crusades harvested 220 and 252 souls for the kingdom! Such a great harvest that we were forced to use the crusade grounds for church today as the physical church structure cannot contain the number of new believers. Praise His holy name!

Be strong and courageous for I have given you the city! The crusades were held in a cattle ranch field. To walk the field, you want to avoid cow patties and tripping over large anthills or clusters of large grass growth. One of the things that have proven to be quite effective in the spread of the Gospel was that of the music, praise, and worship with dancing the choreographed routines. I believe that God worked through the dance, communicating to the parents that they can trust me. I make their children smile and laugh.

Momma Wilma taught on the prayer of petition "contracts" with God. Anita taught on the Holy Spirit, over 220 received the Holy Spirit with evidence of speaking in tongues.

As I was giving the teaching on spiritual warfare relating like that of tornadic attacks on a community. Dark clouds formed overhead as I was speaking of the attacks, but as I was talking of the power of God, the sky opened up to blue sky and the sun shining down.

Praise Him in the middle of the storm.

As we were transitioning from conference to crusade, large dark storm clouds were forming to the east. My flesh did not want it to rain, so I started praying against it. It started to sprinkle. I walked over to the tent and surveyed the scene; as before, the music was playing and the dance team was going to town. The sprinkles started to transition into rain. I was standing under the tent, protected from the rain, looking out at where the move of God happened the previous two days. It was then that I heard a voice, not an audible voice, but I distinctly heard in my spirit.

"Is this what I called you to do?"

I slapped the back of my hand and said, "No, Lord, this is not what You called me to do. I am supposed to be dancing with the children." We are to serve God when it is convenient and when it is inconvenient.

So I proceeded to step into the rain. As before, I started dancing with the children. The rain transitioned to a full force downpour. We continued to dance and praise the Lord. The group of between fifty to sixty people just danced and danced, even forming a human train of dancers, dancing around the compound. The downpour lasted over an hour. I paced myself and paused occasionally for a drink of bottled water. I had jelled my hair, so "drinking" the water rolling down my face was not an option. After, well, over an hour and half, the rain subsided and the crew got the sound system back going. Pastor Isaac began preaching, and I got on the stage with him.

After some fifteen minutes, it started pouring rain again. We just continued praising our God in the middle of this downpour. At this stage of the game, I did not think that I had a dry stitch of clothing. In the distance, I saw some lightning. The engineer inside me considered the metal speaker towers, metal stage, and the truck trailer stage backdrop... But my God! Here in Uganda, He called me to dance in the rain. He will protect us.

We continued our praise. The rains stopped after some thirty to forty-five minutes. Pastor Isaac continued preaching for a little but then passed the mic to me. I felt lead to transition away from a salvation message. Initially, I spoke of Jesus healing the leper. I then spoke of the woman with issue of blood, Zacchaeus climbing the tree to see Jesus, and the four friends who lower the paralytic through the roof. In each case, they each pressed in to get a touch from Jesus.

The woman was unclean. She risked being stoned to death if she were found out. The law required her to yell out "unclean." Her being by herself in public like this was extremely risky. She was desperate, and Jesus was her last hope. She pressed in to get a touch from Jesus.

Zacchaeus jumped up and down trying to see Jesus over the crowd. He pressed in and ran up the road and climbed a tree to see Jesus. When Jesus saw him, He said, "Zacchaeus, come down immediately. I must stay at your house today."

The four friends of the paralytic man, seeing the large crowd pressed in and climbed on the roof, tore a hole in the roof to lower the man. In each case, they wanted a touch from Jesus, so they went above and beyond and pressed in to get that touch from the healer Jesus.

I then directed my message squarely at the crowd in front of me. "When it began to rain, you could have gone home. No one would have thought otherwise about it, but you did not go home. You stayed here because you want a touch from Jesus the healer, either for yourself or you brought a loved one with you. You have stayed here. You have pressed in to get a touch from Jesus. The Holy Spirit is here tonight, so if you need your healing, come forward."

I then called for the pastors to come and pray and lay hands on those who came forward. I came off the stage and started praying and praying. It seemed like I prayed for at least 45 minutes with at least 200 people. But later, David indicated more like over 250 individuals.

Later, I found out that the region had been experiencing a dry season in the middle of their rain season. Their animals were dying because of this drought. They feel the praise dancing was bringing healing to both the people and the land. I have Native American Indian blood running through my veins—a rain dance. No, we are to praise Him in the middle of the storm. God, through this storm, brought healing to His people, and God brought healing and cleansed the land this day. He brought His healing to both. While I was up on the stage dancing and praising my God, I did not know how this simple act could be used as a conduit for so much grace and healing. He is a good, good Father!

On September 30, today was a rest day. I was blown away by the move of God here. I was being blessed with a large harvest. A harvest that I did not plow the ground, sow the seed, water the plant. I did not weed the area. God gave the increase. I just harvested another's labor.

I feel very humbled by being used by God in this way. First, I would like to thank my wife for sending me. Second, I would like to thank the team of brothers and sisters who sowed seeds into this effort and sending me. And for our team, Rex and Wilma, who have been doing this in Uganda for fourteen years. Along with Anita and Bp. Kamanzi David who have been doing the plowing, planting, and watering low these many years. They all have assembled a wonderful support team that works tirelessly behind the scenes. May God richly bless them with wonderful spiritual blessings in the heavenly.

The hand of God has been on this mission trip from the beginning. Bp. Kamanzi David has done an amazing job organizing all this effort. The local church pastors hosting these pastors leadership conferences and facilitating so well with such grace. Collectively between teams A and B, I believe God had brought in a harvest of just over one thousand decisions for Christ and many, many healings thus far. We will get better numbers when all the dust settles. We are at the halfway point. We went into another area of the bush tomorrow. I was told that the Uganda National Band will be greeting us when we would arrive. What a way to honor God and the move that He was doing in our midst. Praise be His holy name.

On October 1, the village we were headed to was way back in the bush country in a mountainous region. The dirt road leading in and out was a very narrow road with steep drop-offs of over a thousand feet. The drive in took about two hours. We were reunited with team B just as we were to head into the village. The people of the village had come out and greeted us on each side of the road. They had banana tree branches that they were waving as we passed by. It almost seemed like Palm Sunday. Also, some had laid articles of clothing down in the path of our van. Ahead of them was the Uganda National Marching Band. This parade procession escorted us into the village. The full contingent of teams A and B was there so we could spread out the teaching responsibilities. God was moving strong, and each message was well received. Again, I spoke on the fivefold ministry, and we prayed for the pastors and ministry leaders. The foundation of prayer that was laid for Uganda all these months was one element of why the soil of hearts is so freshly tilled. Praying for the favor of men, this parade is an evidence of God answering those prayers. Praise His name!

David called me up on stage as well as several of the children. The children and I did the "O Sifuni Mungo" song together. My evangelism message was on comparing and contrasting rich young ruler and Nicodemus. I again explained that Jesus left His palace in heaven and became a man and walked among us. When we gave the altar call, we saw over 250 salvations this night! I also then went into teaching of Christ the healer.

Cameron, who was in the crowd, prayed for someone. The language barrier prevented communication as to about what. It was impressed on Cameron's spirit that the man had back and neck issues. So with the loudspeakers blaring, Cameron prayed for this man's back. Later in the evening, Cameron saw the man as he was testifying for the healing he had received. He was instantly healed of back and neck pain! Praise God! Close to a hundred testified of healings that evening.

A special dispensation of the grace of God had been displayed to me. In 1984, I injured my back at work. My mid back was twisted. In 1990, I was in a car crash. My right sciatic was injured. Since '84, certain movements were limited for me. Since '90, other movements were limited for me. Pain would limit that movement.

All the dancing for the Lord that I have been doing—the twisting, squatting, jumping—would all be limited by pain. In other words, forget it. I would not be able to do it. Since coming to Uganda, I have had no pain. No pain in handling heavy luggage at the airport. No pain in the daily operations of life.

After Friday's teachings, that night John had a dream that I came to his home and prayed for his back. Saturday night, I gave testimony of my back being healed when speaking about our Jesus who is the healer! After the evening came to a close, David took me to John's home, and we prayed for his back. Tuesday evening, I saw John again and he said his back was healed. Praise the name of the Lord!

On October 2, we were joined by another team member, Gary Scrogyns. This day, I went first after the introductory prayers. I taught on spiritual warfare, afterward Gary taught. When we broke for lunch, information of another minister who was to come to Uganda and teach in Kampala but was unable to because of lack of funds. So I was selected to be the sole teacher for the next six days starting the next day. Team A would continue with the current format. Team B was going back out. And team C, consisting of Hamisi, the driver; Pius; and I headed back to Kampala. While in Mbarara, I had seen in passing both Pius and Hamisi. Hamisi had a chicken ranch supplying the region with thousands of eggs a week.

On October 3, well, I am truly thankful for prayers. We arrived in Kampala at the height of rush hour. When we arrived at the church, I was greeted by a smile on every face. I gave the message on the centurion faith and not being double-minded. I was to be filling in for a couple who could not make it. So I would be speaking three times a day for the next five or more days. Luckily, the last three days were at a different venue, so I could use the same material twice.

So I was challenged to develop three to five new messages within the next twenty-four hours. I was in a foreign nation without my computer or any study Bible. My Bible had a very limited concordance. The one saving grace I had was an application on my phone called My Sword. I spent close to four hours in prayer asking God for a fresh word in season. By one in the morning, I had nothing. Well, nothing in the way of a message, but I had everything in the way of peace. I had a peace that cannot be explained. Unlike the night before the SAT exams, a night filled with stress, doubt, fear, and high anxiety, I felt an overwhelming peace about God delivering a message to me the next day. God was in control.

On October 4, good morning from Kampala, Uganda. This was the day that the Lord had made let us rejoice and be glad in it. I woke up to a pounding driving rain. There was nothing quite like the smell after a morning rain. Scientifically, yes, it's the ions in the atmosphere. But to me, it is a reminder that we are blessed every single morning. We are blessed with a new day, a day that can be of our choosing. Do we choose to praise God, or do we choose to be grumpy? I choose to praise God.

This pastors leadership conference theme was shine.

> *Let your light so shine before men, that they may see your good works and glorify your Father in heaven. (Matthew 5:16, NKJV)*

Each session, I would lead in with the story of the fall of man and how the glory of God left Adam and Eve after the fall.

As of eight in the morning, I still did not have a message, but then God gave me a download. First session, I taught on Joshua and the wall of Jericho. I taught of how the glory of the Lord was in the ark of the covenant. We as believers in Christ have the Holy Spirit living in us. We are the temple of the Holy Spirit. Our walk of faith needs to shine God's glory so that others only see Jesus and not our fleshly nature. This lesson lasted an hour and fifteen minutes. The second session was on spiritual warfare. The third was on being doers of the word. Faith without works is dead and following with teaching on Matthew 25:31. Some forty pastors and church leaders were in attendance. I was speaking life into them and their congregations; this is such a humbling experience.

Hamisi my driver, Pius, and Pius's sister, Ester, and I went to dinner at

Chicken Tonight. We had some great fellowship over dinner and dug into the Word of God deeper. After we ate dinner, we drove by Mandela National Stadium. Mandela National Stadium was packed out with a night of prayer for the nation of Uganda. In keeping with the spirit of prayer in the area, our team came back to the hotel and spent an hour in prayer. Praise His holy name.

On October 5, God is so good. As I had been here in the lobby, studying God's Word, preparing my heart for the day...an instrumental had been playing on a continued loop.

Silent night, holy night
All is calm, all is bright
Round yon Virgin, Mother, Mother and Child
Holy infant so tender and mild
Sleep in heavenly peace
Silent night, holy night
All is calm, all is bright
Round yon Virgin, Mother, Mother and Child
Holy infant so tender and mild
Sleep in heavenly peace
Christ, Christ, the Savior is born
Christ, Christ, the Savior
Christ, Christ, the Savior is born

Remember, this was the middle of October! God's grace extended. Last night, Mandela Stadium hosted a prayer, praise, and worship vigil for Kampala and Uganda. My hotel sat within eyesight of it, some two hundred yards or so. I must say, I can still feel the presence and power of the Holy Spirit. So peaceful, even above all the noise of a busy street.

Ministry update reporting from teams A, B, and C. Collectively, this mission had seen over 2,500 decisions for Christ! And God confirming His Word with signs following of many, many healings. *Praise the Lord!*

Well, I still had no new message to teach on as of eight in the morning this day! But I was not stressed; I had been hearing "Silent Night, Holy Night" over and over. My God is faithful. He gave me a message just in time, on Christ, the bridegroom, and we the body being the bride. I downloaded several scriptures and had the pastors turning pages on pages back and forth from Old to New testaments. Again, this teaching was over an hour, yet they were gobbling it up faster than a Thanksgiving turkey. Faith is action. Love is action.

During worship, I was off to the side, praying and praising His name. The second message was developed during worship. This was a short message, only forty-five minutes. The funny thing, as of this writing, I did not remember what I taught. Pius indicated at lunch that he saw me feverishly writing down the message, and he could not believe that the message was that fresh of a download.

After lunch, we cued up the "O Sifuni Mungo" song and called up the children. We all enjoyed this time. It amazed me how this song had been used as such a conduit of His grace and breaking down walls. I then thanked the kids for helping me and gave each one candy.

I taught the fivefold ministry message; again, the pastors affirmed that it was on target for what they needed. We ended praying for the pastors. In the back, I was drawn to a familiar face. The pastor of the first church in Kampala from two weeks ago was visiting. He was speaking with Pius about something. He asked Pius if we could drop by on Sunday afternoon for a children's program.

On October 6, again, I did not have anything fresh from the night before. Right on time, at eight in the morning on Sunday, I received the download. I trust in Him! Psalm 23—He gave me a reference scripture after reference scripture. The pastors were flipping pages all morning long! Over thirty minutes were spent on just the first verse! The Lord is my Shepherd. I shall not want. This teaching lasted close to an hour and half, and I received much positive affirmation afterward.

In the evening on Sunday, we ventured back to the church where the first pastors leadership conference was held at. He wanted me for a children's program they had. We were greeted by some fifty children of ages ranging from five to fourteen. They were singing familiar Christian children songs in English. We exchanged greetings and introductions. They continued to sing. Once complete, they then had some Q&A for me about America.

They then wanted me to sing the "O Sifuni Mungo" song with the kids. These children learned a choreographed dance for the song in the last two weeks. It was a joy and a blessing to see them enjoy a song I have enjoyed for some thirty years.

After I gave the children candies, a young seven-year-old Muslim boy asked if he could be born again. I had the privilege of leading him in the Salvation Prayer! This was without a formal altar call; he felt the call of the Holy Spirit. Praise the Lord.

On October 7, today was a rest day. I went to the market to buy the touristy things to bring home. Pius gave me a guided tour of downtown Kampala. He pointed out points of interest as we drove around. One very disheartening location was the Nile Hotel. This hotel is now called the Serena Hotel. But when it was the Nile Hotel, it was used during the scourge of Idi Amin regime. If one was taken to the Nile, they did not come out alive. In the distance, I saw the Kampala Central Mosque spire. It is the second largest mosque in Africa. Omar Kaddafi assisted in the financing of building it. This day was a much-needed time to relax.

On October 8, today, before we went to teach at the pastors leadership conference, we visited Hamis's daughter at the university. On our way to the university, we drove by an industrial area that was formerly a jungle. When it was a jungle during Idi Amin scourge, this was considered the killing fields. Bodies would be dropped off in this area of the jungle. Once we arrived at the university, we got a tour of the campus and a very extensive tour of the library. One real odd thing that happened while touring the library. I was looking over the engineering books and came across a very thick volume commentary on the book of Matthew. This book had never been catalogued into the library. I am still searching for the meaning of this find. Nothing is by accident with God. I believe I will be taking the book of Matthew into my study room for more in depth study.

The university was founded by George Harry Gasson. He was an Evangelist, teacher, and builder who began his work in Mukono in1906. The year 1906 is the same year our home was built. The year 1906 is the same year that the first church in Kansas that I ever preached at was built and the same year as the Azusa Street Revival in Los Angeles, the rebirth of the modern-day Pentecostal church. Hmmm, something to ponder.

Today, I was attending the last church that I would be ministering at. As I usually do, when I got on sight, I like to pray in the back of the sanctuary. As I was praying in a clockwise direction, several of the kids came alongside me and grabbed my hands. They walked with me as I was praying. At times, I would lean over and pick one up and hold them as I prayed and walked.

I gave the spiritual warfare and centurion faith teachings. I know they are the same messages, but yet they are not. The basic message is consistent, but some points are emphasized more than others. Some points are brand-new while others are not mentioned at all. It is like God is customizing the word to fit that local body.

As we were on our way to Chicken Tonight, I think I gave Hamisi, Pius, and Ester a cause for alarm. We were stuck in traffic. The traffic in Uganda was nothing but chaos. The vehicle of choice in Uganda seemed to be the Toyota passenger van taxi along with the *boda boda*. A *boda boda* is a 250cc motorcycle taxi that often will have three or four passengers hanging on the back. So we were stuck in traffic. The *boda bodas* had left and had not swarmed the empty spaces between the cars yet. We were not moving. So I said, "Chinese fire drill!"

I knew my hosts would not know what I was about to do. I jumped out and ran around the car screaming with my hands waving above my head. On the second lap around, I was shaking hands and blessing the adjacent taxi passengers. When I got back inside the car and I scanned around, all eyes were wide. They could not believe what I had just done. Just as I finished the fire drill, the boda bodas swarmed again. Oh, the fun.

While eating and fellowshipping, I was surprised! What a thrill! Hamisi wanted to be baptized. I get the distinct privilege of baptizing a fellow believer. Hamisi had been my driver for the last week. He converted to Christianity from Muslim in 2010. During the time together, the Holy Spirit was telling him that it was time.

Witnessing this most joyous moment would be his firstborn daughter and his son. Hamisi's sister and her husband and daughter, Pius, my man Friday of this past week would also be there.

On October 9, good morning from Kampala, Uganda. Rejoice in the Lord always. This was one of my last days in Uganda. My last full day of ministry. Boy, what an experience this has been. God's grace abounds.

This was the day that the entire nation of Uganda celebrated independence!

This was what I put together for the baptism of Hamisi. We were gathered here today to witness the baptism of brother Hamisi. In the year 2010, he converted to Christianity from Islam. This last week, Hamisi had been my driver in and around Kampala. He had been there during every teaching to the pastors. In the evenings, he, Pius, and I, we have sat and had fellowship over dinner. We were eating physically but also spiritually.

This became much like the story of Philip in the Acts 8:26–36.

There are so many parallels to this story. Philip was an apostle of Christ. Ethiopian was from Africa. Ethiopian was in his chariot. Ethiopian was a captain of coin. Ethiopian was seeking God, asking questions.

What prevents him from being baptized? I am a disciple of Christ. Hamisi was from Africa. Hamisi drove me in a chariot. Hamisi was a captain of business. Hamisi was seeking God, asking questions

What prevents him from being baptized?

So we were here to baptize Hamisi in the name of the Father, Son, and Holy Spirit.

We went back to the church for one final time of ministry. As usual, I went in the back of the church to pray, asking for direction on which messages to deliver. I heard pretty loudly—Psalm 23 and fivefold. When I went up to the podium and announced that the next message would be on Psalm 23, both Pius and Hamisi expressed great pleasure to hear the Psalm 23 message again.

When I was called to the podium, I did something unusual (even unusual for me). I polled the audience from which their nation of origin was. When I found out that two pastors and several parishioners were from the Congo, I immediately broke into prayer for them and their families. Once I completed the fivefold teaching, I again prayed for these pastors. The pastors from the Congo wanted me to go with them to the Congo. I told them that I did not know if I had that much faith yet.

Somewhere in all of this, I mentioned the "O Sifuni Mungo" song and the folks from the Congo knew it. We tried to sing it together as their native tongue is Swahili. But we could not as both them and I only knew the verses in Swahili. I did not know the verses in English!

Working alongside both Hamisi and Pius this past week had been a true blessing. The sessions before and after the formal teachings at the pastors leadership conferences were a delight. Seeing the spirit flowed during the conference sessions was an awesome sight, but then the sessions afterward were even more blessed. Exploring the questions that the teachings generated by Hamisi, Pius, and occasionally Pius's sister, Ester, were a pure joy.

As we dug even deeper into the things of God, He showed up in the middle of Chicken Tonight. Being around those who hunger and thirst after the things of God just filled my heart with unspeakable joy. The scripture spoke to the Word of God going out and not coming back void but accomplishing that which it was set out to do was amply demonstrated during these sessions.

During some of these sessions as I was expounding on a thought, sometimes I said to myself, "Where did that come from?" A sermon or word I heard from years ago took root and bore fruit today. At the end of each day, our brain "file sorts" our memories, sorting long-term and short-term memories. Our spirit does not have to do that. A word that God has planted in our spirit is always available to us to use. We just need to be in an attitude of the heart to allow His word to flow through us as needed. It is this attitude that enabled me to get the fresh downloads from God to formulate teaching messages on the fly as He directed.

Yes, in the natural, I did not have the normal resources to develop those messages, but in these instances, God takes our "natural" and adds His "super" to our natural, and He makes it supernatural. The Holy Spirit, who is the teacher, brought back remembrances of scriptures that my natural fifty-six-year-old brain might have difficulty recalling. When pressed with a seemingly impossible task of coming up with so many new messages in such a short time, all I could do was trust God. I trusted Him to give me the messages. He came through in time with a timely message for these pastors. I feel so very humbled that God would choose to flow as mightily as He did. Praise His holy name! But really, I was not totally surprised that God came through in my time of need. After all, this entire effort had been covered in the JCP prayer, hours and hours of prayer, for over ten months.

I would not have been able to do this last week without the service of both Hamisi and Pius. His sister, Ester, also was my interpreter on occasion. Ester wanted to be a foreign missionary. I instructed her to first make a vision board that would illustrate what her dreams were. Take a picture of her holding a passport. The first step was to get her passport. Each milestone that she must accomplish prior to becoming a missionary would be put up on the board. Pray those milestones into reality.

On October 10, Gary took us to a Fisherman's Wharf of sorts, Kampala style. With this being the last day in country, Gary wanted to make sure we got a true flavor of the country. He wanted fried fish, no, not fish like from H.Salt Fish and Chips; it's an entire fried fish. He even got Cameron to eat the eyeball of a fried fish. No, thank you.

On the way back to the hotel from the Wharf, we drove past an Asherah pole, or at least a Uganda version of one. Asherah poles are found in many books of the Old Testament, one verse is Deuteronomy 16:21. This particular Asherah pole has a backstory. Some local high school and college students were drunk one evening and wanted to go out on Lake Victoria in a boat. They convinced a boat master to launch. During the night, a storm whipped up and capsized the boat. All aboard the boat perished with the exception of one. The sole survivor was the son of a local provincial king. This king worshipped this Asherah pole. Now the parents of the children who died also worshipped this Asherah pole. These are the principalities and powers, rulers of darkness that we must pray against when we pray over a region.

Back home, on October 13, a stow away from Uganda. After church, I was quick to start unpacking from the trip. Going through the items I brought back, describing each item purchased for the kids and grandkids to Laura was fun. I was throwing trash away from the trip. Shortly afterward, Laura also threw something away. I heard her scream a little. I rushed in and she asked me to look in the trash, asking if I saw a mouse. Yes! A mouse was looking back at me with his beady little eyes! I brought a mouse back from Uganda! I dealt with it quickly and then searched the rest of my luggage. We found that a chocolate bar that I bought in Atlanta was half eaten with the wrappings all shredded. A valuable lesson learned the hard way. When traveling in a foreign land, always store your luggage fully zipped up! Our "visitor" was in my briefcase and got through at least two security scans without incident.

On October 21, I had not received much update as to the healing testimonies beyond those listed here. I am sure they will find their way to me. But for now, this is what I know.

When I was with team A, in all its varied incarnations, each day, the spirit would weave a very beautiful tapestry with all the different teachers and messages. Yes, the messages were repeated, but the areas that they varied between locations was how the Holy Spirt was working all the messages into one unified message for that local body needed for that day.

From all teams reporting, this mission team saw 5,682 decisions for Christ. The local pastors were seeing to it that these new believers were getting into small cell groups for their spiritual growth and maturity. They were getting discipled, so we had no need of worry that these spiritual children were being spiritually orphaned.

In the days following his baptism, Hamisi indicated that his bad cough that he had for months left him the moment he came out of the water. God healed him of it!

Going into this for the first time in Uganda, I had no preconceived notions as to what the rules were and what was expected of me. I had been to Haiti once, two years ago. There we fed over 2,500 orphans, and we were available as prayer team members for four crusades. I did have one opportunity to preach there. On average, the most that I have ever taught in an audience was approximately 30. The notion of teaching/preaching to hundreds somehow did not intimidate me. This entire mission trip had been bathed in so many hours of prayer. I know I can trust my God. I was prepared in spirit, soul, and body for this mission.

Faith is not a feeling.

In the past, when I "felt" God's presence, I would get the Gospel goosebumps. This often occurs when teaching/preaching at different times during the delivery of the message. All through this mission, I rarely "felt" the Gospel goosebumps. The fruit of the teaching/preaching was clearly evident. His Spirit was moving, regardless of whether or not I "felt" it. I had this confidence that I was and am in the will of God. It was standing firm on this knowledge and the knowledge that He would never leave me nor forsake me. This was my faith and not based on a feeling.

When I am blessed to lead someone in the sinner's prayer, the feeling of joy that comes over me is inexpressible. I thought that when God used me to lead hundreds to Christ, the feeling of joy would somehow be enhanced or magnified, but it was not. I mean, what was I thinking? Leading one to Christ is joy inexpressible. How can you top that?

In the past, when I would "feel" the anointing come over me to pray for healing, that feeling would be in my right palm. Prior to Uganda, God had used me as a conduit of His healing on so many occasions. At these times, my right palm would feel like I had applied IcyHot on it. This sensation would intensify and pulsate. Once at work, the anointing came on, so I used an infrared monitor to compare the temperatures of both my palms. The right one was 2.7 degrees cooler when I had the anointing (the engineer in me). By and large during this trip in Uganda, the sensation on my right palm was silent. But yet, many were healed.

I rejoice for those who have come to Christ over the course of this mission trip. I am honored to be a small part of all of that. I also am very honored to have been able to speak life into all those pastors during this time. By teaching, encouraging, exhorting, and loving on them. This is true multiplication. For the pastors will carry the same teaching, encouraging, exhorting, and loving to their congregations.

Faith is not a feeling.
Faith is action.
Faith is doing His will.

Jesus is our commander in chief, chief of the armies of God. Those in any military service are bound to obey the last commandments of their superior officer until we get additional orders.

Our last orders from our commander in chief?

Then Jesus came to them and said, "All authority in heaven and on earth has been given to me. Therefore go and make disciples of all nations, baptizing them in the name of the Father and of the Son and of the Holy Spirit, and teaching them to obey everything I have commanded you. And surely I am with you always, to the very end of the age." (Matthew 28:18–20, NIV)

We need to be about doing His business, regardless of how we "feel".

A PARTING MESSAGE FROM WADE IN THE WATER MINISTRY

As with any race, we must always stay hydrated; but with this race, we are not looking for natural water or Fiji Water—we need to thirst after righteousness. Thirsty?

The *Apollo Saturn V* weighed over 6.5 million pounds at liftoff. The first stage was powered by 5 North American Aviation Rocketdyne F-1 rocket engines. Each engine produced 1.52 million pounds of thrust for a combined thrust of 7.6 million pounds. Each engine had a turbopump that fed it the liquid oxygen and RP-1 (rocket grade kerosene). The engines were so thirsty of the propellants that the pump fed the engine at a rate of 40,282 gallons a minute!

> *Blessed and fortunate and happy and spiritually prosperous (in that state in which the born-again child of God enjoys His favor and salvation) are those who hunger and thirst for righteousness (uprightness and right standing with God), for they shall be completely satisfied! (Matthew 5:6, AMPC)*

We need to be thirsty for right standing with God, thirstier than those powerful rocket engines. Praise His holy name that we can tap into His Dunamis Power to live our daily life! He says that we can do all things through Christ Who strengthens us! Jesus, the real "most interesting man in the world," said it first: "Stay thirsty, my friends."

COMMUNION PRAYER
COMPILED AND WRITTEN BY WANDA WALKER

Jesus said, "I am the living bread which comes down from heaven, if anyone eats of this bread, he will live forever, and the bread I give is My flesh, which I give for the life of the world. He who feeds on Me will live because of Me. This is the bread which comes down from heaven, He who eats this bread will live forever. These words are spirit, and they are life."

I give thanks to You, my Father God, for this bread and this cup and ask You to bless it. Bless it for the use of my spirit, soul, and body. I take and eat of this bread which represents the body of Jesus, which was broken for me. In His body, He bore my sins and my sickness. For Jesus was wounded for my transgressions. He was bruised for my iniquities; the chastisement of my peace was upon Him, and with His stripes I am healed. Every disease, every sickness, every virus, and every pain that touches my body dies instantly. I believe I receive my healing and complete deliverance from all sickness and disease. Body, I command you to line up to God's Word! I refuse any malfunction of my body. I eat this bread in remembrance of Jesus, my Savior, my Lord, my Redeemer, my Healer, my Life-Giver, my Intercessor, my Sanctifier, my Wisdom, my Peace, and my Soon Coming King. (Eat.)

This cup is the New Covenant in His blood. This cup represents the blood of Jesus that He shed for me on the cross of Calvary. The blood of Jesus Christ, Who, through the eternal Spirit, offered up Himself without spot to God. This blood purges my conscience from dead works to serve the Living God. Jesus is the Mediator of the New Covenant, and by His own blood, He entered in once into the holy place, having obtained eternal redemption for me. His blood cleanses me from all my sin and unrighteousness for all my shortcomings and all my lack. His blood cleanses me from my secret faults, keep me back from presumptuous sins: let them not have dominion over me. Thank You, Father, for cleansing me from all my sins. I will drink of this cup, and as often as I drink it, I do in remembrance of Jesus, my Savior, my Lord, my Redeemer, my Healer, my Life-Giver, my Intercessor, my Sanctifier, my Wisdom, my Peace, and my Soon Coming King. (Drink.)

As often as I eat this bread and drink from this cup, I show the Lord's death till He returns for His bride. If I show forth His death, I will also show forth His life! My Father, I receive your promises. I have eternal life, and You shall raise me up in these last days. You dwell in me and I in You. I put on the Lord Jesus Christ! I put on the new man who after God is created in righteousness and true holiness. I take on the mind of Christ. I think quickly and accurately in every situation and every circumstance that comes my way. I take on God's wisdom and knowledge to do all things through Christ Who strengthens me!

I hold fast the confession of my faith without wavering. I cast not away, therefore, my confidence or boldness, which has great recompense of reward.

Thank You, Father, for the New Covenant because You put Your laws into my mind and You write them in my heart. My sins and iniquities, You will remember them no more. Therefore, Father, I come boldly into your thrown room of grace by the blood of Jesus Christ. I draw near with a true heart in full assurance of faith, having my heart sprinkled from an evil conscience and my body washed with the pure water of the Word. I am clean by Your Word. Thank You, Father, for Your grace.

JERICHO CROSS PRAYER MANUAL

Our life should be a life based on prayer. Our life is a walk of faith in the God of Abraham, Isaac, and Jacob. Our life should be filled with faith-filled prayers to the God of Abraham, Isaac, and Jacob Whose desire it is for us to have an abundant life filled with everything, above and beyond we can ask or even think. Our prayers should not sound like, "Oh, God, please, please do this, that, or the other thing." Our prayers need be based on what we know to be God's will and promises for our life. Our God does not change, and His promises do not expire. All God's promises are yes and amen! We have been adopted into the family of God through His Son, Jesus Christ. The blood shed on the cross gains us access to all things pertaining to that which was promised to the nation of Israel as they continued to obey the Word of God.

We know that it is God's will that all mankind be restored to relationship to Him through the atoning blood of Jesus, bringing forgiveness of all sins. We know that Jesus died so that we could be reconciled back to God in our entirety, spirit, soul (mind, will, and emotions), and body. When we are born again, our spirit is made alive in Christ and we are saved. We are being saved as we are being transformed by the renewing of our mind through the Word; we are working out our salvation with fear and trembling. And we will be saved once our time on earth has come to an end and we are then with Him in eternity. So we pray in faith that all come to Him to be saved, thanking Him for the work He is doing right now in the unseen realms to bring whomever we are focused on to the saving knowledge of Jesus Christ. As we pray for them, we bind whatever forces that might be working against the will and Word of God; we also then loose the heavenly hosts to war on their behalf. We loosen the warring angels to protect and the ministering angels to bring love and comfort to those with whom we are praying for. We thank the Holy Spirit for healing, teaching, and comforting us and our fellow travelers.

We pray with the faith of a mustard seed; we pray in faith, knowing that God hears our prayers that line up with His will and Word as we walk in perpetual forgiveness to our fellow travelers.

Now faith is the substance of things hoped for, the evidence of things not seen. For by it the elders obtained a good testimony.

(Hebrews 11:1–2, NKJV)

Now faith is the assurance (the confirmation, the title deed) of the things [we] hope for, being the proof of things [we] do not see and the conviction of their reality [faith perceiving as real fact what is not revealed to the senses]. For by [faith trust and holy fervor born of faith] the men of old had divine testimony borne to them and obtained a good report. (AMPC)

The fundamental fact of existence is that this trust in God, this faith, is the firm foundation under everything that makes life worth living. It's our handle on what we can't see. The act of faith is what distinguished our ancestors, set them above the crowd. (MSG)

Now faith brings our hopes into reality and becomes the foundation needed to acquire the things we long for. It is all the evidence required to prove what is still unseen. This testimony of faith is what previous generations were commended for. (TPT)

From this point forward, we operate in faith! Every prayer we pray is with the understanding that our prayers do not just pass over our lips and then they bounce off the ceiling of our prayer closet and back at us, but they are heard—nay, they eco in the throne room of grace at the foot of our Lord and Savior Jesus Christ as He sits and reigns on His glorious throne. He dispatches His warring angels when needed as well as His ministering angels. With this said, we understand that we are doing battle on our knees in the realms of the spirit world. Understanding that we do not do battle with conventional weapons like guns and bombs—no, we do not even use the nuke option in the natural. No, we go full nuke in the spiritual on our knees!

For though we walk (live) in the flesh, we are not carrying on our warfare according to the flesh and using mere human weapons. For the weapons of our warfare are not physical [weapons of flesh and blood], but they are mighty before God for the overthrow and destruction of strongholds, [Inasmuch as we] refute arguments and theories and reasonings and every proud and lofty thing that sets itself up against the [true] knowledge of God; and we lead every thought and purpose away captive into the obedience of Christ (the Messiah, the Anointed One), Being in readiness to punish every [insubordinate for his] disobedience, when your own submission and obedience [as a church] are fully secured and complete. (2 Corinthians 10:4–5, AMPC)

The world is unprincipled. It's dog-eat-dog out there! The world doesn't fight fair. But we don't live or fight our battles that way—never have and never will. The tools of our trade aren't for marketing or manipulation, but they are for demolishing that entire massively corrupt culture. We use our powerful God-tools for smashing warped philosophies, tearing down barriers erected against the truth of God, fitting every loose thought and emotion and impulse into the structure of life shaped by Christ. Our tools are ready at hand for clearing the ground of every obstruction and building lives of obedience into maturity. (MSG)

For although we live in the natural realm, we don't wage a military campaign employing human weapons, using manipulation to achieve our aims. Instead, our spiritual weapons are energized with divine power to effectively dismantle the defenses behind which people hide. We can demolish every deceptive fantasy that opposes God and break through every arrogant attitude that is raised up in defiance of the true knowledge of God. We capture, like prisoners of war, every thought and insist that it bow in obedience to the Anointed One. Since we are armed with such dynamic weaponry, we stand ready to punish any trace of rebellion, as soon as you choose complete obedience. (TPT)

Knowing all this, let us pray.

World Harvest Church Leadership
World Harvest Enid and World Harvest Stillwater

Pastors Brad and Tamy Mendenhall
Pastors Mike and Tamara Sturgeon
[Insert your church and leadership]

Brothers and sisters, pray for us. (1 Thessalonians 5:25, NIV)

We will pray for pastors. Included in this prayer are thirty categories to pray. As we pray for WH pastors, we are also praying for the other churches and pastors in Enid and the Garfield County. We pray for our church leadership as standing in proxy for the rest of the churches and pastors in Enid. These are thirty prayers that we specifically pray in the JCP, but given that they are thirty, this also affords us to pray one prayer a day for our pastors so that each day, we pray a prayer of protection over our pastors. I would also suggest that these thirty prayers, as you pray them once a day, also pray them over yourself as you are praying for pastor. This way, as you pray for pastor, they are standing in proxy for you as well! How about that for full 360 degrees of coverage in prayer! Again, this is just a suggestion, not being legalistic or anything.

1. Pray for the Personal Needs of My and Your Pastor

MY PASTOR HAS A STRONG MARRIAGE

I thank You and praise You, Heavenly Father, for protecting my pastors Brad and Tamy's marriage. I thank You that You are keeping them strong and strengthening them individually as well as a couple. I thank You that they make a weekly priority to have a date night to celebrate their relationship. I thank You that they guard this date night from any intrusions. I thank You that they model Christ's relationship with the church found in Ephesians 5, they follow that pattern with each other. I thank You that my pastor tenderly loves and cherishes their spouse. I thank You that they respect and encourage their husband/wife, submitting one to another. I thank You, Father, that their love for You spills over into their love for one another. I thank You that they do not take each other for granted, that every day they wake anew with the idea of pursuing each other's affection. In the name of Jesus, I plead the blood of Jesus over my pastor's marriage. I draw a hedge of protection around them, and no harm will come nigh their dwelling. I thank You for hearing my prayers. In the precious name of Jesus I pray. Amen!

So husbands ought to love their own wives as their own bodies; he who loves his wife loves himself. For no one ever hated his own flesh, but nourishes and cherishes it, just as the Lord does the church. For we are members of His body, of His flesh and of His bones. "For this reason a man shall leave his father and mother and be joined to his wife, and the two shall become one flesh." This is a great mystery, but I speak concerning Christ and the church. Nevertheless let each one of you in particular so love his own wife as himself, and let the wife see that she respects her husband." (Ephesians 5:28–33, NKJV)

PRAYER FOR HEDGES OF PROTECTION FOR MY PASTOR

I thank You and praise You, Father God, for building a hedge of protection around my pastors Brad and Tamy's marriage. I thank You that they are operating with discernment when they minister and that they are aware of the potential for any improper relationships. In the name of Jesus, I come against the Jezebel spirit from influencing them in there walk with You, Lord. I thank You that they are able to discern and see the warning signs of the divisiveness that can come when individuals sow seeds of discord. I thank You that their family time is protected from interruptions.

For this reason a man shall leave his father and mother and be joined to his wife, and the two shall become one flesh' So then, they are no longer two but one flesh. Therefore what God has joined together, let not man separate. (Matthew 19:5–6, NKJV)

For the weapons of our warfare are not carnal but mighty in God for pulling down strongholds, casting down arguments and every high thing that exalts itself against the knowledge of God, bringing every thought into captivity to the obedience of Christ. (2 Corinthians 10:4–5, NKJV)

MY PASTOR HAS A STRONG FAMILY

Lord Jesus, I thank You and praise You for my pastors Brad and Tamy. I thank You that their children are protected from the adversary. I pray against the pressures of the ministry from impacting their family time. I thank You that the children are not discouraged or embittered against their parents for them answering Your call. I thank You that my pastors are providing godly leadership in the home, based on scriptural truth. I thank You that my pastors raise their children in the love and respect of the Lord.

Fathers, don't exasperate your children, but raise them up with loving discipline and counsel that brings the revelation of our Lord. (Ephesians 6:4, TPT)

Fathers, don't exasperate your children by coming down hard on them. Take them by the hand and lead them in the way of the Master. (MSG)

Children, do what your parents tell you. This delights the Master no end. Parents, don't come down too hard on your children or you'll crush their spirits. (Colossians 3:20–21, MSG)

Let the children respect and pay attention to their parents in everything for this pleases our Lord Jesus. And fathers, don't have unrealistic expectations for your children or else they may become discouraged. (TPT)

MY PASTOR IS KEEPING A BALANCED LIFE

Lord Father, I thank and praise You that my pastors Brad and Tamy are making wise lifestyle choices to protect their health and the temple of the Holy Spirit. I thank You that they are focused on the areas of exercise, eating moderately, and getting sufficient rest. I thank You, Lord, that my pastors make time daily for relaxation and renewal to balance the stress of ministry. I thank You that they make time in their schedule for short mini vacations as well as extended vacations.

Or do you not know that your body is the temple of the Holy Spirit who is in you, whom you have from God, and you are not your own? For you were bought at a price; therefore glorify God in your body and in your spirit, which are God's. (1 Corinthians 6:19–20, NKJV)

Therefore I run thus: not with uncertainty. Thus I fight: not as one who beats the air. But I discipline my body and bring it into subjection, lest, when I have preached to others, I myself should become disqualified. (1 Corinthians 9:26–27, NKJV)

I don't know about you, but I'm running hard for the finish line. I'm giving it everything I've got. No sloppy living for me! I'm staying alert and in top condition. I'm not going to get caught napping, telling everyone else all about it and then missing out myself. (MSG)

For that reason, I don't run just for exercise or box like one throwing aimless punches, but I train like a champion athlete. I subdue my body and get it under my control, so that after preaching the good news to others I myself won't be disqualified. (TPT)

MY PASTOR HAS FINANCIAL PROVISION AND WISDOM

I thank You and praise You, Father God, that You own the cattle on a thousand hills; thus, You provide for the financial needs of my pastors Brad and Tamy and their family. I thank You that they will be wise stewards of both personal finances and church funds and that they seek Your face when making the big decisions concerning the direction the church is taking and the impact that has on the church's finances. I thank You that my pastors strongly believe and practice the concept of sowing and reaping, in that they are faithful tithers and are faithful to sow into other ministries. I thank You that my pastors are blessed, and in that blessing, they in turn bless others. I praise Your holy name for my pastors. Thank You.

And my God shall supply all your need according to His riches in glory by Christ Jesus. (Philippians 4:19, NKJV)

I am convinced that my God will fully satisfy every need you have, for I have seen the abundant riches of glory revealed to me through the Anointed One, Jesus Christ! (TPT)

Let your conduct be without covetousness; be content with such things as you have. For He Himself has said, "I will never leave you nor forsake you. (Hebrews 13:5, NKJV)

If anyone teaches otherwise and does not consent to wholesome words, even the words of our Lord Jesus Christ, and to the doctrine which accords with godliness, he is proud, knowing nothing, but is obsessed with disputes and arguments over words, from which come envy, strife, reviling, evil suspicions, useless wranglings of men of corrupt minds and destitute of the truth, who suppose that godliness is a means of gain. From such withdraw yourself. Now godliness with contentment is great gain. For we brought nothing into this world, and it is certain we can carry nothing out. And having food and clothing, with these we shall be content. But those who desire to be rich fall into temptation and a snare, and into many foolish and harmful lusts which drown men in destruction and perdition. (1 Timothy 6:3–11, NKJV)

I have been young, and now am old; Yet I have not seen the righteous forsaken, Nor his descendants begging bread. (Psalm 37:25, NKJV)

I once was young, now I'm a graybeard—not once have I seen an abandoned believer, or his kids out roaming the streets. (MSG)

Do not lay up for yourselves treasures on earth, where moth and rust destroy and where thieves break in and steal. (Matthew 6:19,

NKJV)

I have shown you in every way, by laboring like this, that you must support the weak. And remember the words of the Lord Jesus, that He said, 'It is more blessed to give than to receive. (Acts 20:35, NKJV)

MY PASTOR HAS A GUARDED HEART

I am very thankful that my pastors Brad and Tamy use discernment in use of e-mail, the Internet, and other media. I thank You, God, for guarding their hearts concerning the use of idle, free time. I continue in a thankful heart that my pastors are walking morally pure and that they put on the whole armor of God so that they will never fall into sexual temptation. I am thankful that my pastors take every thought captive and bring them into obedience to Christ. I am thankful that they walk—no, chase after righteousness in the spirit and not walk according to the flesh and lustful desires. In the name of Jesus, I bind the Jezebel spirit and any other foul spirit that is trying to influence and take down my pastors. I bind you and cast you to the foot of the cross; I loosen the warring angels on my pastors' behalf to protect them from the schemes of the adversary. I loosen the ministering angels to minister to the needs of my pastors. I thank You, Heavenly Father, for hearing my prayers and dispatching the heavenly hosts on behalf of my pastors. I praise Your name!

Let us walk properly, as in the day, not in revelry and drunkenness, not in lewdness and lust, not in strife and envy. But put on the Lord Jesus Christ, and make no provision for the flesh, to fulfill its lusts. (Romans 13:13–14, NKJV)

Finally, my brethren, be strong in the Lord and in the power of His might. Put on the whole armor of God, that you may be able to stand against the wiles of the devil. For we do not wrestle against flesh and blood, but against principalities, against powers, against the rulers of the darkness of this age, against spiritual hosts of wickedness in the heavenly places. (Ephesians 6:10–12, NKJV)

Because it is written, "Be holy, for I am holy." (1 Peter 1:16, NKJV)

For the weapons of our warfare are not carnal but mighty in God for pulling down strongholds, casting down arguments and every high thing that exalts itself against the knowledge of God, bringing every thought into captivity to the obedience of Christ. (2 Corinthians 10:4–5, NKJV)

2. Pray for the Spiritual Needs of My and Your Pastor

MY PASTOR IS PURSUING JESUS

I thank You and praise You, Heavenly Father, for my pastors Brad and Tamy's personal walk with You. I am thankful that You abide in them as they abide in You. I am so thankful that they continue building on their passion for You, the Christ. I am thankful that their spirit man is nourished and strengthened in their personal quiet time with Father God. I am thankful that their soul (mind, will, and emotions) is being renewed and transformed by the washing of the water through the Word. I am thankful for their prayer time and time in the Word of God, that this time is increasing above and beyond that which is required for their sermon preparation. I pray that they will spend more time in the Word of God than reading Christian books and articles. I am thankful that their delight is in the law of the LORD and they meditate on Your law day and night. I pray that they are very selective in the Christian books and articles they consume.

The next morning, Jesus got up long before daylight, left the house while it was dark, and made his way to a secluded place to give himself to prayer. (Mark 1:35, TPT)

Always be eager to present yourself before God as a perfect and mature minister, without shame, as one who correctly explains the Word of Truth. (2 Timothy 2:15, TPT)

MY PASTOR HAS STRONG CHARACTER AND INTEGRITY

Father God, I am thankful that my pastors, Brad and Tamy, are taking very proactive steps in cultivating a strong character full of uncompromised integrity. I am so thankful to You, Father, that they actively walk in such a way as to be far and above, beyond reproach. I am thankful their testimony is genuine, authentic, and transparent. I am thankful that as they walk this walk of faith in You that they have accountability partners that help them when they are in need. I am thankful that they are pursuing strong character and integrity and they find them in You, our Heavenly Father.

Now the purpose of the commandment is love from a pure heart, from a good conscience, and from sincere faith. (1 Timothy 1:5,

NKJV)

> *Moreover he must have a good testimony among those who are outside, lest he fall into reproach and the snare of the devil. (1 Timothy 3:7, NKJV)*

MY PASTOR HAS DEEP FRIENDSHIPS

I am thankful that my pastors Brad and Tamy do not walk in the counsel of the ungodly, nor stand in the way of sinners, nor sit in the seat of the scornful. Father God, I am thankful and praise You that for bringing godly friends and encouragers to my pastors Brad and Tamy's lives. These friends are agents sent by You to strengthen them for the ministry and provide meaningful fellowship and times of rest. I am thankful that these friends are there to edify, build, and strengthen my pastors in the ways everlasting by Your Word.

> *But I trust in the Lord Jesus to send Timothy to you shortly, that I also may be encouraged when I know your state. For I have no one like-minded, who will sincerely care for your state. For all seek their own, not the things which are of Christ Jesus. But you know his proven character, that as a son with his father he served with me in the gospel. (Philippians 2:19–22, NKJV)*

PROTECTION FROM EVIL FOR MY PASTOR

I thank You and praise You, Father God, for providing divine protection over my pastors Brad and Tamy from the evil plans, plots, and schemes of the adversary, Satan. I call on the heavenly host of warring angels to be dispatched to protect my pastors. I plead the blood of Jesus over my pastors and draw a hedge of protection around them in Jesus's name. I am thankful that they are not corrupted as they rub shoulders with the world in the course of ministry.

> *Because you have made the Lord, who is my refuge, Even the Most High, your dwelling place, No evil shall befall you, Nor shall any plague come near your dwelling. (Psalm 91:9–10, NKJV)*

> *No weapon formed against you shall prosper, And every tongue which rises against you in judgment You shall condemn. This is the heritage of the servants of the Lord, And their righteousness is from Me," Says the Lord. (Isaiah 54:17, NKJV)*

Now whom you forgive anything, I also forgive. For if indeed I have forgiven anything, I have forgiven that one for your sakes in the presence of Christ, lest Satan should take advantage of us; for we are not ignorant of his devices. (2 Corinthians 2:10–11, NKJV)

Let him turn away from evil and do good; Let him seek peace and pursue it. For the eyes of the Lord are on the righteous, And His ears are open to their prayers; But the face of the Lord is against those who do evil. (1 Peter 3:11–12, NKJV)

The Lord also will be a refuge for the oppressed, A refuge in times of trouble. And those who know Your name will put their trust in You; For You, Lord, have not forsaken those who seek You. (Psalm 9:9–10, NKJV)

And when the tempter came to him, he said, If you are the Son of God, command that these stones be made bread. But he answered and said, It is written, Man shall not live by bread alone, but by every word that proceeds out of the mouth of God. (Matthew 4:3–4, NKJV)

MY PASTOR HAS A FRESH ANOINTING

Dear Lord, Heavenly Father, I am so very thankful that You are pouring a fresh divine anointing on my pastors Brad and Tamy's lives and ministry. I thank You and praise You that this fresh anointing is energizing their entire being, spirit, soul, and body to be bold witnesses of the Gospel of Jesus Christ. I am thankful that You are working powerfully in their lives and that it is very evident both in their personal spiritual lives as You and Your Word are being poured out into the spiritual lives of the congregation.

But we all, with unveiled face, beholding as in a mirror the glory of the Lord, are being transformed into the same image from glory to glory, just as by the Spirit of the Lord. (2 Corinthians 3:18, NKJV)

The Spirit of the Lord is upon Me, Because He has anointed Me To preach the gospel to the poor; He has sent Me to heal the brokenhearted, To proclaim liberty to the captives And recovery of sight to the blind, To set at liberty those who are oppressed. (Luke 4:18, NKJV)

And when they had gone over, Elijah said to Elisha, Ask what

I shall do for you before I am taken from you. And Elisha said, I pray you, let a double portion of your spirit be upon me. He said, You have asked a hard thing. However, if you see me when I am taken from you, it shall be so for you—but if not, it shall not be so. As they still went on and talked, behold, a chariot of fire and horses of fire parted the two of them, and Elijah went up by a whirlwind into heaven. And Elisha saw it and he cried, My father, my father! The chariot of Israel and its horsemen! And he saw him no more. And he took hold of his own clothes and tore them in two pieces. He took up also the mantle of Elijah that fell from him and went back and stood by the bank of the Jordan. (2 Kings 2:9–13, AMPC)

MY PASTOR HAS CLEAR BIBLICAL VISION

I thankful to You, Father God, for giving my pastors Brad and Tamy a crystal clear biblical vision of what You want to see in Your local body of Christ. I am thankful that You are guiding my pastors step by step in what it will take to attain that vision of this local body of Christ. You are giving my pastors the wisdom to make the right choices for who are the colaborers in Christ at the church. I am thankful that You are revealing Your glory to them and that they will be able to communicate that vision clearly and confidently to the local body of Christ. I am thankful that You are bringing all the necessary resources to bare in fulfilling that vision. You are bringing the people, and You are bringing the finances to make Your vision for the local body of Christ a reality.

Where there is no revelation, the people cast off restraint; But happy is he who keeps the law. (Proverbs 29:18, NKJV)

And the Lord answered me and said, Write the vision and engrave it so plainly upon tablets that everyone who passes may [be able to] read [it easily and quickly] as he hastens by. (Habakkuk 2:2, AMPC)

MY PASTOR HAS THE MIND OF CHRIST

I thank You and praise You, Father, that my pastors, Brad and Tamy, think biblically in all that they do. I am thankful that they take on the mind of Christ as they meditate on Your Word day and night. I am thankful that they pursue You with every fiber of their beings. I am thankful that they abide in Christ as Christ abides in them. I am thankful and I praise You that they meditate on Your Word day and night.

But he who is spiritual judges all things, yet he himself is rightly judged by no one. For "who has known the mind of the Lord that he may instruct Him?" But we have the mind of Christ." (1 Corinthians 2:15–16, NKJV)

MY PASTOR IS SEEKING GOD'S WILL

I am very thankful that my pastors, Brad and Tamy, earnestly seek God's will and that they are committed to instant and complete obedience to Your will. I am thankful that they are eagerly ready to see a mighty work of God in the power and might of the Holy Spirit in and through their ministry to You and their sheep. I am thankful that Your Word is a lamp unto their feet and a light unto their path as they seek Your will and guidance for their lives and ministry.

Then He said to them all, "If anyone desires to come after Me, let him deny himself, and take up his cross daily,[a] and follow Me. For whoever desires to save his life will lose it, but whoever loses his life for My sake will save it." (Luke 9:23–24, NKJV)

For though we walk in the flesh, we do not war according to the flesh. For the weapons of our warfare are not carnal but mighty in God for pulling down strongholds, casting down arguments and every high thing that exalts itself against the knowledge of God, bringing every thought into captivity to the obedience of Christ. (2 Corinthians 10:3–5, NKJV)

MY PASTOR IS IN GROWING FAITH

I am thankful that my pastors Brad and Tamy are followers of Jesus Christ in faith and they have a passionate love for You, Father God. I am thankful that they do not give in to worries, fears, and do not have an anxious spirit. I thank You that they grow in faith daily. I thank You that they walk boldly in faith in every endeavor that they take in You. I thank You that You bring opportunities before them where they can exercise their faith and You confirm Your Word in power with signs, wonders, and miracles following.

But we all, with unveiled face, beholding as in a mirror the glory of the Lord, are being transformed into the same image from glory to glory, just as by the Spirit of the Lord. (2 Corinthians 3:18, NKJV)

We are bound to thank God always for you, brethren, as it is fitting, because your faith grows exceedingly, and the love of every one of you all abounds toward each other, so that we ourselves boast of you among the churches of God for your patience and faith in all your persecutions and tribulations that you endure, which is manifest evidence of the righteous judgment of God, that you may be counted worthy of the kingdom of God, for which you also suffer. (2 Thessalonians 1:3–5, NKJV)

But you, dear friends, carefully build yourselves up in this most holy faith by praying in the Holy Spirit, staying right at the center of God's love, keeping your arms open and outstretched, ready for the mercy of our Master, Jesus Christ. This is the unending life, the real life! (Jude 20–21, MSG)

But you, dear friends, carefully build yourselves up in this most holy faith by praying in the Holy Spirit, staying right at the center of God's love, keeping your arms open and outstretched, ready for the mercy of our Master, Jesus Christ. This is the unending life, the real life! (TPT)

3. Pray for the Leadership Needs of My and Your Pastor

MY PASTOR IS GROWING IN HUMILITY

Lord, Heavenly Father, I am thankful that my pastors Brad and Tamy are humble; they are very authentic and transparent in their faith. I am thankful that they are not given to pride, envy, or hypocrisy. I am thankful that You have given them pure motives and they give You, Father God, all the glory for every gain or victory. I am thankful that they operate in the understanding that as they decrease, You increase. I am thankful that they have a heart that only wants to glorify Your holy name.

He has shown you, O man, what is good; And what does the Lord require of you But to do justly, To love mercy, And to walk humbly with your God? (Micah 6:8, NKJV)

My only boast is in the crucifixion of the Lord Jesus, our Messiah. In him I have been crucified to this natural realm; and the natural realm is dead to me and no longer dominates my life.

(Galatians 6:14, TPT)

MY PASTOR IS USING TIME WISELY

Lord Jesus, I am thankful and I praise You that my pastors Brad and Tamy are using wise time management in their day-to-day tasks. I am thankful that they seek Father God's perspective for their schedules, guarding their time against unnecessary interruptions. I am thankful that they use Your discernment when ministering with people in need, that they are skillful and tactful, operating in love while drawing conversations to closure when someone is not as time-conscious. I am thankful that my pastors are skillful in delegating ministry needs to the proper persons within the congregation with the giftings that would satisfy that ministry's needs. I am thankful that they operate in Your wisdom in every activity of ministry.

So teach us to number our days, That we may gain a heart of wisdom. (Psalm 90:12, NKJV)

See then that you walk circumspectly, not as fools but as wise, redeeming the time, because the days are evil. (Ephesians 5:15–16, NKJV)

Walk in wisdom toward those who are outside, redeeming the time. (Colossians 4:5, NKJV)

MY PASTOR IS LEADING AS A SHEPHERD

I praise God for my pastors Brad and Tamy's leadership, and I thank the Father that they make godly decisions. I am thankful that they follow Jesus's example in that they have His shepherd's heart. I am thankful that they would leave the ninety-nine to find the one. I am thankful that my pastors always speak the truth in love. I am thankful that they know the shepherd's heart in that sometimes sheep can be dumb and need to be lovingly disciplined with the rod of correction. I thank You that their words are wrapped in wisdom, prevalent with peace, forged in forgiveness, lavished in love, and laced with grace toward their sheep (parishioners).

And Your servant is in the midst of Your people whom You have chosen, a great people, too numerous to be numbered or counted. Therefore give to Your servant an understanding heart to judge Your people, that I may discern between good and evil. For who is able to judge this great people of Yours?" The speech pleased the Lord, that Solomon had asked this thing. Then God said to him:

"Because you have asked this thing, and have not asked long life for yourself, nor have asked riches for yourself, nor have asked the life of your enemies, but have asked for yourself understanding to discern justice, behold, I have done according to your words; see, I have given you a wise and understanding heart, so that there has not been anyone like you before you, nor shall any like you arise after you. (1 Kings 3:8–12, NKJV)

Shepherd the flock of God which is among you, serving as overseers, not by compulsion but willingly, not for dishonest gain but eagerly; nor as being lords over those entrusted to you, but being examples to the flock. (1 Peter 5:2–3, NKJV)

And I will give you shepherds according to My heart, who will feed you with knowledge and understanding. (Jeremiah 3:15, NKJV)

Having then gifts differing according to the grace that is given to us, let us use them: if prophecy, let us prophesy in proportion to our faith; or ministry, let us use it in our ministering; he who teaches, in teaching; he who exhorts, in exhortation; he who gives, with liberality; he who leads, with diligence; he who shows mercy, with cheerfulness. Let love be without hypocrisy. Abhor what is evil. Cling to what is good. Be kindly affectionate to one another with brotherly love, in honor giving preference to one another; not lagging in diligence, fervent in spirit, serving the Lord; rejoicing in hope, patient in tribulation, continuing steadfastly in prayer; distributing to the needs of the saints, given to hospitality. (Romans 12:6–13, NKJV)

MY PASTOR IS GROWING IN DISCERNMENT

I am so thankful to You, Father, and I praise You that my pastors, Brad and Tamy, will counsel and teach with discernment through the wise use of the scripture. I thank You, Father, that they exude wisdom in every word of advice that they handle out and that every word is laced with grace and love from the throne room of grace. I pray a hedge of protection from the effects of sinful or negative attitudes that they encounter as they counsel others. In the name of Jesus, I bind any sinful and negative attitudes and speech that would try to bring my pastors down. I call forth the Holy Spirit to comfort my pastors and keep them from harm by these types of negative and sinful attitudes expressed to them. I thank You that they are growing in discernment, not only as it relates to ministering Your grace to others, but also that this same discernment can also protect them from attacks from the adversary. Thank You that You hear our prayers and are acting on them as we speak. Praise Your holy name, Jesus.

If any of you is deficient in wisdom, let him ask of the giving God [Who gives] to everyone liberally and ungrudgingly, without reproaching or faultfinding, and it will be given him. Only it must be in faith that he asks with no wavering (no hesitating, no doubting). For the one who wavers (hesitates, doubts) is like the billowing surge out at sea that is blown hither and thither and tossed by the wind. (James 1:5–6, AMPC)

And if anyone longs to be wise, ask God for wisdom and he will give it! He won't see your lack of wisdom as an opportunity to scold you over your failures but he will overwhelm your failures with his generous grace. Just make sure you ask empowered by confident faith without doubting that you will receive. For the ambivalent person believes one minute and doubts the next. Being undecided makes you become like the rough seas driven and tossed by the wind. You're up one minute and tossed down the next. (TPT)

MY PASTOR IS FULL OF HEALING AND JOY

In the name of Jesus, I call forth the healing balm oil of the Holy Spirit to heal any hurts that my pastors have suffered in the ministry of our Lord Jesus Christ. I thank You for guarding their hearts from back talking and bitterness in the church. I thank You that they serve You, the Lord, with gladness. I thank You that they encourage the congregation to worship God with a joyful, surrendered spirit. I thank You that they demonstrate their joyful worship before You our Father. Praise You that they operate in healing and joy on a daily basis.

To grant [consolation and joy] to those who mourn in Zion—to give them an ornament (a garland or diadem) of beauty instead of ashes, the oil of joy instead of mourning, the garment [expressive] of praise instead of a heavy, burdened, and failing spirit—that they may be called oaks of righteousness [lofty, strong, and magnificent, distinguished for uprightness, justice, and right standing with God], the planting of the Lord, that He may be glorified. (Isaiah

61:3, AMPC)

But He was wounded for our transgressions, He was bruised for our iniquities; The chastisement for our peace was upon Him, And by His stripes we are healed. (Isaiah 53:5, NKJV)

THE GREATEST COMMANDMENT

In the name of Jesus, I thank You that my pastors Brad and Tamy love the God of Israel with all their hearts, souls, minds, and strength and that this love is demonstrated by them to all who they encounter. I thank You that God's Holy Spirit will continue to work in their hearts in power and might and they are led by the Holy Spirit in everything that they do. I thank You, Father, that my pastors have a deep love for You, a love that grows deeper with each passing day. I thank You that this love for You is demonstrated by their unwavering desire to see the great commandment fulfilled in their lifetime as they love all unconditionally throughout the days, weeks, months, and years to come.

You shall love the LORD your God with all your heart, with all your soul, and with all your strength. (Deuteronomy 6:5, NKJV)

But seek first the kingdom of God and His righteousness, and all these things shall be added to you. (Matthew 6:33, NKJV)

MY PASTOR IS FEARING GOD

Lord Father, I thank You and praise You that my pastors Brad and Tamy focus on the Word of God and walk in the fear (respect) of the Lord; this is a reverential type of fear, acknowledging Your power and might. This reverence for You, Abba Father, is stronger than any fear of man. It is based in this reverential type of fear that drives them to hear from You as they prepare their messages. I pray that they will seek to please You, Father God, rather than men, as they pursue holiness rather than the praise of men. I thank You and praise You that my pastors preach the uncompromised Word of Father God out of reverential respect and fear of You.

The fear of the Lord leads to life, And he who has it will abide in satisfaction; He will not be visited with evil. (Proverbs 19:23, NKJV)

Be diligent to present yourself approved to God, a worker who does not need to be ashamed, rightly dividing the word of truth. (2

Timothy 2:15, NKJV)

*I charge you therefore before God and the Lord Jesus Christ,
who will judge the living and the dead at[a] His appearing and His
kingdom: Preach the word! Be ready in season and out of season.
Convince, rebuke, exhort, with all longsuffering and teaching. (2
Timothy 4:1–2, NKJV)*

*But without faith it is impossible to please Him, for he who
comes to God must believe that He is, and that He is a rewarder of
those who diligently seek Him. (Hebrews 11:6, NKJV)*

MY PASTOR IS COURAGEOUS IN PREACHING

I praise You thank You, Father God, for giving my pastors Brad and Tamy such a courageous attitude while preaching in the pulpit as they proclaim Christ and His kingdom. I come against any spirit of lack of self-confidence that may try to derail my pastors as they prepare and then present the Gospel of Jesus Christ. I bind that spirit in the name of Jesus, and I cast it to the foot of the cross. In the name of Jesus, I call forth the Holy Spirit to empower my pastors with the wisdom, love, compassion, and grace from the throne room of heaven as they speak Your Word in power. I thank You that You have given my pastors a courage and boldness to deliver Your Word in power and might. I thank You that my pastors have the boldness of Peter on the Day of Pentecost as they deliver Your prophetic Word in the power of the Holy Spirit. I thank You, Father God, that they preach with insight, transparency, and humility in the power of the Holy Spirit and that that Word is confirmed with signs, wonders, and miracles.

*To them God willed to make known what are the riches of the
glory of this mystery among the Gentiles: which is Christ in you,
the hope of glory. Him we preach, warning every man and teaching
every man in all wisdom, that we may present every man perfect
in Christ Jesus. To this end I also labor, striving according to His
working which works in me mightily. (Colossians 1:27–29, NKJV)*

*For God has not given us a spirit of fear, but of power and of
love and of a sound mind. (2 Timothy 1:7, NKJV)*

*For I want you to know what a great conflict I have for you
and those in Laodicea, and for as many as have not seen my
face in the flesh, that their hearts may be encouraged, being knit*

together in love, and attaining to all riches of the full assurance of understanding, to the knowledge of the mystery of God, both of the Father and of Christ, in whom are hidden all the treasures of wisdom and knowledge. Now this I say lest anyone should deceive you with persuasive words. For though I am absent in the flesh, yet I am with you in spirit, rejoicing to see your good order and the steadfastness of your faith in Christ. (Colossians 2:1–5, NKJV)

The Spirit of the Lord is upon Me, Because He has anointed Me To preach the gospel to the poor; He has sent Me to heal the brokenhearted, To proclaim liberty to the captives And recovery of sight to the blind, To set at liberty those who are oppressed. (Luke 4:18, NKJV)

Men of Israel, hear these words: Jesus of Nazareth, a Man attested by God to you by miracles, wonders, and signs which God did through Him in your midst, as you yourselves also know Him, being delivered by the determined purpose and foreknowledge of God, you have taken by lawless hands, have crucified, and put to death; whom God raised up, having loosed the pains of death, because it was not possible that He should be held by it. (Acts 2:22–24, NKJV)

Therefore let all the house of Israel know assuredly that God has made this Jesus, whom you crucified, both Lord and Christ." Now when they heard this, they were cut to the heart, and said to Peter and the rest of the apostles, "Men and brethren, what shall we do?" Then Peter said to them, "Repent, and let every one of you be baptized in the name of Jesus Christ for the remission of sins; and you shall receive the gift of the Holy Spirit. For the promise is to you and to your children, and to all who are afar off, as many as the Lord our God will call. (Acts 2:36–39, NKJV)

MY PASTOR HAS THE GREAT COMMISSION TATTOOED ON HIS HEART

I am most thankful to You, my Heavenly Father, that my pastors Brad and Tamy have a passion to answer the great commission of Christ. I thank You that they are committed to personal interpersonal evangelism, interpersonal discipleship, and the equipping of the saints to the work of the ministry. I give You all the praise, honor, and glory, Father God, for giving them a heart to develop a thriving missions program in our church. I thank You for instilling in their spirit the desire to reach the lost at any cost—to reach the lost in Judea, Jerusalem, Samaria, and to the ends of the earth. I thank You for giving my pastors creative "outside-the-box" ideas in reaching the lost. I thank You for giving my pastors the insight on how to make the seemingly impossible possible as they depend on You, Jehovah Jireh, to provide for all the resources for the outreach.

> *Go therefore and make disciples of all the nations, baptizing them in the name of the Father and of the Son and of the Holy Spirit, teaching them to observe all things that I have commanded you; and lo, I am with you always, even to the end of the age." Amen. (Matthew 28:19–20, NKJV)*

> *Later He appeared to the eleven as they sat at the table; and He rebuked their unbelief and hardness of heart, because they did not believe those who had seen Him after He had risen. And He said to them, "Go into all the world and preach the gospel to every creature. He who believes and is baptized will be saved; but he who does not believe will be condemned. And these signs will follow those who believe: In My name they will cast out demons; they will speak with new tongues." (Mark 16:14–17, NKJV)*

> *For there is no distinction between Jew and Greek, for the same Lord over all is rich to all who call upon Him. For "whoever calls on the name of the Lord shall be saved." How then shall they call on Him in whom they have not believed? And how shall they believe in Him of whom they have not heard? And how shall they hear without a preacher? And how shall they preach unless they are sent? As it is written: "How beautiful are the feet of those who preach the gospel of peace, Who bring glad tidings of good things!" But they have not all obeyed the gospel. For Isaiah says, "Lord, who has believed our report?" So then faith comes by hearing, and hearing by the word of God." (Romans 10:12–17, NKJV)*

MY PASTOR DAILY PRACTICES PERSONAL PRAYER, PRAISE, AND WORSHIP

God, my Heavenly Father, I thank You for my pastors, Brad and Tamy, who live a life full of prayer, praise, and worship. I thank You that they will lead by example during their prayer time. I thank You that they worship by raising holy hands in praise, worship, and adoration of You, our Heavenly Father. I thank You and praise You, Jesus, that they practice being in Your presence daily, moment by moment, as they abide in You and You abide in them. I praise and thank You that they teach the congregation how to walk in a close relationship with You, the Father. I thank You that their worship and prayers are powerful in the spirit.

Lord, You have been our dwelling place in all generations. Before the mountains were brought forth, Or ever You had formed the earth and the world, Even from everlasting to everlasting, You are God. You turn man to destruction, And say, "Return, O children of men." For a thousand years in Your sight Are like yesterday when it is past, And like a watch in the night. (Psalm 90:1–4, NKJV)

Now in the morning, having risen a long while before daylight, He went out and departed to a solitary place; and there He prayed. (Mark 1:35, NKJV)

Rejoice always, pray without ceasing, in everything give thanks; for this is the will of God in Christ Jesus for you. (1 Thessalonians 5:16–18, NKJV)

These all continued with one accord in prayer and supplication, with the women and Mary the mother of Jesus, and with His brothers. (Acts 1:14, NKJV)

MY PASTOR TRUSTS GOD IN CONFLICT

Lord Father, I thank You that my pastors Brad and Tamy trust You during the storm and are not given in to discouragement. In the name of Jesus, I come against the lying wagging tongues of the gossipers within the church. Those who are wolves in sheep clothing, whose sole goal is to bring division within the local body of Christ, speaking lies against the pastors and others in church leadership. In the name of Jesus, I bind those lying lips and call forth the Holy Spirit to communicate His grace into their lives, so they can see the error of their ways. I call on the Holy Spirit to bring comfort to my pastors and church leadership in Jesus's name. I thank You that my pastors are able to deal with inevitable criticism and conflict with Your wisdom, love, and grace. I thank You that they commit themselves into your hands, oh, Lord God, Who judges righteously.

Desperate, I throw myself on you: you are my God! Hour by hour I place my days in your hand, safe from the hands out to get me. Warm me, your servant, with a smile; save me because you love me. Don't embarrass me by not showing up; I've given you plenty of notice. Embarrass the wicked, stand them up, leave them stupidly shaking their heads as they drift down to hell. Gag those loudmouthed liars who heckle me, your follower, with jeers and catcalls. (Psalm 31:18, MSG)

And can you believe it? they kept right on sinning; all those wonders and they still wouldn't believe! So their lives dribbled off to nothing, nothing to show for their lives but a ghost town. When he cut them down, they came running for help; they turned and pled for mercy. They gave witness that God was their rock, that High God was their redeemer, But they didn't mean a word of it; they lied through their teeth the whole time. They could not have cared less about him, wanted nothing to do with his Covenant. (Psalms 78:36, MSG)

But their repentance lasted only as long as they were in danger; they lied through their teeth to the true God of Covenant. So quickly they wandered away from his promises, following God with their words and not their hearts! Their worship was only flattery. (TPT)

Also look at Proverbs 6:16–19, 10:18, 20:19, 26:28, 29:5; Jeremiah 23:16–17, 27:9, 10; Matthew 7:15; 2 Thessalonians 2:9–13; 1 Timothy 4:7, 6:20; 2 Timothy 2:16; 2 Peter; 1 John 3–5; Revelation 12:10.

Who, when He was reviled, did not revile in return; when He suffered, He did not threaten, but committed Himself to Him who judges righteously; who Himself bore our sins in His own body on the tree, that we, having died to sins, might live for righteousness— by whose stripes you were healed. For you were like sheep going astray, but have now returned to the Shepherd and Overseer of your souls. (1 Peter 2:23–25, NKJV)

But I say to you who hear: Love your enemies, do good to those who hate you, bless those who curse you, and pray for those who spitefully use you. (Luke 6:27–28, NKJV)

MY PASTOR HAS A SERVANT'S HEART

I pray for my pastors Brad and Tamy. I thank You, Father, that they practice servant leadership through getting into the trenches and getting their hands dirty, so to say. I thank You, like Jesus, humbled himself and left heaven to become a man, so my pastors lead by example and are humble as they serve the needs of the local body of Christ. Just as Christ came, not to be served but to serve, our pastors know the heart of Christ and serve the body of Christ. I thank You that they edify the congregation in serving others motivated by and with God's agape, unconditional love.

But Jesus called them to Himself and said to them, "You know that those who are considered rulers over the Gentiles lord it over them, and their great ones exercise authority over them. Yet it shall not be so among you; but whoever desires to become great among you shall be your servant. And whoever of you desires to be first shall be slave of all. For even the Son of Man did not come to be served, but to serve, and to give His life a ransom for many." (Mark 10:42–45, NKJV)

For you, brethren, have been called to liberty; only do not use liberty as an opportunity for the flesh, but through love serve one another. For all the law is fulfilled in one word, even in this: "You shall love your neighbor as yourself. (Galatians 5:13–14, NKJV)

With goodwill doing service, as to the Lord, and not to men, knowing that whatever good anyone does, he will receive the same from the Lord, whether he is a slave or free. (Ephesians 6:7–8, NKJV)

After that, He poured water into a basin and began to wash the disciples' feet, and to wipe them with the towel with which He was girded. Then He came to Simon Peter. And Peter said to Him, "Lord, are You washing my feet?" Jesus answered and said to him, "What I am doing you do not understand now, but you will know after this." Peter said to Him, "You shall never wash my feet!" Jesus answered him, "If I do not wash you, you have no part with Me." Simon Peter said to Him, "Lord, not my feet only, but also my hands and my head!" (John 13:5–9, NKJV)

Let nothing be done through selfish ambition or conceit, but in lowliness of mind let each esteem others better than himself. Let each of you look out not only for his own interests, but also for the interests of others. Let this mind be in you which was also in Christ Jesus, who, being in the form of God, did not consider it robbery to be equal with God, And being found in appearance as a man, He humbled Himself and became obedient to the point of death, even the death of the cross. Therefore God also has highly exalted Him and given Him the name which is above every name, that at the name of Jesus every knee should bow, of those in heaven, and of those on earth, and of those under the earth, and that every tongue should confess that Jesus Christ is Lord, to the glory of God the Father. (Philippians 2:3–8, NKJV)

MY PASTOR HAS A HEART FOR REVIVAL

I thank You, Jesus, and I pray that my pastors Brad and Tamy are seeking God the Father for personal revival. I thank You that they seek Your face and desire a deeper understanding and touch from Your Holy Spirit to bring about the revolutionary change that transforms their walk with You, Father God. I thank You that the wind of Holy Spirt is rushing into their lives entirely, spirit, soul, and body, bringing them deeper revelation into Your nature, transforming them from glory to glory. I am thankful that they desire the same revival in my church and my community and my region and are bringing those prayers into Your throne room of grace.

When the Day of Pentecost had fully come, they were all with one accord in one place. And suddenly there came a sound from heaven, as of a rushing mighty wind, and it filled the whole house where they were sitting. Then there appeared to them divided tongues, as of fire, and one sat upon each of them. And they were all filled with the Holy Spirit and began to speak with other tongues, as the Spirit gave them utterance. (Acts 2:1–4, NKJV)

And with many other words he testified and exhorted them, saying, "Be saved from this perverse generation." Then those who gladly received his word were baptized; and that day about three thousand souls were added to them. (Acts 2:40–41, NKJV)

The humble shall see this and be glad; And you who seek God, your hearts shall live. (Psalm 69:32, NKJV)

When I shut up heaven and there is no rain, or command the locusts to devour the land, or send pestilence among My people, if My people who are called by My name will humble themselves, and pray and seek My face, and turn from their wicked ways, then I will hear from heaven, and will forgive their sin and heal their land. Now My eyes will be open and My ears attentive to prayer made in this place. (2 Chronicles 7:13–15, NKJV)

MY PASTOR WORKS WHOLEHEARTEDLY

I very thankful that my pastors Brad and Tamy strive for personal excellence in every aspect of their daily lives. I thank You, Lord Father, that You are moving mountains on my pastors behalf to make the work of the day easier less challenging and removing any strife. I am also thankful that my pastors are "all in"; just as Christ was "all in," my pastors are doing what it takes to present You to the world in all Your love, grace, patience, kindness, goodness, and forgiveness.

And whatever you do, do it heartily, as to the Lord and not to men, knowing that from the Lord you will receive the reward of the inheritance; for you serve the Lord Christ. (Colossians 3:23–24, NKJV)

As His divine power has given to us all things that pertain to life and godliness, through the knowledge of Him who called us by glory and virtue, by which have been given to us exceedingly great and precious promises, that through these you may be partakers of the divine nature, having escaped the corruption that is in the world through lust. (2 Peter 1:3–4, NKJV)

Trust in the Lord with all your heart, And lean not on your own understanding; In all your ways acknowledge Him, And He shall direct your paths. (Proverbs 3:5–6, NKJV)

MY PASTOR MINISTRY TEAM WORKS IN UNITY

I pray for the spiritual unity between our pastors and within the church staff as well as among the spiritual leadership of the church (elders, deacons, etc.), I thank You, Heavenly, Father that all the church staff puts aside and checks all petty pride and selfish motives at the door. I thank

You that every staff member as well as all ministry volunteers operate in the fruits of the spirit as defined in Galatians 5. I thank You, Father, that the enemy is not allowed to create divisions, strife, or misunderstanding among the church leaders. In the name of Jesus, I come against the plans and schemes of the adversary and call them laid to waste in the garbage can. I thank You that the church staff is driven and motivated by Your love as they operate with each individual gifting, their strengths are complementing each other, and unity brings out each person's strengths and gifting for the furtherance of the Gospel of Jesus Christ so that Christ is glorified.

But the fruit of the Spirit is love, joy, peace, longsuffering, kindness, goodness, faithfulness, gentleness, self-control. Against such there is no law. (Galatians 5:22–23, NKJV)

If it is possible, as much as depends on you, live peaceably with all men. (Romans 12:18, NKJV)

Therefore let us pursue the things which make for peace and the things by which one may edify another. (Romans 14:19, NKJV)

Now I plead with you, brethren, by the name of our Lord Jesus Christ, that you all speak the same thing, and that there be no divisions among you, but that you be perfectly joined together in the same mind and in the same judgment. (1 Corinthians 1:10, NKJV)

MY PASTOR HAS A HEALTHY CHURCH BODY

I am thankful that pastors Brad and Tamy do not have to worry and stress about the little stuff. I thank You that my pastors have no worries about how things are going to get done in the ministry. I praise Your name, ABBA Father, that my pastors operated in wisdom in choosing who works in the volunteer ministry. I thank You Lord, that World Harvest will never have a lack of people ready, willing, and able to do the work of the ministry. I am very grateful that World Harvest has the right leaders in place full of the Holy Spirit and are operating in the Fivefold Ministry. World Harvest has a local church body full of doers of the Word and not just hearers of the Word. I thank You, Jesus, that my local body of Christ lives, operates, and preaches the Gospel of Jesus Christ in the power of the Holy Spirit and that You confirm Your Word with signs following.

And the apostles went out announcing the good news

everywhere, as the Lord himself consistently worked with them, validating the message they preached with miracle-signs that accompanied them! (Mark 1620, TPT)

So Christ himself gave the apostles, the prophets, the evangelists, the pastors and teachers, to equip his people for works of service, so that the body of Christ may be built up until we all reach unity in the faith and in the knowledge of the Son of God and become mature, attaining to the whole measure of the fullness of Christ. (Ephesians 4:11–13, NIV)

CHURCHES IN ENID, OKLAHOMA

Evangel Assembly of God
Enid First Assembly of God
Calvary Assembly of God
Central Assembly of God
Bethel Baptist Church
Bethlehem Baptist Church
Oakwood Christian Church
Bible Baptist Church
Salvation Army Church
Calvary Baptist Church
Chisholm Trial Cowboy
Emmanuel Baptist Church
First Baptist Church
First Indian Baptist Church
First Missionary Baptist Church
Garland Road Baptist Church
Gospel Light Baptist Church
Liberty Southern Baptist Church
Progressive Baptist Church
Temple Baptist Church
The Oasis
Trinity Baptist Church
Full Gospel Tabernacle Church
Forgotten Ministries
Hallmark Independent Baptist Church
Grace Bible Church

Victory Bible Church
St. Francis Xavier Parish
St. Gregory the Great
Cedar Ridge Wesleyan Church
Central Christian Church
Enid Seventh-day Adventist
Awakening the Fire Ministries
Christian Church of the Covenant
Faith Center Fellowship
Living Word Fellowship
World Harvest Church
University Place Christian
Zoe Bible Church
Iglesia Cristiana El Shaddai
North Garland Church of Christ
Church of Christ
Marshallese United Church of Christ
Enid Church of God
West Side Church of God
Community Church of the Plains
St Matthews Episcopal Church
House of Prayer
Cornerstone Evangelical Free Church
Oakwood Christian Church
Grace World Outreach Church
Saint Paul Lutheran Church
Faith Lutheran Church
Redeemer Lutheran Church
Trinity Lutheran Church
Grace Mennonite Church
Mennonite Brethren Church
Yad El Ministries Messianic Jewish
Free Methodist Church
First United Methodist Church
Bethany United Methodist Church
New Hope United Methodist
Christ United Methodist Church

Willow View United Methodist Church
First Church of the Nazarene
Maine Nazarene Church
Anew Church
Calvary Chapel of Enid
Christ Community Church
Korean Church of Grace
Covenant Life Worship Center
Covenant Life Christian Fellowship
Peace Korean United Methodist
Driftwood Fellowship
Sonrise Christian Fellowship
Abundant Life Family Church
First Presbyterian Church
Seventh Day Adventist Church
Evangelistic Center Church
Willow Road Christian Church
Sojourn Church
West Willow Community Church
Victory Christian Center
House of Prayer
Vance Air Force Base Chapel
Cornerstone Evangelical Free
Davis Park Christian Church
Abundant Life Family Center
Institute for Rural Church
United Pentecostal Church
Crabtree Correctional Facility
Grace Tabernacle Church of the Lord Jesus Christ
Family Faith Church of the Brethren
Philadelphia Seventh Day Adventist Church
First Love Church
United Pentecostal Church
Enid Reformed Church
West Side Baptist Church
Your Family Church

JERICHO LAP 1

FAMILY

Husbands
Wives
Ex-Husbands
Ex-Wives
Children
Children of Divorce
Grandparents
Great-Grandparents
Child Abuse
Caregivers

HUSBANDS AND WIVES

This is a prayer for husbands and wives to strengthen the holy bond of marriage. If you are the husband, you can pray this prayer in the first person; likewise, if you are the wife, pray the wife's prayer in the first person. Or if you have a particular couple you are interceding for, then insert their names. It is written in third person, directed to a given couple; but by doing it this way, that couple is also standing in proxy for other marriages that may come in mind.

HUSBANDS

Lord Father, I lift up this couple in prayer today to strengthen their marriage. This is a prayer of *faith* proclaiming the finished work that Christ has already accomplished in this couple evoking Hebrews 11:1.

Lord Father, today, I lift up the husband in prayer. I thank You and praise Your holy name that he wakes up each day with a desire to follow You! I thank You that the husband's desire is to abide in You as You abide in him. I thank You, Heavenly Father, that the husband loves You—the Lord his God—with every passion of his heart, with all the energy of his being, and with every thought that is within him. I thank You, Heavenly Father, that the fruit produced by the Holy Spirit within him is divine love in all its varied expressions: joy that overflows his heart expressed to his wife, peace that subdues his wife, patience that endures life's challenges, kindness in action to his wife, a life full of virtue, faith that prevails, gentleness of heart to his wife, and strength to his spirit.

I thank You, Father, that the husband is quick to hear and slow to anger, that he does not let the sun go down on his anger but that he prays first, seeking Your face before reacting, so that he can respond in love to resolve differences. I thank You that he listens twice as much as he speaks. And that he inclines his ear to hear what You, Father God, have to say. I am thankful that the husband fills his home with Your praises. I am thankful that the husband is quick to praise his wife, far quicker to praise than to criticize his wife. I thank You that the husband realizes that he is the protector of his wife in all areas of her being. I thank You that the husband protects her physical life. I thank You that he protects her virtue. I thank You that he protects her self-esteem, self-image, and self-worth. I thank You that the husband's words are always filled with praise, grace, gentle kindness, and love.

I thank You that the husband continues to pursue his wife, he continues to woo her, and that he places her in high esteem for the jewel that she is. I thank You that he continues to fan the flames of passion and romance by doing the little things in life for her. Yes, the occasional gifts, flowers, and greeting cards—yes, he continues to do those things. I am thankful he is also doing the little things like taking the trash out or changing a light bulb—these things done for her without her asking more than once. I thank You that the husband is in tune with the needs of his wife that he naturally does things for her before she even knows that they need to be done. I thank You that he does all in an attitude of love and self-sacrifice.

I thank You that the husband is considerate of his wife, giving her tenderness, and he pays her honor in treating her as an equal.

I thank You that the husband demonstrates love for his wife with the same tender devotion that Christ demonstrated to us, his bride. For Christ died for us. He sacrificed himself to make us holy and pure, cleansing us through the showering of the pure water of the Word of God. I thank You, Father, that everything the husband does for his wife is designed to make her a mature believer, until she becomes a source of praise to You, Father God, glorious and radiant, beautiful and holy, without fault or flaw. I thank You that the husband is loving and caring for his wife, the same way he loves and cares for his own body, for to love his own wife is to love his own self. No one abuses his own body but pampers it—serving and satisfying its needs. Likewise, I am thankful that the husband serves his wife and seeks to satisfy all his wife's needs. I am thankful that the husband is gracious to his wife just as he is gracious to himself.

I am thankful that both the husband and wife are submitted to Your Holy Word and to the will of You, Father God. I am thankful this mutual submission to the Word of God motivates the mutual submission to one another as husband and wife, seeking God's wisdom and will in every decision they make. I thank You, Heavenly Father, that the husband realizes his purpose and roll as the priest of the household and steps up to that responsibility in being the example of Christ in his household. Leading his wife to the foot of the cross in all humility, honor, praise, and adoration to You, the Risen King.

I am thankful that both husband and wife can share tender moments of vulnerability one with another knowing that together, they are stronger than they are individually. I am thankful that they come together in prayer as they fight whatever challenges come their way, on their knees before You, Father God.

I thank You for hearing my prayers, in the powerful name of Jesus I pray, amen.

> *In the same way you married men should live considerately with [your wives], with an intelligent recognition [of the marriage relation], honoring the woman as [physically] the weaker, but [realizing that you] are joint heirs of the grace (God's unmerited favor) of life, in order that your prayers may not be hindered and cut off. [Otherwise you cannot pray effectively.] (1 Peter 3:7, AMPC)*

> *Husbands, you in turn must treat your wives with tenderness, viewing them as feminine partners who deserve to be honored, for they are co-heirs with you of the "divine grace of life," so that nothing will hinder your prayers. (TPT)*

> *The same goes for you husbands: Be good husbands to your wives. Honor them, delight in them. As women they lack some of your advantages. But in the new life of God's grace, you're equals. Treat your wives, then, as equals so your prayers don't run aground. (MSG)*

> *Out of respect for Christ, be courteously reverent to one another.*

(Ephesians 5:21, MSG)

And out of your reverence for Christ be supportive of each other in love. (TPT)

Be subject to one another out of reverence for Christ (the Messiah, the Anointed One). (AMPC)

Submitting to one another in the fear of God. (NKJV)

WIVES

Dear Lord, Heavenly Father, I now lift up the wife. I thank You and praise You that she wakes up each day with a desire to follow You! I thank You that the wife's desire is to abide in You as You abide in her. I thank You that the wife loves the Lord her God with every passion in her heart, with all the energy of her being, and with every thought that is within her. I thank You, Heavenly Father, that the fruit produced by the Holy Spirit within her is divine love in all its varied expressions: joy that overflows her heart expressed to her husband, peace that subdues her husband, patience that endures life's challenges, kindness in action to her husband, a life full of virtue, faith that prevails, gentleness of heart to her husband, and strength to her spirit.

I thank You, Father, that the wife is quick to hear and slow to anger, that she does not let the sun go down on her anger but that she prays first, seeking Your face before reacting, so that she can respond in love to resolve differences. I thank You that she listens twice as much as she speaks. And that she inclines her ear to hear what You, Father God, has to say. I am thankful that the wife fills her home with Your praises. I am thankful that the wife is quick to praise her husband, far quicker to praise than to criticize her husband. I thank You that the wife's words are always filled with praise, grace, and love.

I thank You that the wife is always understanding and supportive of her husband. I thank You, Heavenly Father, that just as the wife is respectful and reverent to You, so is the wife to her husband. I am thankful that the wife is devoted to her husband in everything. I am thankful that the wife sets her husband up for success and not for failure. I am thankful that the wife builds her husband's confidence up.

I am thankful that both husband and wife can share tender moments of vulnerability one with another knowing that together, they are stronger than they are individually. I am thankful that they come together in prayer as they fight whatever challenges come their way, on their knees before Father God.

> *Wives, understand and support your husbands in ways that show your support for Christ. The husband provides leadership to his wife the way Christ does to his church, not by domineering but by cherishing. So just as the church submits to Christ as he exercises such leadership, wives should likewise submit to their husbands. (Ephesians 5:22–23, MSG)*

> *For wives, this means being supportive to your husbands like you are tenderly devoted to our Lord, for the husband provides leadership for the wife, just as Christ provides leadership for his church, as the Savior and Reviver of the body. In the same way the church is devoted to Christ, let the wives be devoted to their husbands in everything. (TPT)*

> *However, let each man of you (without exception) love his wife as (being in a sense) his very own self; and let the wife see that she respects and reverences her husband (that she notices him, regards him, honors him, prefers him, venerates, and esteems him; and that she defers to him, praises him, and loves and admires him exceedingly. (Ephesians 5:33, AMP)*

I thank You that husbands and wives are praying daily for their marriages. I thank You that they seek after You with passion and they pray for wisdom. I thank You that they are diligent in communicating with You their needs and their hearts' desire in faith! I thank You that they are finding hope in You! I thank You that husbands lead and love their family in reverence to You, Lord, and that wives respect and support their husbands. I thank You that children are raised with a great example of marriage being lived out right in front of them. I pray, Lord, for healing in marriages that are in despair or on the verge of separation. Let loose Your graceful and powerful love into the hearts of husbands and wives. I pray for a revolution in marriages in Jesus's name. *Amen!*

As a closing prayer for marriages, I thank You that You are giving the husband and wife strength and please grant them an extra dose of energy to take care of all the priorities in their lives. I pray that they would be diligent to follow through with caring for their responsibilities. I also pray that they take adequate time to rest and rejuvenate their bodies so that they can keep going strong. I pray that they always remember You are with them. I pray that they remain humble and thankful for Your strength that sustains them. I pray that Your will is done in their lives. Help them to avoid wrestling with thoughts of inadequacy. Please help them to never neglect their priorities in Jesus's name. Amen! I thank You that the husband and wife are receiving a special dose of wisdom and grace to operate in their callings as husband and wife, that they receive a double anointing when they need it the most. In Jesus's name, we pray and thank You for hearing our prayers.

> *Live joyfully with the wife whom you love all the days of your vain life which He has given you under the sun. (Ecclesiastes 9:9, NKJV)*

> *Wives, submit to your own husbands, as is fitting in the Lord. (Colossians 3:18, NKJV)*

> *He who finds a wife finds a good thing, And obtains favor from the Lord. (Proverbs 18:22, NKJV)*

Dear Heavenly Father, I lift marriages up to You. I pray especially over husbands and wives who struggle with an addiction to pornography. Lord, I thank You that You are revealing to them how dangerous this stronghold is. In the name of Jesus, I come against that Jezebel spirit that has its grips on marriages. You foul spirit that wants to choke a marriage like a boa constrictor, I bind you in the name of Jesus, and cast you to the foot of the cross! I thank You Father God, that You are breaking the bondage of pornography in marriages in Jesus's name! I thank You that You're are giving husbands and wives the strength to overcome this temptation through the power of the Holy Spirit. I thank and praise Your holy name that You are sending people to encourage them and keep them accountable so as to not to stumble. I thank You that You are bringing to marriages that have been struggling with this issue. Victory in Jesus's name. Amen! I thank You that You are bringing holiness back into this marriage that had been under the bondage of pornography. I thank You that the love of Jesus is being brought back into this marriage. I thank You that any bitterness and unforgiveness that built up as a result of this sin is healed in the name of Jesus. I thank You that You are bringing this marriage back to wholeness and oneness and unity in the name of Jesus.

> *Jesus said, "Moses wrote this command only as a concession to*

208

your hardhearted ways. In the original creation, God made male and female to be together. Because of this, a man leaves father and mother, and in marriage he becomes one flesh with a woman— no longer two individuals, but forming a new unity. Because God created this organic union of the two sexes, no one should desecrate his art by cutting them apart." (Mark 10:5–9, MSG)

And to the husbands, you are to demonstrate love for your wives with the same tender devotion that Christ demonstrated to us, his bride. For he died for us, sacrificing himself to make us holy and pure, cleansing us through the showering of the pure water of the Word of God. All that he does in us is designed to make us a mature church for his pleasure, until we become a source of praise to him—glorious and radiant, beautiful and holy, without fault or flaw. Husbands have the obligation of loving and caring for their wives the same way they love and care for their own bodies, for to love your wife is to love your own self. No one abuses his own body, but pampers it—serving and satisfying its needs. That's exactly what Christ does for his church! He serves and satisfies us as members of his body. For this reason a man is to leave his father and his mother and lovingly hold to his wife, since the two have become joined as one flesh. Marriage is the beautiful design of the Almighty, a great and sacred mystery—meant to be a vivid example of Christ and his church. So every married man should be gracious to his wife just as he is gracious to himself. And every wife should be tenderly devoted to her husband. (Ephesians 5:25–32, TPT)

But because of [the temptation to participate in] sexual immorality, let each man have his own wife, and let each woman have her own husband. (1 Corinthians 7:2 (AMP)

Perhaps. But because of the danger of immorality, each husband should have sexual intimacy with his wife and each wife should have sexual intimacy with her husband. (TPT)

A prayer for ex-husbands and ex-wives to reconcile and live peacefully apart in forgiveness and brotherly/sisterly love.

First and foremost, Dear Lord Heavenly Father, I now lift up the ex-husband and ex-wife. I thank You and praise You that individually they wake up each day with a desire to follow You! I thank You that their desire is to abide in You as You abide in them individually. I thank You that they love the Lord their God with every passion in their hearts, with all the energy of their beings, and with every thought that is within them. I thank You, Heavenly Father, that the fruit produced by the Holy Spirit within them is divine love in all its varied expressions: joy that overflows their individual hearts, peace that subdues, patience that endures life's challenges, kindness in action to their ex-husband or ex-wife, a life full of virtue, faith that prevails, gentleness of heart to their ex-husband or ex-wife, and strength to their spirits. In the name of Jesus, I come against any bitterness and unforgiveness that may still be present between these ex-spouses. I bind that and cast it to the foot of the cross. I call forth the Holy Spirit to minister to each ex-spouse and bring Your comfort, Your healing, and Your grace to each ex-spouse in Jesus's name. I thank You that the ex-spouses are actively praying for one another with all diligence and respectful attitude. I thank You that when they speak with each other, they are mindful of the ex-spouse and only speak words of edification to one another. I am thankful that each ex-spouse only speaks of praise of their ex-spouse in front of their children. I am thankful that You are working in their individual lives to bring about forgiveness and reconciliation to one another.

> Do two walk together except they make an appointment and have agreed? (Amos 3:3, AMPC)

> Finally, all [of you] should be of one and the same mind (united in spirit), sympathizing [with one another], loving [each other] as brethren [of one household], compassionate and courteous (tenderhearted and humble). (1 Peter 3:8 (APMC)

> Little children, let us not love [merely] in theory or in speech but in deed and in truth (in practice and in sincerity). (1 John 3:18, AMPC)

> Beloved children, our love can't be an abstract theory we only talk about, but a way of life demonstrated through our loving deeds. (TPT)

> Beloved, let us love one another, for love is (springs) from God; and he who loves [his fellowmen] is begotten (born) of God and is coming [progressively] to know and understand God [to perceive and recognize and get a better and clearer knowledge of Him]. (1

John 4:7, AMPC)

*Living as becomes you with complete lowliness of mind
(humility) and meekness (unselfishness, gentleness, mildness),
with patience, bearing with one another and making allowances
because you love one another. (Ephesians 4:2, AMPC)*

*Let no foul or polluting language, nor evil word nor
unwholesome or worthless talk [ever] come out of your mouth,
but only such [speech] as is good and beneficial to the spiritual
progress of others, as is fitting to the need and the occasion, that it
may be a blessing and give grace (God's favor) to those who hear
it. (Ephesians 4:29, AMPC)*

*For if you forgive people their trespasses [their reckless
and willful sins, leaving them, letting them go, and giving up
resentment], your heavenly Father will also forgive you. (Matthew
6:14, AMPC)*

*Have not I commanded you? Be strong, vigorous, and very
courageous. Be not afraid, neither be dismayed, for the Lord your
God is with you wherever you go. (Joshua 1:9, AMPC)*

*Strength! Courage! Don't be timid; don't get discouraged. God,
your God, is with you every step you take. (MSG)*

*Then he answered and spoke to me, saying, This is the word of
the LORD to Zerubbabel, saying, Not by might, nor by power, but
by my spirit, said the LORD of hosts. (Zechariah 4:6)*

In the name of Jesus, I stand against unforgiveness and bitterness between the ex-husband and ex-wife. In the name of Jesus, I call forth laborers in the field to minister to each individual that extends Your grace, love, healing, and forgiveness, into their hearts and spirits. I plead the blood of Jesus over this couple and thanking You that You are bringing reconciliation between them as they continue to walk in Your grace, love, and forgiveness. You through the power of the Holy Spirit are removing the scales off of their eyes to see the workings that You are making in the life of their ex-spouse. I thank You that their heart is being softened to see that You are working in the life of the ex-spouse. I thank You that as they individually come closer to You, they realize that by working together, they are stronger for their children.

If one or both have not remarried, I pray for a reconciliation of their marriage. I thank You for complete forgiveness and reconciliation and restoration of trust between them.

CHILDREN

Lord Jesus, You said in Your Word to not prevent or block a child from coming unto You. I thank You that the parents train up their children in the ways that they should go, and in the end, that child will not depart from the ways of their teaching. I thank You that the parents operate in the fruits by the Holy Spirit operating in divine love in all its varied expressions: joy that overflows in their hearts as expressed to their children, peace that subdues their children, patience that endures life's challenges, kindness in action to their children, a life full of virtue, faith that prevails, gentleness of heart to their children, and strength to their spirit in working with all areas of their children's lives. I am thankful that the father does not provoke his children to anger and wrath but that he lovingly disciplines and counsels the children in the ways of Christ.

Lord Jesus, I lift up each and every teacher that has influence on the children. I thank You that they take their jobs seriously and reverently. I thank You that the teachers realize that they have responsibility to teach truth and that they are accountable for what they teach. They are accountable, not just to the state, not just to the parents. I thank You that they are becoming more and more into the realization that they are accountable to You, our Heavenly Father. I thank You that the teachers understand that they are accountable for every idle word they say to the children and, as such, they seek and pursue Your truth. The teachers seek and pursue You, the Author of the truth, for You are the way, the truth, and the life.

In the name of Jesus, I call forth laborers into the field to minister the Good News of the Gospel of Jesus Christ to the children. In Jesus's name I bind any demonic forces that would plan and scheme to bring harm to the children, and I loosen the heavenly host of warring angels to bring a hedge of protection around the children. With the blood of Jesus, I draw a hedge of protection around the children, and I am thankful that God hears my prayers in the throne room of His grace. In the name of Jesus, I am thankful that the children are protected from the evils of this world as they are exposed to so much these days. I am thankful that their virtue and innocence are

212

being guarded by their parents as well as the heavenly hosts of warring and ministering angels. I thank You, Father God, for giving the children wisdom when selecting friends to play with and just hang around with. I thank You that You are directing the right kind of friend into their paths—friends that will edify them and encourage them to follow You! I thank You that the children will come and follow You, Jesus Christ. I thank You that when they grow up, as adults they will still continue to serve You! In the name of Jesus I pray. Amen!

Train up a child in the way he should go, And when he is old he will not depart from it. (Proverbs 22:6, NKJV)

Behold, children are a heritage from the Lord, The fruit of the womb is a reward. Like arrows in the hand of a warrior, So are the children of one's youth. Happy is the man who has his quiver full of them; They shall not be ashamed, But shall speak with their enemies in the gate. (Psalm 127:3–5, NKJV)

And you, fathers, do not provoke your children to wrath, but bring them up in the training and admonition of the Lord. (Ephesians 6:4, NKJV)

Fathers, don't exasperate your children by coming down hard on them. Take them by the hand and lead them in the way of the Master. (MSG)

Children, obey your parents in the Lord, for this is right. "Honor your father and mother"—which is the first commandment with a promise-- "so that it may go well with you and that you may enjoy long life on the earth. (Ephesians 6:1–3, NKJV)

CHILDREN OF DIVORCE

If children are involved, I thank You that the parents peacefully coexist coming into agreement on parenting the children. I thank You, Father, that the children are not used as a pawn against one another. I thank You that both parents acknowledge the other parents rights and love for the children and that both encourage their children to have a relationship with the ex-spouse. I am thankful that the parents are seeking to resolve conflict and bring harmony back to the family in communicating with the children about forgiveness. I am thankful that just as You have worked in the hearts of both parents, so too You will work in the hearts of the children. I am thankful that You are working in the hearts and minds of the children and bringing healing to them from hurts resulting from the divorce. I am thankful that You are sending laborers into the field to minister to these hurting children. May Your Holy Spirit wrap His loving caring arms around them and give comfort to their hurting hearts. May they realize that the divorce was not any of their faults, not a result of anything that they have done or said. In the name of Jesus, I come against any spirit of depression, anxiety, helplessness, and hopelessness in the children. In the name of Jesus, I come against the lying spirits that would try to convince the children that they are less than, lies about self-worth, self-esteem, lies of self-loathing. I bind those spirits in Jesus's name and cast them to the foot of the cross. I come against the spirit of suicide in the name of Jesus. I bind you and cast you to the foot of the cross in the name of Jesus! In the name of Jesus, I draw a hedge of protection around the children; the enemy cannot harm them! I loosen the ministering angels to minister to the children. I loosen the Holy Spirit to comfort, heal, and bring the children into an understanding about the divorce. I am thankful and praising Your holy name that You, Father God, are bringing forgiveness to the hearts of the children extended to both parents for the divorce.

> *That the older men be sober, reverent, temperate, sound in faith, in love, in patience; the older women likewise, that they be reverent in behavior, not slanderers, not given to much wine, teachers of good things that they admonish the young women to love their husbands, to love their children, to be discreet, chaste, homemakers, good, obedient to their own husbands, that the word of God may not be blasphemed. (Titus 2:2–5, NKJV)*

GRANDPARENTS AND GREAT-GRANDPARENTS

Dear Lord, we lift up the glory generation—or as some would say, the forgotten generation—the generation that encompass our elders. We know that more than fifty million Americans are likely to spend their last days in some type of extended-care facility and not with family. We know that 75 percent will be women. We are saddened that 60 percent of those in an elder-care home will never have a visitor. In the name of Jesus, we come against those statistics! We call on the heavenly hosts, the ministering angels, and the Holy Spirit to remind the family members that they have family wasting away in there. We thank You that the family members hear

Your voice and start visiting their family wherever they may be. May these last days of the glory generation be filled with the joy that only family members can bring. May their fleeting moments still under the sun be filled with the joy, laughter, love, and memories that only family can bring. Father, I thank You that parents are bringing their children to visit the child's grandparents and great-grandparents so that the legacy of love in the family can continue to be passed on from generation to generation.

Father, I thank You that the nurses and other caregivers at these facilities grow to realize the value in these precious souls and they treat them with the care and respect that they deserve! I thank You, Father God, that You are sending workers into the fields of these facilities and tend to the glory generation. Lord Father, in the name of Jesus, I come against Alzheimer's and dementia for robbing these lovely souls of their memories! Alzheimer's and dementia, you are a curse from the pit of hell. You are only names; my Bible states that every knee will bow and every tongue will confess that Jesus Christ is Lord. Jesus is Lord over all, that means Alzheimer's and dementia, you must bow to the foot of the cross. I pray for you to be gone! In the name of Jesus! By His stripes we *were healed*! Minister Your love and grace to these tender people. We lift up all those who are in these local facilities.

Arbors Senior Living Center
Brookdale
Burgundy Place
The Commons (UMC)
Enid Senior Care
Greenbrier Residential Living
Clay Hall Senior Residences

Honor (respect, obey, care for) your father and your mother, so that your days may be prolonged in the land the Lord your God gives you. (Exodus 20:12, AMP)

Don't be harsh or impatient with an older man. Talk to him as you would your own father, and to the younger men as your brothers. Reverently honor an older woman as you would your mother, and the younger women as sisters. Take care of widows who are destitute. If a widow has family members to take care of her, let them learn that religion begins at their own doorstep and that they should pay back with gratitude some of what they have received. This pleases God immensely. You can tell a legitimate widow by the way she has put all her hope in God, praying to him constantly for the needs of others as well as her own. But a widow who exploits people's emotions and pocketbooks—well, there's nothing to her. Tell these things to the people so that they will do the right thing in their extended family. Anyone who neglects to care for family members in need repudiates the faith. That's worse than refusing to believe in the first place. (1 Timothy 5:1–4, MSG)

CHILD ABUSE

Hurting people hurt people. Physical abuse is more about anger and exerting control over another person than it is anything else. Lord Father, You know the intents of the heart of mankind. You know what the hurt and pain that the assaulter is dealing with. You know exactly the motives of the assaulter. Whether it is that the assaulter was psychologically, emotionally, physically, or sexually abused as a child, we do not know, but we know You do. Lord Jesus, we thank You that You are sending ministering angels to minister to the abuser. Lord Jesus, change the heart, cause them to understand that the only way for them to truly gain control over their lives is to give You control over every aspect of their lives. I pray for the salvation of the souls of the abuser right now in the name of Jesus. I pray that the Holy Spirit reveals Himself to the abuser, right now, so as to stop the assault from happening, right now in the name of Jesus. Cause the assaulter to stop and then to turn to Jesus, the only true answer to the pain in their heart. I thank You, Jesus, for hearing my prayers. I thank You that You are bringing healing to the entire person of the former abuser. You are bringing healing to the spirit, soul, and body of the former abuser. I thank You that You are bringing peace to their soul. In the name of Jesus, I call the cycle of abuse to be broken. I come against the curse of abuse that is on the former abusers family to be canceled and broken in Jesus's name. Thank You, Jesus.

I lift up the victim of child abuse. In the name of Jesus, I come against any anxiety, fear, condemnation, depression, and thoughts of suicide that is coming against the victim, right now! I bind those lies from the pit of hell, and I cast them to the foot of the cross! I call on the Holy Spirit, Who is the Comforter, to bring comfort to this victim. The Holy Spirit, Who is the revealer of truth, I call on the Holy Spirit to convey the truth to this victim—that they are not to blame for this abuse. In the name of Jesus, I call forth for laborers to enter into the field to minister God's grace, love, and forgiveness to this victim. I thank You that Your pure unconditional love is being demonstrated to this victim and that their heart is being turned over to Christ as Savior and Lord. We thank You, Jesus. that You are bring full healing to the victim, spirit, soul, and body! No shame and no fear because You give them power, love, and a sound mind.

MEDICAL PROFESSION CAREGIVERS

Dear Heavenly Father, I lift up all who work in the medical professions, all those who work in the healing arts. I ask that You protect them. I ask that they operate in wisdom. I draw a hedge of protection around them and pour the blood of Jesus over them. I pray divine health over each and every one of them, and I ask that you bless them abundantly for the sacrifices that they have so graciously given. I thank You, Father God, for the talents that You have blessed them with. I pray protection over their families, and I proclaim that no sickness will befall their household. In the mighty name of Jesus, *amen*!

JERICHO LAP 2

CITY OF ENID, GARFIELD COUNTY, AND THE STATE OF OKLAHOMA

First and foremost, I cast the same prayers over the civic leaders, as I did for the husband and wife as individuals. I pray for the civic leaders, judges, peace officers, first responders, educators, and every other city employee of the city of Enid, employee of Garfield County, and of the region and state. I thank God as He is sending laborers into the field to minister to each and every person in leadership over the city of Enid. If they are not believers in Christ, I thank You, Father, that they will be surrendering their lives to Jesus Christ as Lord and Savior. I thank You, Father God, that the Holy Spirit guides them in all that they say and do. I thank You that they operate in wisdom, Your wisdom, in every endeavor that they pursue for the city. I am thankful that there resides no motive of selfish gain in our civic leaders, and I am thankful that they have a heart to serve the community in all humility and grace. I thank You, Father, that just as they manage their personal finances with integrity, so they are managing the city finances with the same level of integrity. I pray God's good, pleasing, and perfect will be worked out in their lives. I am thankful that they submit all their plans to Jehovah God to seek His will as to how they are to lead the city of Enid. In the name of Jesus, I come against the dominion of darkness that has rule and reign over the city of Enid and Garfield County, Oklahoma. In the name of Jesus, by the authority that He has bestowed on me as a believer in Jesus Christ, I come against the principalities, against powers, against the rulers of the darkness of this world, against spiritual wickedness in high places that are over this region of Garfield County and the state of Oklahoma. In the name of Jesus, I bind them from influencing the civic leaders of the region and state. I bind them and cast them to the foot of the cross of Calvary. In the precious and holy name of Jesus, I loosen the warring angels to do battle on the behalf of the civic leaders. I pray that You, Father God, send laborers into the field to minister to the civic leaders, ministering Your wisdom, love, and grace. I also loosen the ministering angels to bring Your influence on the lives of the civic leaders.

> *Let every soul be subject to the governing authorities. For there is no authority except from God, and the authorities that exist are appointed by God. Therefore whoever resists the authority resists the ordinance of God, and those who resist will bring judgment on themselves. For rulers are not a terror to good works, but to evil. Do you want to be unafraid of the authority? Do what is good, and you will have praise from the same. For he is God's minister to you for good. But if you do evil, be afraid; for he does not bear the sword in vain; for he is God's minister, an avenger to execute wrath on him who practices evil. Therefore you must be subject, not only because of wrath but also for conscience' sake. For because of this you also pay taxes, for they are God's ministers attending continually to this very thing. Render therefore to all their due: taxes to whom taxes are due, customs to whom customs, fear to whom fear, honor to whom honor. Owe no one anything except to love one another, for he who loves another has fulfilled the law. (Romans 13:1–8, NKJV)*

> *And Jesus answered and said to them, "Render to Caesar the things that are Caesar's, and to God the things that are God's." And they marveled at Him." (Mark 12:17, NKJV)*

> *The binding scripture—Matthew 12:28–29, 16:19.*

CIVIC LEADERS IN ENID, OKLAHOMA

Enid, OK, Mayor Bill Shewey
Council Ronald Janzen
Council Derwin Norwood
Council Ben Ezzell
Council Jonathan Waddell
Council Tammy Wilson
Council George Pankonin
Police Chief Brian O'Rourke
Fire Chief Joe Jackson
Garfield County Judges
Judge Hladik, Dennis
Judge Woodward, Paul K
Judge Newby, Tom
Judge Justin Eilers
Judge Lovell, Brian N.
Judge Jason Seigars
Enid Board of Education
HS principal
Emerson Middle School principal
Longfellow Middle School principal
Waller Middle School principal
Eisenhower Elementary Principal
Adams Elementary School principal
Coolidge Elementary School principal
Garfield Elementary School principal
Glenwood Elementary School principal
Hoover Elementary School principal
McKinley Elementary School principal
Monroe Elementary School principal
Prairie View Elementary School principal
Taft Elementary School principal

STATE OF OKLAHOMA

Governor Kevin Stitt
Lt. Governor Matt Pinnell AG E. Mike Hunter
State Senate
Senator Jim Inhofe
Senator James Lankford
US Rep. Tom Cole
US Rep. Kevin Hern
US Rep. Frank Lucas
US Rep. Markwayne Mullin
US Rep. Kendra Horn

JERICHO LAP 3

UNITED STATES OF AMERICA

First and foremost, I cast the same prayers over the civic leaders of this nation as I did for the husband and wife as individuals. I pray for the civic leaders of this nation, judges, peace officers, first responders, educators, and every other federal employee of the United States of America. I thank God as He is sending laborers into the field to minister to each and every person in leadership over the United States of America. If they are not believers in Christ, I thank You, Father, that they will be surrendering their lives to Jesus Christ as Lord and Savior. I thank You, Father, God that the Holy Spirit guides them in all that they say and do. I thank You that they operate in wisdom, Your wisdom, in every endeavor that they pursue for this nation. I am thankful that there resides no motive of selfish gain in our civic leaders, and I am thankful that they have a heart to serve the community in all humility and grace. I thank You, Father, that just as they manage their personal finances with integrity, so they are managing the national finances with the same level of integrity. I pray God's good, pleasing, and perfect will be worked out in their lives. I am thankful that they submit all their plans to Jehovah God to seek His will as to how they are to lead our nation. In the name of Jesus, I come against the dominion of darkness that has rule and reign over this nation. In the name of Jesus, by the authority that He has bestowed on me as a believer in Jesus Christ, I come against the principalities, against powers, against the rulers of the darkness of this world, against spiritual wickedness in high places that are over this nation, the United States of America. In the name of Jesus, I bind them from influencing the civic leaders of this nation, I bind them and cast them to the foot of the cross of Calvary. In the precious and holy name of Jesus, I loosen the warring angels to do battle on the behalf of the civic leaders. I pray that You, Father God, send laborers into the field to minister to the civic leaders, ministering Your wisdom, love, and grace. I also loosen the ministering angels to bring Your influence on the lives of the civic leaders.

I lift up an additional prayer for our president, Lord Father, I thank You that he operates in Your wisdom in all matters pertaining to this nation. I pray that he surrounds himself with godly council, men and women of God whose desire is only to serve You first then this nation. I thank You, our Father, that President Trump seeks Your face daily in prayer and in Your Word. When I was praying for husbands and fathers, Lord Jesus, I was also praying for our president. Those words in those prayers are also being applied to our president. In the name of Jesus, I plead the blood of Jesus over my president, Trump, and I draw a hedge of protection over him and his entire family. In the name of Jesus, I come against every plan and scheme of the adversary that is against him. I come against every lie from the pit of hell that is being propagated by Satan's accomplices, the mass media. I call forth their lying lips to be silenced in the name of Jesus. I loosen Your Holy Spirit to minister to those individuals that are unwittingly involved in these attacks on our president, the spirit of truth, to be showered on them so they see the errors of their ways and confess Jesus as their Lord and Savior. I loosen Your warring angels to protect the president. I also loosen the ministering angels to minister to him in Your truth.

> *Let every soul be subject to the governing authorities. For there is no authority except from God, and the authorities that exist are appointed by God. Therefore whoever resists the authority resists the ordinance of God, and those who resist will bring judgment on themselves. For rulers are not a terror to good works, but to evil. Do you want to be unafraid of the authority? Do what is good, and you will have praise from the same. For he is God's minister to you for good. But if you do evil, be afraid; for he does not bear the sword in vain; for he is God's minister, an avenger to execute wrath on him who practices evil. Therefore you must be*

subject, not only because of wrath but also for conscience' sake.
For because of this you also pay taxes, for they are God's ministers
attending continually to this very thing. Render therefore to all
their due: taxes to whom taxes are due, customs to whom customs,
fear to whom fear, honor to whom honor. Owe no one anything
except to love one another, for he who loves another has fulfilled
the law. (Romans 13:1–8, NKJV)

And Jesus answered and said to them, "Render to Caesar the
things that are Caesar's, and to God the things that are God's."
And they marveled at Him." (Mark 12:17, NKJV)

US GOVERNMENT

President Donald Trump
FL Melania Trump
Vice President Mike Pence
Karen Pence
Sec. of State Mike Pompeo
Sec. of the Treasury Steve Mnuchin
Sec. of Defense Patrick Shanahan
Attorney General Matthew Whitaker

US SUPREME COURT

I pray that God guides the justices of the Supreme Court. That they
judge rightly according to biblical principles. That they put aside political
ideologies and judge according to existing law and to not make new law
from their own bias. I pray that they judge according to the original intent
of the Founding Documents, the Constitution, Amendments, and Federalist
Papers. I pray that God sends laborers to minister to each and every justice.
I pray that the Holy Spirit guides them in all that they do. I pray that if they
do not know Christ as their personal Lord and Savior, that laborers will be
sent to minister the Gospel of Jesus Christ in the right way that would break
down the barriers to bring them into repentance and forgiveness under the
blood of Jesus.

John G. Roberts Jr., chief justice of the US
Anthony M. Kennedy
Clarence Thomas
Ruth Bader Ginsburg

Stephen G. Breyer

Samuel Anthony Alito

Sonia Sotomayo

Elena Kagan

Neil Gorsuch

Brett Kavanaugh

US Army, US Navy, US Marines, US Air Force and US Coast Guard

For the continued prayer for the city of Enid and, by proxy, the state of Oklahoma and the United States of America, we speak with the authority given us in the scripture. There are demonic forces in the spirit world that we do not see that have been dedicated to the task of attacking a specific area and subject matter. We will attempt to cover some of the major strongholds that Satan has on the lives of Enid, Oklahoma, and the USA. But feel free to cover any and all that God lays on your heart. If you come up with an additional subject matter, find one of the categories below that that subject will fit with and pray at that time so we maintain unity of the Spirit.

> *And when He had called His twelve disciples to Him, He gave them power over unclean spirits, to cast them out, and to heal all kinds of sickness and all kinds of disease. (Matthew 10:1, NKJV)*

> *Heal the sick, raise the dead, cleanse those who have leprosy, drive out demons. Freely you have received; freely give. (Matthew 10:8, NKJV)*

The binding scripture—Matthew 12:28–29, 16:19.

JERICHO LAP 4

SEXUAL SIN (LUST)
THE JEZEBEL SPIRIT
ADDICTION TO PORN
SEXUAL ASSAULT
HUMAN TRAFFICKING
ABORTION

By the authority of the blood of Christ shed on the cross of Calvary, we come against the sensual spirits of adultery and sexual addiction in Jesus's name! In Jesus's name, we come against the evil principalities that tempt mankind in the sexual realm. We call forth the heavenly warring angels to fight against the evil prince who is responsible for sexual temptation. We come against the evil powers and bind them in Jesus's holy name! We say that you must yield to the name of Jesus! We come against spiritual hosts of wickedness in the heavenly places, and we call forth the warring angels who have responsibility over these differing evil powers to do battle in the spiritual realms in Jesus's name. Jezebel, get Your hands off of marriages in the name of Jesus!

I pray especially for those who struggle with an addiction to pornography. Lord, I thank You that You are revealing to them how dangerous this stronghold is. I thank You that You are breaking the bondage of pornography in marriages in Jesus's name! I thank You that You are giving husbands and wives the strength to overcome this temptation. I thank and praise Your holy name that You are sending people to encourage them and keep them accountable so as to not to stumble. I thank You that You are bringing those who have been struggling with this issue victory in Jesus's name. Amen! I thank You that You are removing the shame that existed under the bondage of pornography and You are bringing restoration and healing to the spirit and mind of that former slave to pornography. I thank You that the love of Jesus is being brought back into this marriage. I thank You that any bitterness and unforgiveness and self-loathing that built up as a result of this sin is healed in the name of Jesus. I thank You that You are bringing this person back to wholeness in the name of Jesus.

Lord, I thank You that You are revealing yourself in very personal ways to those involved in the pornography industry so that they turn their hearts to You, O Lord! I thank You that one by one, those who are in the porn industry are realizing that they have God-shaped vacuum inside their hearts that only You can fill, Lord Jesus. Holy Spirit, reveal to them that the emptiness they feel inside can only be answered in the person of Jesus Christ. Point them to a faith filled church that can bring them healing to their spirit, soul, and body. Thank You that one by one, hearts are being turned back to You, Jesus, and full healing is being brought to them through You!

Hurting people hurt people. Sexual assault is more about anger and exerting control over another person than it is really about a sexual act. Lord Father, You know the intents of the heart of mankind. You know what the hurt and pain that the assaulter is dealing with. You know exactly the motives of the assaulter. Whether it is that the assaulter was psychologically, emotionally, physically or sexually abused as a child, we do not know, but we know You do. Lord Jesus, we thank You that You are sending ministering angels to minister to the assaulter. Lord Jesus, change the heart, cause them to understand that the only way for them to truly gain control is to give You control over their lives. I pray for the salvation of the souls of the assaulter right now in the name of Jesus. I pray that the Holy Spirit reveals Himself to the abuser, right now, so as to stop the assault from happening, right now in the name of Jesus. Cause the assaulter to stop and then to turn to Jesus, the only true answer to the pain in their heart. I thank You, Jesus, for hearing my prayers. I thank You that You are bringing healing to the entire person of the former abuser. You are bringing healing to the spirit, soul, and body of the former abuser. I thank You that You are bringing peace to their soul. In the name of Jesus, I call the cycle of abuse to be broken. I come against the curse of abuse that is on the former abusers family to be canceled and broken in Jesus's name. Thank You, Jesus.

I lift up the victim of sexual assault. I call on the Holy Spirit, Who is the Comforter, to bring comfort to this victim. The Holy Spirit, Who is the revealer of truth, I call on the Holy Spirit to convey the truth to this victim that they are not to blame for this sexual assault. In the name of Jesus, I call forth for laborers to enter into the field to minister God's grace, love, and forgiveness to this victim. I thank You that Your pure unconditional love is being demonstrated to this victim and that their heart is being turned over to Christ as Savior and Lord. We thank You, Jesus, and praise Your holy name that You are bringing full healing to the victim, spirit, soul, and body! I thank You and praise You that they have no shame and no fear because You give them power, love, and a sound mind.

Lord, I thank You that You are sending laborers into the field to minister to those who are in the bondage of sex trafficking. Lord Jesus, make a way where there is no way; those who are holding the victim hostage, allow them to grow sloppy in dealing with the victim, give the victim courage to escape the bondage of sex trafficking. Remove the shame and stigma associated with being a victim of this crime. I thank You that You are sending laborers into the field to rescue these persons in bondage in sex trafficking. I thank You that Your grace, love, and forgiveness is effectively being communicated to these victims and that they are turning their hearts to You, Jesus and Savior and Lord. I thank You that You are bringing full and complete healing to these victims.

Dear Lord Jesus, we lift up the young female who is faced with a crisis pregnancy. We lift her up during this time of extreme need. I thank You, Jesus, for sending laborers into the field to minister Your love, grace, and forgiveness to this young woman. I thank You and praise You that Your love, grace, and forgiveness casts out all shame from this situation. I thank You that You are using this crisis pregnancy to bring her to the saving knowledge and grace of Jesus Christ. I thank You that the Holy Spirit is speaking to her right now. Just like the blood of Cain was crying out to God, may the blood of the innocents cry out to this young woman testifying to the saving grace of Jesus. In the name of Jesus, I bind the lying lips of the adversary and those of organizations like Planned Parenthood. I thank You that ministries like Journey House Pregnancy Resource Center are in existence to counsel, guide, and inform these young woman about the truth of what abortion is, but more, they share the truth of God's love and mercy. I thank You that these young women are realizing that adoption is a very positive option. I thank You, Father, that You are giving her the strength to make the right decision.

Dear Lord Jesus, I lift up the woman who has had an abortion. Father God, forgive her of this poor choice that she made. Forgive her of the fear and self-loathing that she walked in. Thank You for Your grace as she turns to You for forgiveness. Let her not forget to forgive herself. I pray that she turns and seeks Your face and asks for forgiveness. I pray that she realizes that her mess can be turned into a message to others who have gone through this. Holy Spirit, I thank You that You are bringing comfort and healing to her hurting heart. In the name of Jesus, I pray. Amen.

No temptation has overtaken you except such as is common to man; but God is faithful, who will not allow you to be tempted beyond what you are able, but with the temptation will also make the way of escape, that you may be able to bear it. (1 Corinthians 10:13, NKJV)

Flee sexual immorality. Every sin that a man does is outside the body, but he who commits sexual immorality sins against his own body. (1 Corinthians 6:18, NKJV)

To keep you from the evil woman, From the flattering tongue of a seductress. Do not lust after her beauty in your heart, Nor let her allure you with her eyelids. For by means of a harlot. A man is reduced to a crust of bread; And an adulteress will prey upon his precious life. Can a man take fire to his bosom, And his clothes not be burned? Can one walk on hot coals, And his feet not be seared? So is he who goes in to his neighbor's wife; Whoever touches her shall not be innocent. (Proverbs 6:24–29, NKJV)

You have heard that it was said to those of old, 'You shall not commit adultery. But I say to you that whoever looks at a woman to lust for her has already committed adultery with her in his heart. (Matthew 5:27–28, NKJV)

Marriage is honorable among all, and the bed undefiled; but fornicators and adulterers God will judge. (Hebrews 13:4, NKJV)

Do you not know that the unrighteous will not inherit the kingdom of God? Do not be deceived. Neither fornicators, nor idolaters, nor adulterers, nor homosexuals, nor sodomites, nor thieves, nor covetous, nor drunkards, nor revilers, nor extortioners will inherit the kingdom of God. And such were some of you. But you were washed, but you were sanctified, but you were justified in the name of the Lord Jesus and by the Spirit of our God. (1 Corinthians 6:9–11, NKJV)

For this is the will of God, your sanctification: that you should abstain from sexual immorality; that each of you should know how to possess his own vessel in sanctification and honor, not in passion of lust, like the Gentiles who do not know God. (1 Thessalonians 4:3–5, NKJV)

Additional scriptural reference—Deuteronomy 23:17–18; Leviticus 17:7; Proverbs 5:1–14; Proverbs 15:27; Ezekiel 16:15, 28; Hosea 4:13–19; Judges 2:17; Ezekiel 16; 1 Corinthians 6:13–16; Philippians 3:19; Galatians 5:19; James 4:4; 1 Timothy 6:7–14;

The binding scripture—Matthew 12:28–29, 16:19.

JERICHO LAP 5

ALCOHOL ADDICTION
DRUG ADDICTION

Lord Jesus, we lift up the alcoholic. We thank You, Father, that You are sending laborers into the field to minister to the alcoholic. We thank You that Your love, grace, and forgiveness is being demonstrated to the alcoholic through these, Your ministers. By the authority of the blood of Christ shed for me on the cross of Calvary, we come against the spirits of alcohol addiction in Jesus's name! We know that alcohol can never take away the pain of whatever it is that the alcoholic is trying to drown out. We come against the demonic powers that bring men and women into the bondage of addiction. In the name of Jesus, we bind those spirits and cast them to the foot of the cross; you must yield to the power of the blood of Jesus. We pray that the power of the Holy Spirit would consume those who yield to Christ and cleanse the body of the addicted, drive out the chemical dependency from their bodies. Replace the physical need for the chemical for a need and thirst for the righteousness of Christ. We thank You that lives are being changed and the chains of addiction are being broken in the name of Jesus.

We know that some translations translate the Greek word pharmakeia as "witchcraft," and that in witchcraft potions and concoctions are used for mind-altering experiences. Not being a Greek scholar, I cannot definitively say "yes" or "no" on this. My prayer will proceed to err on the side of caution and assume that the witchcraft inference is more true than false.

We do know and can definitively conclude that like alcohol, drugs are mind-altering substances that alter behavior in the human, making them more susceptible to suggestion. The inhibitions come down, and caution is thrown to the wind while under the influence of drugs. By the authority of the blood of Christ shed for me on the cross of Calvary, we come against the spirits of drug addiction in Jesus's name! We come against the demonic powers of witchcraft that casts the spells to bring men and women into bondage of addiction. In the name of Jesus, we bind those spirits and cast them to the foot of the cross; you must yield to the power of the blood of Jesus. We pray that the power of the Holy Spirit would consume those who yield to Christ and cleanse the body of the addicted, drive out the chemical dependency from their bodies. Replace the physical need for the chemical for a need and thirst for the righteousness of Christ. We thank You that lives are being changed and the chains of addiction are being broken in the name of Jesus.

But if I cast out demons by the Spirit of God, surely the kingdom of God has come upon you. Or how can one enter a strong man's house and plunder his goods, unless he first binds the strong man? And then he will plunder his house. (Matthew 12:28–29, NKJV)

And I will give you the keys of the kingdom of heaven, and whatever you bind on earth will be bound in heaven, and whatever you loose on earth will be loosed in heaven. (Matthew 16:19, NKJV)

Now the doings (practices) of the flesh are clear (obvious): they are immorality, impurity, indecency, Idolatry, sorcery, enmity, strife, jealousy, anger (ill temper), selfishness, divisions (dissensions), party spirit (factions, sects with peculiar opinions, heresies), Envy, drunkenness, carousing, and the like. I warn you beforehand, just as I did previously, that those who do such things shall not inherit the kingdom of God. (Galatians 5:19–21, AMPC)

It is obvious what kind of life develops out of trying to get your own way all the time: repetitive, loveless, cheap sex; a stinking accumulation of mental and emotional garbage; frenzied and joyless grabs for happiness; trinket gods; magic-show religion; paranoid loneliness; cutthroat competition; all-consuming-yet-never-satisfied wants; a brutal temper; an impotence to love or be loved; divided homes and divided lives; small-minded and lopsided pursuits; the vicious habit of depersonalizing everyone into a rival; uncontrolled and uncontrollable addictions; ugly parodies of community. I could go on. This isn't the first time I have warned you, you know. If you use your freedom this way, you will not inherit God's kingdom. (MSG)

The cravings of the self-life are obvious: Sexual immorality, lustful thoughts, pornography, chasing after things instead of God, manipulating others, hatred of those who get in your way, senseless arguments, resentment when others are favored, temper tantrums, angry quarrels, only thinking of yourself, being in love with your own opinions, being envious of the blessings of others, murder, uncontrolled addictions, wild parties, and all other similar behavior. Haven't I already warned you that those who use their "freedom" for these things will not inherit the kingdom realm of God! (TPT)

Therefore let us not sleep, as others do, but let us watch and be sober. (1 Thessalonians 5:6, NKJV)

Be sober, be vigilant; because your adversary the devil walks about like a roaring lion, seeking whom he may devour. (1 Peter 5:8, NKJV)

Therefore gird up the loins of your mind, be sober, and rest your hope fully upon the grace that is to be brought to you at the revelation of Jesus Christ. (1 Peter 1:13, NKJV)

Nor thieves, nor covetous, nor drunkards, nor revilers, nor extortioners will inherit the kingdom of God. (1 Corinthians 6:10, NKJV)

Additional scriptural reference—Ephesians 5:18, Proverbs 20:1, Proverbs 23:29–34, Isaiah 5:22, 1 Thessalonians 5:8.

The binding scripture—Matthew 12:28–29, 16:19.

JERICHO LAP 6

DISCOURAGEMENT
DESPAIR
DEPRESSION
ANXIETY
SUICIDE

Lord Jesus, I pray for anyone, anywhere, suffering from depression right now. In the mighty name of Jesus, by these prayers, in the spiritual realms, I reach down and I pull you out of that sink hole of discouragement, despair, depression, anxiety, and suicide. As in Ezekiel 16:6, "I passed by you and saw you lying in your blood, and I said to you as you lay in your blood: Live! Yes, I said to you as you lay in your blood: Live!" so too I say, "Live!" In the name of Jesus, I come against that spirit of suicide; I come against that whispering, lying voice of the devil and his demons. In Jesus's mighty name, I say, "Shut up! Close those lips, in Jesus's name." I speak now directly to you, child of God, "It's not over yet, there's hope for your future, for the Word of our Lord says that He has a future and a hope for you!" I now speak life over you in name of Jesus. You shall not die, but you shall live, for He came to give us life and life abundantly. God, our Heavenly Father, wants to bless you beyond even your wildest dreams. So stay, my brother, my sister, you and your life will be celebrated for generations to come. God is not done with you yet; the best in life still awaits you.

By the authority of the blood of Christ shed on the cross of Calvary, I come against the spirits of despair, discouragement, depression, anxiety, and suicide in Jesus's name! In the name of Jesus, I come against the spirit of confusion and dejection in your life. In the name of Jesus, live and not die. In the name of Jesus, I come against the spirit of despair and depression in your life. In the name of Jesus, I come against the spirit fear in you right now. In the name of Jesus, I come against every form of panic or anxiety attack that is coming on you right now. In the name of Jesus, I come against the spirit of shame that is hovering over you right now. In the name of Jesus, I come against the spirit of guilt and condemnation that has burrowed deep into your spirit and soul—begone in the name of Jesus. In the name of Jesus, I come against that spirit of frustration that is over you. In the name of Jesus, I come against that spirit of inferiority that weighs you down like an anchor. In the name of Jesus, I come against any force, both internal and external, that wants take away your peace and tranquility.

I thank Jesus that God's peace that passes all human understanding is now operating in your life. I thank Jesus that His hands have lifted you up and out of that pit of despair and depression. I pray that whatever is responsible for your pain, be destroyed now in Jesus's mighty name. I thank You, Jesus, that the pain they are carrying—be it emotional, medical, relational, financial, or even marital—is lifted off of their life. I pray for divine intervention for their life today in Jesus's name. I thank You, Jesus, that the Son of righteousness will rise with healing on His wings over them and drip them with heavenly medicines of comfort, healing, peace, and restoration. Holy Spirit, I ask that You wrap Your loving arms around them and give them that very comforting hug. I thank You that the sweet presence of the Holy Spirit overshadows them right now in Jesus's name. I thank You that You are sending laborers into the field to minister to these who have been suffering under the bondage of depression. May they come to the saving knowledge of Jesus Christ and make Him their Savior and Lord. May the Holy Spirit come on them in power and grace to help them in this hour of need. These things we thank You, Heavenly Father, for hearing our prayers and answering them in Jesus's name.

And the Lord, He is the One who goes before you. He will be with you, He will not leave you nor forsake you; do not fear nor be dismayed. (Deuteronomy 31:8, NKJV)

The righteous cry out, and the Lord hears, And delivers them out of all their troubles. The Lord is near to those who have a broken heart, And saves such as have a contrite spirit. (Psalm 34:17, NKJV)

Yet when holy lovers of God cry out to him with all their hearts, the Lord will hear them and come to rescue them from all their troubles. (TPT)

I waited patiently for the Lord; And He inclined to me, And heard my cry. He also brought me up out of a horrible pit, Out of the miry clay, And set my feet upon a rock. And established my steps. He has put a new song in my mouth Praise to our God; Many will see it and fear, And will trust in the Lord. (Psalm 40:1–3, NKJV)

I waited patiently for the Lord; And He inclined to me, And heard my cry. He also brought me up out of a horrible pit, Out of the miry clay, And set my feet upon a rock, And established my steps. He has put a new song in my mouth— Praise to our God; Many will see it and fear, And will trust in the Lord. (MSG)

I waited and waited and waited some more, patiently, knowing God would come through for me. Then, at last, he bent down and listened to my cry. He stooped down to lift me out of danger from the desolate pit I was in, out of the muddy mess I had fallen into. Now he's lifted me up into a firm, secure place and steadied me while I walk along his ascending path. A new song for a new day rises up in me every time I think about how he breaks through for me! Ecstatic praise pours out of my mouth until everyone hears how God has set me free. Many will see his miracles; they'll stand in awe of God and fall in love with him! (TPT)

But You, O Lord, are a shield for me, My glory and the One who lifts up my head. I cried to the Lord with my voice, And He heard

232

me from His holy hill. (Psalm 3:3–4, NKJV)

But you, God, shield me on all sides; You ground my feet, you lift my head high; With all my might I shout up to God, His answers thunder from the holy mountain. (MSG)

But in the depths of my heart I truly know that you, Yahweh, have become my Shield; You take me and surround me with yourself. Your glory covers me continually. You lift high my head when I bow low in shame. I have cried out to you, Yahweh, from your holy presence. You send me a Father's help. (TPT)

Why are you cast down, O my soul? And why are you disquieted within me? Hope in God; For I shall yet praise Him, The help of my countenance and my God. (Psalm 42:11, NKJV)

Why are you down in the dumps, dear soul? Why are you crying the blues? (MSG)

Fix my eyes on God—soon I'll be praising again. He puts a smile on my face. He's my God."

So I say to my soul, "Don't be discouraged. Don't be disturbed. For I know my God will break through for me." Then I'll have plenty of reasons to praise him all over again. Yes, living before his face is my saving grace!" (TPT)

Yes, all of you be submissive to one another, and be clothed with humility, for "God resists the proud, But gives grace to the humble." Therefore humble yourselves under the mighty hand of God, that He may exalt you in due time, casting all your care upon Him, for He cares for you." (1 Peter 5:6–7, NKJV)

So be content with who you are, and don't put on airs. God's strong hand is on you; he'll promote you at the right time. Live carefree before God; he is most careful with you. (MSG)

If you bow low in God's awesome presence, he will eventually exalt you as you leave the timing in his hands. Pour out all your worries and stress upon him and leave them there, for he always tenderly cares for you. (TPT)

These things I have spoken to you, that in Me you may have peace. In the world you will have tribulation; but be of good cheer,

I have overcome the world. (John 16:33, NKJV)

I've told you all this so that trusting me, you will be unshakable and assured, deeply at peace. In this godless world you will continue to experience difficulties. But take heart! I've conquered the world. (MSG)

And everything I've taught you is so that the peace which is in me will be in you and will give you great confidence as you rest in me. For in this unbelieving world you will experience trouble and sorrows, but you must be courageous, for I have conquered the world! (TPT)

Finally, brethren, whatever things are true, whatever things are noble, whatever things are just, whatever things are pure, whatever things are lovely, whatever things are of good report, if there is any virtue and if there is anything praiseworthy—meditate on these things. (Philippians 4:8, NKJV)

Summing it all up, friends, I'd say you'll do best by filling your minds and meditating on things true, noble, reputable, authentic, compelling, gracious—the best, not the worst; the beautiful, not the ugly; things to praise, not things to curse. (MSG)

So keep your thoughts continually fixed on all that is authentic and real, honorable and admirable, beautiful and respectful, pure and holy, merciful and kind. And fasten your thoughts on every glorious work of God, praising him always. (TPT)

For I am persuaded that neither death nor life, nor angels nor principalities nor powers, nor things present nor things to come, nor height nor depth, nor any other created thing, shall be able to separate us from the love of God which is in Christ Jesus our Lord. (Romans 8:38–39, NKJV)

None of this fazes us because Jesus loves us. I'm absolutely convinced that nothing—nothing living or dead, angelic or demonic, today or tomorrow, high or low, thinkable or unthinkable—absolutely nothing can get between us and God's love because of the way that Jesus our Master has embraced us. (MSG)

So now I live with the confidence that there is nothing in the universe with the power to separate us from God's love. I'm convinced that his love will triumph over death, life's troubles, fallen angels, or dark rulers in the heavens. There is nothing in our present or future circumstances that can weaken his love. There is no power above us or beneath us—no power that could ever be found in the universe that can distance us from God's passionate love, which is lavished upon us through our Lord Jesus, the Anointed One! (TPT)

Beloved, do not think it strange concerning the fiery trial which is to try you, as though some strange thing happened to you; but rejoice to the extent that you partake of Christ's sufferings, that when His glory is revealed, you may also be glad with exceeding joy. (1 Peter 4:12–13, NKJV)

Friends, when life gets really difficult, don't jump to the conclusion that God isn't on the job. Instead, be glad that you are in the very thick of what Christ experienced. This is a spiritual refining process, with glory just around the corner. (MSG)

Beloved friends, if life gets extremely difficult, with many tests, don't be bewildered as though something strange were overwhelming you. Instead, continue to rejoice, for you, in a measure, have shared in the sufferings of the Anointed One so that you can share in the revelation of his glory and celebrate with even greater gladness! (TPT)

The steps of a good man are ordered by the Lord, And He delights in his way. Though he fall, he shall not be utterly cast down; For the Lord upholds him with His hand. (Psalm 37:23–24, NKJV)

Stalwart walks in step with God; his path blazed by God, he's happy. If he stumbles, he's not down for long; God has a grip on his hand. (MSG)

The steps of the God-pursuing ones follow firmly in the footsteps of the Lord, and God delights in every step they take to follow him. If they stumble badly they will still survive, for the Lord lifts them up with his hands. (TPT)

Fear not, for I am with you; Be not dismayed, for I am your God.

I will strengthen you, Yes, I will help you, I will uphold you with My righteous right hand. (Isaiah 41:10, NKJV)

Don't panic. I'm with you. There's no need to fear for I'm your God. I'll give you strength. I'll help you. I'll hold you steady, keep a firm grip on you. (MSG)

See also Matthew 16:19.

JERICHO LAP 7

SATAN AND HIS DEMONS

By now, given that we have touched on so many areas of human existence and prayed for them, the following is a general blanket prayer to cover anything we may have missed along the way:

By the authority given me by the blood that was shed on the cross at Calvary and in the Word of God, in Jesus's name, we come against the evil principalities (Prince over Enid and Garfield County), we call forth the heavenly warring angel, the Heavenly Prince over Enid and Garfield County to bring the evil prince captive. We come against the evil powers and bind them in Jesus's holy name! We come against the rulers of the darkness of this age and say that you must yield to the name of Jesus! We come against spiritual hosts of wickedness in the heavenly places, and we call forth the warring angels who have responsibility over these differing evil powers in Jesus's name. Not by my own authority, but in the authority of Him Who paid the blood price on the cross. In the name of Jesus Christ of Nazareth, I bind any and all evil spirits over this region and cast you to the foot of the cross at Calvary. I loosen the warring angels and ministering angels to go on God's behalf to do the work in the spirit realm. I call forth the power of the Holy Spirit to work in the lives of mankind.

Father God, I pray for unity and peace over this region and let every prejudice and ethnicity and stereotype and religious and political view rip it apart… We lift up a banner of prayer and a blood barrier of hundreds of miles around Enid.

We pray for unity and peace over every pastor and over every church because we know there is one head over one body—His church; and Jesus said, "I have many sheep in other pastures." So it is here in Enid too! Father God, I pray that angels of peace and unity are dispatched over Enid to drive out hate, drive out separation that divides your body of believers, and that we will never allow the devil's hateful plans and schemes that divide into our community again… Father God, we repent for our actions and sins that divide, and we forgive in the same way… In the mighty name of Jesus!

Amen.

I ask that laborers go into the field for the harvest is ripe but the workers are few, I thank You, Heavenly Father, for hearing all these prayers as we have come boldly into Your throne room of grace. I thank You, Father God, and I give You all the praise, honor, and glory for the work You have done and are doing in these lives we have lifted to You. In the name of Jesus we pray, and all God's children, say, "*Amen.*"

But if I cast out demons by the Spirit of God, surely the kingdom of God has come upon you. Or how can one enter a strong man's house and plunder his goods, unless he first binds the strong man? And then he will plunder his house. (Matthew 12:28–29, NKJV)

But if it's by God's power that I am sending the evil spirits packing, then God's kingdom is here for sure. How in the world do you think it's possible in broad daylight to enter the house of an awake, able-bodied man and walk off with his possessions unless you tie him up first? Tie him up, though, and you can clean him out. (MSG)

On the other hand, if I drive out demons by the power of the Spirit of God, then the end of Satan's kingdom has come! Who would dare enter the house of a mighty man and steal his property? First he must be overpowered and tied up by one who is stronger than he. Then his entire house can be plundered and every possession stolen. (TPT)

And I will give you the keys of the kingdom of heaven, and whatever you bind on earth will be bound in heaven, and whatever you loose on earth will be loosed in heaven. (Matthew 16:19, NKJV)

And that's not all. You will have complete and free access to God's kingdom, keys to open any and every door: no more barriers between heaven and earth, earth and heaven. A yes on earth is yes in heaven. A no on earth is no in heaven. (MSG)

Assuredly, I say to you, whatever you bind on earth will be bound in heaven, and whatever you loose on earth will be loosed in heaven. "Again I say to you that if two of you agree on earth concerning anything that they ask, it will be done for them by My Father in heaven. For where two or three are gathered together in My name, I am there in the midst of them. (Matthew 18:18–20, NKJV)

Take this most seriously: A yes on earth is yes in heaven; a no on earth is no in heaven. What you say to one another is eternal. I mean this. When two of you get together on anything at all on earth and make a prayer of it, my Father in heaven goes into action. And when two or three of you are together because of me, you can be sure that I'll be there. (MSG)

Receive this truth: Whatever you forbid on earth will be considered to be forbidden in heaven, and whatever you release on earth will be considered to be released in heaven. Again, I give you an eternal truth: If two of you agree to ask God for something in a symphony of prayer, my heavenly Father will do it for you. For wherever two or three come together in honor of my name, I am right there with them! (TPT)

The thief comes only in order to steal and kill and destroy. I came that they may have and enjoy life, and have it in abundance (to the full, till it overflows.) (John 10:10, AMP)

Then the seventy returned with joy, saying, "Lord, even the demons are subject to us in Your name." And He said to them, "I saw Satan fall like lightning from heaven. Behold, I give you the authority to trample on serpents and scorpions, and over all the power of the enemy, and nothing shall by any means hurt you. Nevertheless do not rejoice in this, that the spirits are subject to you, but rather rejoice because your names are written in heaven." (Luke 10:19–20, NKJV)

This girl followed Paul and us, and cried out, saying, "These men are the servants of the Most High God, who proclaim to us the way of salvation." And this she did for many days. But Paul, greatly annoyed, turned and said to the spirit, "I command you in the name of Jesus Christ to come out of her." And he came out that very hour. (Acts 16:17–18, NKJV)

Then He appointed twelve, that they might be with Him and that He might send them out to preach, and to have power to heal sicknesses and to cast out demons. (Mark 3:14–15, NKJV)

Now the Spirit expressly says that in latter times some will depart from the faith, giving heed to deceiving spirits and doctrines of demons, speaking lies in hypocrisy, having their own conscience seared with a hot iron. (1 Timothy 4:1, NKJV)

The Holy Spirit has explicitly revealed: At the end of this age, many will depart from the true faith one after another, devoting themselves to spirits of deception and following demon-inspired revelations and theories. (TPT)

For though we walk (live) in the flesh, we are not carrying on our warfare according to the flesh and using mere human weapons. For the weapons of our warfare are not physical [weapons of flesh and blood], but they are mighty before God for the overthrow and destruction of strongholds, [Inasmuch as we] refute arguments and theories and reasonings and every proud and lofty thing that sets itself up against the [true] knowledge of God; and we lead every thought and purpose away captive into the obedience of Christ [the Messiah, the Anointed One]. (2 Corinthians 10:3–5, AMPC)

The world is unprincipled. It's dog-eat-dog out there! The world doesn't fight fair. But we don't live or fight our battles that way—never have and never will. The tools of our trade aren't for marketing or manipulation, but they are for demolishing that entire massively corrupt culture. We use our powerful God-tools for smashing warped philosophies, tearing down barriers erected against the truth of God, fitting every loose thought and emotion and impulse into the structure of life shaped by Christ. (MSG)

For although we live in the natural realm, we don't wage a military campaign employing human weapons, using manipulation to achieve our aims. Instead, our spiritual weapons are energized with divine power to effectively dismantle the defenses behind which people hide. We can demolish every deceptive fantasy that opposes God and break through every arrogant attitude that is

raised up in defiance of the true knowledge of God. We capture,
like prisoners of war, every thought[d] and insist that it bow in
obedience to the Anointed One. (TPT)

Additional scriptural references—Exodus 7:11, 8:7, 9:11, 22:18; Leviticus
19:26; Deuteronomy 18:11; 1 Samuel 15:23; Isaiah 2:6, 19:3, 47:13;
Jeremiah 10:2; Hosea 4:12; Micah 5:12; Galatians 5:20; Revelation 9:21,
18:23, 21:8, 22:15.

Glossary of Bible Translations used are the following:

(ASV) American Standard Version
(AMP) Amplified Bible
(AMPC) Amplified Bible, Classic Edition
(AKJV) Authorized King James Version
(CEV) Contemporary English Version
(ESV) English Standard Version
(GNT) Good News Translation
(ISV) International Standard Version
(KJV) King James Version
(MSG) The Message
(NASB) New American Standard Bible
(NCV) New Century Version
(NIV) New International Version
(NKJV) New King James Version
(NLT) New Living Translation
(TPT) The Passion Translation

Additional Reading:

The Believer's Authority
Kenneth E. Hagin

Plans Purposes & Pursuits
Kenneth E. Hagin

The Beauty of Spiritual Language
Jack Hayford

Why Tongues
Kenneth E. Hagin

The following book—when I started writing the *Keys to the Kingdom*, I told my pastor of the shock wave cone; he indicated he read something similar in a book by Mark Matterson. He later bought one for me. Well, I started reading it and found it to be awesome, but I stopped reading at around page 30, as I wanted the Holy Spirit to give me fresh divine inspiration. I do find it interesting that this book was released in 2016, the same year that God gave me the JCP. So when I press "send" on the final version of this manuscript, I will begin again reading the following book: *The Circle Maker* by Mark Matterson.

CPSIA information can be obtained
at www.ICGtesting.com
Printed in the USA
FSHW020246120221
78470FS